The Next Great Bull Market

*How to Pick Winning Stocks
and Sectors in the New
Global Economy*

Matthew McCall

WILEY

John Wiley & Sons, Inc.

Published by John Wiley & Sons, Inc., Hoboken, New Jersey.
Published simultaneously in Canada.

For general information on our other products and services or for technical support, please contact our Customer Care Department within the United States at (800) 762-2974, outside the United States at (317) 572-3993 or fax (317) 572-4002.

Wiley also publishes its books in a variety of electronic formats. Some content that appears in print may not be available in electronic books. For more information about Wiley products, visit our web site at www.wiley.com.

Library of Congress Cataloging-in-Publication Data:

McCall, Matthew, 1976–

 The next great bull market : how to pick winning stocks and sectors in the new global economy / Matthew McCall.

  p. cm.
 Includes index.
 ISBN 978-0-470-44089-6 (hardback)
  1. Speculation. 2. Stocks—Prices—Forecasting. 3. Investment analysis. I. Title.
HG6041.M383   2009
332.63'22--dc22

                                                                    2009027777

Printed in the United States of America
10 9 8 7 6 5 4 3 2 1

I wish to dedicate this book to my late friend Adam Horvath, who lost his battle with cancer in 2009. Adam will always be in my heart and in the hearts of many. I can only wish that this book will touch and encourage people as much as Adam did during his 33 years in this world.

Contents

Foreword

As I type this riding high in the friendly skies in late July 2009, the S&P 500 stands at around 994.

It stood at 954 in late July 1997.

40 index points in 12 years. Whoopee.

Sounds pretty dismal, doesn't it? Those of you who believed you were playing the game right: You know buying and holding stocks for the "long term" did not grow your financial wealth for more than a decade. Many hold retirement plans and 401(k)s down 30–50 over 60 percent from the original value of securities purchased.

So Matt's book here—*The Next Great Bull Market*—sounds a wee bit audacious, no?

If you judge the world from the perspective that "investing in stocks" means investing in U.S.-traded securities *only*, you may have a point.

But . . . if you have arrived at the conclusion, as Matt has, that investing in the post–2008/2009 crash means investing in the world's biggest and most powerful commercial and industrial transformations— what we like to call "ChangeWaves" at my research firm ChangeWave Research—then you indeed *should* be expecting to benefit greatly from the "Next Great Bull Market."

How on earth can one make such a statement?

Because while the developed world—the United States, Europe, Australia, and Canada—were imploding under a wall of incredibly bad investments in incredibly overvalued mortgage and debt securities that existed under the rubric of "sub-prime mortgages" and "collateralized debt obligations" et al.—there was some pretty amazing stuff going on in the emerging economies of the rest of the world.

Hundreds of millions of citizens were lifted out of one dollar-a-day poverty. Hundreds of millions—in China, in India, in Brazil, in other Asian countries—even old-line Communists in Russia.

Put together into a cohort of "new middle class," an entire new civilization was born to the world while our "economy on steroids" boomed and then historically crapped out.

Five hundred million-plus new middle class consumers now have the same dream our parents had and fought for—a sustainably prosperous life for themselves and their children. Hundreds of millions of people all over the world wake up every day dedicated to getting real roofs over their heads, real education for their children, some extra cash to travel and see the world, watch high-definition TVs, and soon have family cars.

Imagine 500 million people moving from 1950s-style America or post-war Europe to the twenty-first century—and skipping the 1980s and 90s!

In sheer numbers the ascension of the New World Middle Class has the greatest impact on our new world economy than *whatever* happens in the next 3, 6, or 12 months in the United States or Europe.

Now look: In a $50 trillion-plus world GDP, the United States *still* creates and consumes 25 percent. Europe, for all its "socialist democrat" sclerosis, is still a 300-million-block of consumers and manufacturers that account for 20 percent of the world GDP.

But when it comes to growth, the emerging giants account for 80 percent of GDP growth in the last 10 years.

And *that*, my friends, is the investment game we will play in the twenty-first century—slicing and dicing up that developing and emerging country growth.

As we start to recover from the greatest recession since the Great Depression, the developed world must face what I will euphemistically call the "Great Restructuring."

It's a polite way to say that after a 15-year economic party, the hangover is brutal and will take *years* to recover from. When we do, we will have a more sustainable economy, and hopefully one that has learned a lesson or two about the horrors of debt-fueled faux prosperity.

But while we take the bitter and painful medicine of the "Great Restructuring," here is what the emerging world is doing: *growing* like an economic cancer U.S. 2010 GDP growth, *less* than 2.5 percent U.S., 1 percent Europe, 8 percent China, and 6 percent BRICs.

- U.S. consumer GDP: back to 66 percent GDP versus 72 percent in 2006.
- Household savings rate: 5 to 7 percent versus 1 to −2 percent in 2001 to 2007.
- Home equity extraction: $90 to $125 billion versus $650 billion in 2006.
- Variable pay contraction: top 10 percent earners down at 30 percent from 2006 levels.
- Top 10 percent of U.S. earners produce 75 percent of *taxable* income.
- Household net worth top 20 percent: down 45 percent from 2007 peak.

Meanwhile . . .

The United States has succeeded in its great historic mission: to globalize the world's economies.

The investment world *is* now different from what it has ever been.

- In the last 10 years, the Internet revolution accelerated this transfer of knowledge and power exponentially—mostly for the good of the world.
- The share of people living on one dollar a day has plummeted from 40 percent in 1981 to 18 percent in 2004 and is estimated to drop to 12 percent by 2015.
- The global economy has more than doubled in size over the last 15 years and is now approaching $54 trillion!
- Global trade has grown by 133 percent in the same period.
- One hundred and twenty-five counties have averaged over 4 percent GDP growth for the last five years—including 20 African countries.
- Eighty percent of world GDP growth for the last five years has come from the BRICs.

In short, the Next Great Bull Market is going to come from the companies and industries in countries that best figure out how to feed, clothe, house, entertain, employ, and provide modern health care to the Great New World Middle Class.

If the United States ever gets serious again about creating an environment that promotes capitalism and entrepreneurism, *we* may even get back to over 3 percent growth rates. (Okay, a guy can have a dream, can't he?)

So welcome to the Next Great Bull Market.

It will *not* be a buy-and-hold market because by definition there will be booms and busts. It *will* be a market where trillions of dollars in new wealth will be created from the high-value, high-growth industries of the twenty-first century, not the past.

Matt has done a great job in giving you a primer on how to grow *your* wealth in this new environement.

Just promise me you won't give it all back this time, okay?

Tobin Smith, Chairman & CEO
ChangeWave Capital LLC

Preface

The basis for this book was established even before the 2008 recession began to send stocks into a bear market. It just so happens that the bear market created one of the most amazing buying opportunities of the last hundred years. Stocks have fallen to levels that investors have only dreamed about and it is now time to take advantage of bargain basement prices and prepare for the Next Great Bull Market.

This book has something to offer anyone who has money invested in the stock market or plans on investing at some point in the future. The nimble day trader will find fresh and exciting stock ideas that they may have overlooked in the past. The active investor who takes a long-term approach will have his eyes opened to investment themes such as lithium that is used for the new electric cars. The active investor will eventually read about the next big thing, but by then it will be too late to make money off the idea. I introduce a number of ideas in this book that can create long-term investment opportunities for any portfolio.

I expect the majority of readers are weekend investors who look at their statements when the market is moving higher, but in 2008 put their unopened portfolio statements right into the filing cabinet. It is human nature to get discouraged with investing as the stock market falls to new lows. Unfortunately for many, that is the best time to buy stocks for the long term. After reading this book, investors will take a new perspective on what took place in 2008 and 2009 and realize the bear market is a buying opportunity that will result in huge profits for those willing to go against the crowd and buy when stocks are low.

The body of the book is dedicated to several major investment themes I feel will lead the Next Great Bull Market. The themes range from the popular to sectors that Wall Street has yet to embrace. Wouldn't you like to be in the first wave of investors before the big money begins pushing the stocks higher? My goal was to discuss a range of themes because I believe both types of investments will flourish when the bull market begins.

What differentiates this book from many others that concentrate on investment themes is my willingness to offer specific investments for each theme. A number of authors and investment advisers have great macro-investment themes regarding how to invest. At the end of the day, however, when the time comes to pick individual stocks and make money for readers and clients, they fail.

There are over 50 individual stock and ETF ideas throughout the book for investors who would like to pursue investing in a theme they believe will be profitable in the future. I cannot guarantee each investment idea in this book, but after extensive research, I have included what I feel are the best of the best for smart investors to consider.

During the 1982 to 2000 bull market, the S&P 500 increased its value by 15 times. I am sure anyone in the market during that amazing time made money, however they kept up with the market or beat the market. My goal is not to simply follow the market, but rather beat the performance of the market with what I consider less risk. How do I accomplish this? I call it *conversification*. It is a mix between concentrating on sectors I believe will outperform and diversification throughout the top-rated sectors.

I explain conversification in more detail in Chapter 14. A quick example, however, will get you thinking in the right frame of mind before delving into the book. One of the investment themes in the book has to do with water turning into a commodity that will be very profitable during the Next Great Bull Market. Your portfolio should concentrate on water investments, but at the same time diversify within the sector. To accomplish this diversification, an investor can spread the money dedicated to water investments into water utilities, water infrastructure stocks, and landowners with large amounts of watershed. The end result is a concentrated investment approach that is not reliant on one niche area, and diversification is thereby created.

I believe the new investment strategies, along with specific investment recommendations in this book, can make you a successful investor in the years ahead. If there is one thing I want you take away from the book, it's that money can be made in the stock market and the end of investing is not here, nor will it occur anytime in the near future. When everyone is doubting the rewards of investing is the exact time you should be putting more money into the stock market.

By thinking outside the box, an investor increases the probability of making money by an astronomical amount. When an investor follows the crowd and bases a new purchase on the cover of a magazine, the rate of success is well below average. The big moves have already been made when the stock has made the cover. In this book, I think outside the box to attempt to identify the stocks that will be featured by the national media. Once everyone jumps on the lithium bandwagon, it is too late to make the big money and that is why you will hear about it in this book first!

Just a quick note on the media before I allow you to jump into the first chapter. Yes, you can consider me a member of the financial media with television spots several times per week, but in my mind I am still an investment adviser who thinks independently. That said, the majority of people who work for financial networks are paid to generate ratings, and how do you get ratings? Well, of course, by either promoting the extremes on both the bullish and bearish sides. With this in mind, please do not base your investment decisions on what you hear on television or read in the newspaper. You are obviously smarter than that because you are reading this book and attempting to learn how to make money on your own.

In conclusion, I thank you for taking the time to read this, my second book. I have 100 percent faith that it will be a learning experience that will be fun along the way. As always, happy investing and may profits rain down upon you.

Acknowledgments

I wish to give my thanks to John Wiley & Sons for helping facilitate my second book. I wish in particular to express my gratitude to Kevin Commins and Meg Freeborn for their hard work on helping me make this book one I am very proud to put my name on to. I also want to thank the amazing people of Fox News Channel and Fox Business Network for their support of my books and for allowing me to share my market thoughts with the world.

From Day One of my career in finance, there have been people along the way who have supported me and believed in what I was trying to accomplish. They range from old bosses to my first clients at Penn Financial Group to my loyal subscribers of *The ETF Bulletin* newsletter. There are two people in particular whom I wish to thank here—thanks to Mike Quaresimo and Mark Whistler for being early influences in my investment career.

This book was based on thought and ideas that have been accumulated over the years and I wish to thank my family for their support along the way. In particular, I wish to thank my lovely wife Marsha for her patience and encouragement during the writing of this book.

Chapter 1

Welcome to the New Global Economy

W hen scholars look back at the current global situation they will pinpoint the year 2007 as the year the new global economy was created. Not only because the U.S. and most global stock markets ended a bull market and began a downturn that was rivaled only by the Great Depression of the 1930s, but also because it brought to light a major global shift in the way the economy, stock market, and basic everyday living has been altered. After the global recession that many felt was almost a depression, we now look at the world in a different manner. Even more important for you as a reader of this book is how investing in the global stock market changed and what you need to know to take advantage of one of the greatest buying opportunities in recent history.

I introduce a number of major investment themes in the pages to come that will take advantage of the new global economy. The paradigm shift in the way investors must now approach investing has reached the mainstream media, however few have realized what exactly it entails. I explain how the recession and subsequent changes to the global land-scape have affected investment strategies that have worked in the past. The key word in that sentence is past; just because you were able to buy a stock and hold it for decades in the past, does not mean it will work in the future.

As a matter of fact, there is a section later in this chapter that breaks down the old buy-and-hold strategy and introduces a new variation. The days of buying the stock of the biggest names on Wall Street and riding the ups and downs is over. It is clear the ups and down will occur, but the end result that involves the stock always moving higher over time is no longer a sure thing. Watching companies such as Lehman Brothers, Bear Stearns, and General Motors disappear within a couple years of each other was the much needed wake-up call for what I call lazy investors.

Recession = Opportunity

During the 2008–2009 recession, it was not uncommon for individual stocks to lose 80 percent of their market capitalization in a matter of months. Profit that took investors years, if not a decade or more, to realize was gone in a blink of an eye. Investors saw their retirement accounts cut in half in 12 months and naturally began to panic as talk of another Great Depression was making its way through the media. When the market is hitting highs, all the talking heads blab about is how stocks will never pull back. The exact opposite occurs during a bear market, and just as people overreact during a bull market, they overreact even more dramatically during a sell-off.

In simple terms, the selling begets selling and there was a point in time during the fourth quarter of 2008 when it was difficult to find anyone interested in buying stocks. The mass panic sent the U.S. stock market to its lowest level in a decade and the buy-and-hold strategy was beginning to be questioned by investors. Even active investors who attempt to time the market using technical and fundamental analysis were throwing in the towel as they watched their accounts plummet at a pace more rapid than the 2000 technology bubble.

The early 2000s sell-off had sent the S&P 500 lower by approximately 50 percent over a three-year period. From the top in late 2007, the S&P 500 fell 50 percent in a matter of one year. The swift magnitude of the sell-off that occurred during the most recent bear market is a reason investors were so shell-shocked. And the selling did not end there; by the time the index bottomed in March 2009 the damage was at 57 percent.

Vulture Investing

A vulture is a scavenger bird that feeds mainly on the carcasses of dead animals. Vulture investors are similar in that they prey on stocks that are thought by many to be dead. The goal of a vulture investor is to swoop down and pick up beaten-down stocks from the carnage. Bear markets and recessions have triggered feasting frenzies for vulture investors, and the most recent scenario was no different. Even Warren Buffett, the largest shareholder of Berkshire Hathaway (NYSE: BRK-A) and one of the greatest investors of all time, turned into a vulture in 2008. The Oracle of Omaha traded in his value investing playbook and transformed into a vulture investor as opportunities arose in the financial sector he could not pass up.

From the high in early 2000 to the low in 2002, the NASDAQ Composite fell a remarkable 78 percent. Along the way, many of the once mega-cap technology stocks that made up the index either disappeared or were priced for certain bankruptcy. This is when vulture investors are at their best. They realize Wall Street has priced a number of stocks for future bankruptcy and the goal of the vulture investor is to find the precious gems among the carnage.

Internet company Akamai Technologies (NASDAQ: AKAM) fell from a high of more than $340 per share in early 2000 to a low of 56 cents in October 2002. A loss of 99.87 percent of its value is another way of saying goodbye to Akamai stock forever. But, vulture investors who were able to sift through the carnage and find the stock for less than one dollar and look at the future of the company were rewarded. Over the next four years, the price of Akamai's stock gained over 7,000 percent and a mere $5,000 investment at $1 per share would have netted you over a quarter of a million dollars (see Figure 1.1).

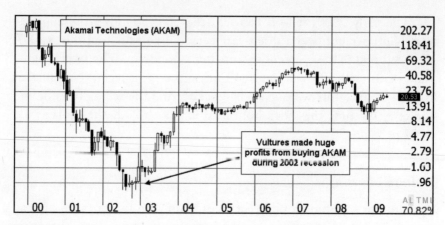

Figure 1.1   Vultures Feasted on Akamai Technologies in 2002 under $1
SOURCE: TeleChart2007® or StockFinder® chart, courtesy of Worden Brothers, Inc.

Maybe you never heard of Akamai or the company Research in Motion, which was not likely a household name in 2002. A few years have passed and Research in Motion (NASDAQ: RIMM) is one of the hot stocks once again as the maker of the BlackBerry (also known as the CrackBerry). It traded as low as $1.39 per share in 2002 before the vultures feasted on the beaten-down shares. The price for one share of Research in Motion skyrocketed within six years to nearly $150. The vultures who did their homework, took some above-average extra risk, and practiced patience, are now reaping the benefits of owning a part of one of the leading makers of smartphones in the world (see Figure 1.2).

As mentioned earlier, even Warren Buffett took on the role of a vulture investor in 2008 and 2009 when he began picking up shares of beaten down financial stocks such as Goldman Sachs (NYSE: GS), US Bancorp (NYSE: USB), and Wells Fargo (NYSE: WFC). Goldman Sachs was not trading at the bankruptcy levels as the previous examples, though the stock had fallen from $250 per share down to $47 in just over 12 months. Wells Fargo and US Bancorp both fell into the single digits and at one point in early 2009 it felt as if all major banks and investment firms would disappear.

I myself was a vulture with my personal money for a very short period of time in November of 2008. Citigroup (NYSE: C) fell to a fresh 16-year low on November 21, 2008, and hit a low of $3.05 intra-day. It happened to be a Friday, and of course there were all types of

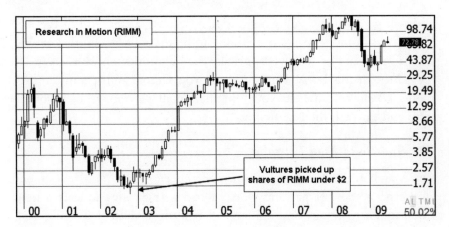

Figure 1.2 Research in Motion rises on the popularity of the BlackBerry
SOURCE: TeleChart2007® or StockFinder® chart, courtesy of Worden Brothers, Inc.

rumors about a government bailout or even bankruptcy over the weekend. I did not think that was the case and bought shares of Citigroup at $4.02 per share. The next Monday the stock opened at $6.12 and I quickly sold at $6.00 for a profit of nearly 50 percent. Over the next two weeks, the stock went as high as $9 and in early March 2009 traded as low as 99 cents before finding a bottom.

Granted, I was a short-term vulture, but I saw a dead stock lying on Wall Street and felt it was good enough to nibble at. A little luck never hurt either and I was able to bank a large, short-term profit. Another situation I can remember like it was yesterday was sitting in the studio for the Fox Business Network on March 4, 2009, with anchor Tracy Byrnes. We were on a commercial break and I looked at her and said, "How can I not buy GE (General Electric) at $6"? One month later, GE doubled in price and as of May 2009, the stock has no intentions of ever going back to $6 again.

The GE situation was a case in which the vulture investor inside me saw the carnage, but did not have the fortitude to go with my investing instincts that have gotten me to where I am today. This *shoulda, woulda, coulda* attitude is one that most investors will harp on and will always talk about as the big fish they almost caught. I like to do this from time to time, but it really gets you nowhere and the more productive approach is to learn from it and move on. The next time a GE situation arises, I will not question my instinct and knowledge of the market and will go with the vulture inside me. Because, at the end of the day, 99 percent of investors are not willing to be the vulture and that is why such a small number of investors make the big money on Wall Street.

Through this book, I introduce to you sectors and specific investments I believe can help you join that small percentage of investors who end up with the big money.

The Andrew Jackson Portfolio

On March 6, 2009, when it appeared the economic and investment landscape could not get any worse, I had a crazy idea to start a new stock index to track some of our fallen leaders. With that being said, I wanted to become a vulture and look for opportunities in companies Americans are familiar with. At the same time I wanted to make it fun, interesting, and relatable to all investors and noninvestors. The creation was the Andrew Jackson Portfolio.

The stock index was created with nine stocks that could be bought for less than $20. If you have not yet found the correlation, Andrew Jackson, the seventh president of the U.S., is featured on the $20 bill. For a total of $20, an investor would be able to buy one share of all the nine stocks that make up the Andrew Jackson Portfolio.

The original constituents of the portfolio are listed in Table 1.1 with their starting price on March 6, 2009.

Table 1.1 Andrew Jackson Portfolio

Stock	Symbol	Purchase Price 3/6/09 Closing Price
American International Group	AIG	$0.35
Advanced Micro Devices	AMD	$2.14
Bank of America	BAC	$3.14
Citigroup	C	$1.03
Eastman Kodak	EK	$2.24
Ford	F	$1.70
General Electric	GE	$7.06
General Motors	GM	$1.45
Office Depot	ODP	$0.68
Total Cost		**$19.79**

What began as part fun and part investment strategy took off like I would have never imagined. Within one day I was receiving interview requests from around the U.S. and the phones in the office did not stop ringing with people wanting to send me a $20 bill! Unfortunately I could not do that for them, but offered up my assistance to get them on the right path. Within two months the Andrew Jackson Portfolio was up over 170 percent!

When the portfolio was created there was the thought that one if not more of the stocks could file bankruptcy and leave the holder of that stock with nothing more than frown on their face. I was also right in that thinking because a few months later General Motors filed for bankruptcy. As of July 2009 it does not appear that the remaining eight stocks are in danger of filing for bankruptcy, although AIG does have some major issues remaining. As of August 6, 2009, exactly five months after the portfolio was created, the gain had ballooned to 184 percent even when with taking into consideration the General Motors bankruptcy.

Sometime you are not trying to be a vulture and you are. Keep in mind that when the situation in the investment world or in life in general appear to be at their worst, it is most likely the bottom and investors need to turn positive and begin thinking positive. What that means in the investment world is buy, buy, buy!

The Train Has Not Left the Station

On March 9, 2009, the S&P 500 hit an intraday low of 666, the lowest levels since 1996. The market found its bottom on that day and began a rally that caught nearly everyone on Wall Street by surprise. The doom and gloom was in full force during the first week of March and no one was crazy enough to jump in front of the large short sellers pushing stocks lower. But just when you think there is no end in sight to the selling, the market surprises everyone and does the exact opposite. The short sellers were forced to cover their short positions and a massive short squeeze occurred in the following weeks.

The S&P 500 gained more than 37 percent over the next two months and it appeared that the lows of March would be the bottom of the bear market. Most individual investors were selling stock in February and March and or the most part gave up on investing. But after the parabolic rise of the market over the following two months, investors were once again lured back into stocks. The feeling among the majority of individual investors I deal with on a regular basis was one of great fear that they may miss the next bull market train.

It is a natural human emotion to want to buy when the market is going higher and sell when stocks are falling. That strategy is called trend investing, which is covered later in this chapter, and can be used in certain market situations. To be successful using a trend investing strategy, however, an investor must limit her emotions when making decisions. Keeping your emotions in check is something that is much easier said than done.

When this book was getting ready to go to print, the market was well off the lows of March 2009 and investors' confidence had turned dramatically bullish. The consumer confidence reading, as reported by The Conference Board, moved up to 54.9 in May from a low of 25.3 in February. Keep in mind this reading is based on a survey of only 5,000 households, so we have to take it for what it is worth. That being said, the big jump from February is a move that cannot be ignored and is likely tied to the strong performance of the stock market in March and April.

The great improvement of the consumer confidence number and my own unscientific study of my clients and subscribers indicate investors have made a reversal from extremely negative to somewhere between hopeful and positive. What is amazing about the drastic change is that it took less than three months for investors to quickly forget about multi-year lows and, more important, the fear they felt. For months, I felt more like a cross between a shrink and a counselor on a suicide hotline than an investment adviser. I can honestly say that I have never experienced anything like it and hopefully will not have to deal with such fear again—it was mentally draining. At one point, I was on the verge of panicking along with the masses; thankfully, I was able to separate the emotion from my investment decisions for my clients.

Now is time to tie in the great reversal in consumer sentiment with the train analogy. The reason the consumer confidence spiked is that as quickly as investors are willing to jump off the train, they want to climb back on with the first sign of positive news. The problem occurs because investors make knee-jerk decisions when jumping off the train and do the same when trying to get back into the market. Putting cash back into the stock market is not a decision that should be taken lightly and needs to have concrete evidence behind the decision. The feeling I had in mid-May was that of euphoria; investors were beginning to worry that the train had left the station and the next train may never arrive. They were, and are, wrong!

Trend Investing

In the world of investments, the word *trend* can be defined in various ways, depending on whom you ask. To the day trader, a trend is how a stock is moving over the last few hours. A swing trader may view a trend as the direction in which the market or a stock is moving over a longer period such as a week or two. The average investor, when asked to define a trend, looks at the market as a whole and will often go along with past performance over the last year, if not longer.

Within the world of investing, a trend can be defined as the general direction of a stock or the overall market. The time frame, as mentioned before, will vary according to whom you ask and what their investment goals are. I focus throughout this book on trends that will have a massive impact on society as a whole, over a significant period of time. Because of the effect long-term trends will have on the world, there will be specific investment themes that will benefit. Ultimately, once you have finished reading this book, you will have a sufficient knowledge of the trends I believe will alter the way we all live in the future and, more importantly, how to profit from the changes.

The majority of investors, whether they will admit it or know it, invest in trends every day. Buying shares of Apple (NYSE: AAPL) a few years ago because you loved the iPod when it was introduced and felt that everyone would eventually be rocking out with the tiny music machine is an example of trend investing. The purchase of Apple covered several investment themes, such as mobile electronics and the growth of the consumer (see Figure 1.3).

At the time of the iPod introduction, the trend was for the U.S. consumer to spend above and beyond his means, and all disposable income was earmarked for discretionary spending. It is clear that an

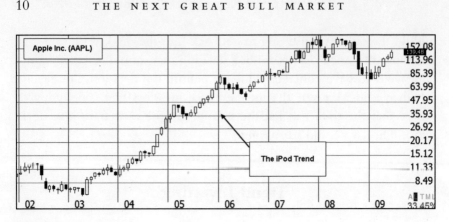

Figure 1.3   Apple Inc.
SOURCE: TeleChart2007® or StockFinder® chart, courtesy of Worden Brothers, Inc.

iPod is not a necessity (even though to some it may be) and therefore with an attractive price point would become a major success. Then there is the product itself, which was compact and very mobile for the user who is always on the move. By making the iPod small in size, it became the new face of mobile electronics.

The growth of the consumer and the mobile electronics trends remain in play, but they are getting closer to maturity as far as investment opportunities are concerned.

Buy and Hold versus Buy and Ignore

The buy-and-hold theory has been the core investment strategy for most readers of this book; that is, until now. After finishing the book you will realize the buy-and-hold strategy was, in reality, a buy-and-ignore strategy. When a new stock is purchased for the long term, it does not mean you should hold the stock for all eternity. For buy-and-ignore investors, a stock is never sold under any circumstance. The company may change management, alter its business model, have to defend itself against a lawsuit, or even see its stock price fall 80 percent. All of these situations are okay for the buy-and-ignore investor because the stock was purchased as a long-term investment.

I would wager that everyone has at one point in time fallen victim to the buy-and-ignore trap. Even the best of companies that no one in the investment community or beyond would ever imagine disappearing have done just that. Bethlehem Steel, once a powerful force in our nation and abroad, was a Dow Jones Industrial Average component until the early 1990s. Many elderly investors owned shares of Bethlehem Steel, including my grandfather who worked at the company, and never imagined the once-thriving steel company's stock price would fall to zero.

For a more recent example, we can turn to a company that has been at the forefront of automobile production in the United States for decades, General Motors (GM). An investor could have bought GM in 1984 for $25 per share and 25 years later that same share of GM could fetch you just over one dollar as it trades on the Pink Sheets and the company is in bankruptcy. The common shares of GM will be eventually deemed worthless and shareholders will be left with a stock certificate that is merely a memento of the past. That is a loss of over 95 percent of your investment over a 25-year time as of June 2009, and if shareholders refuse to sell, it will be a 100 percent loss. To keep things in perspective, the S&P 500 Index gained 500 percent during the same period. In Figure 1.4, the performance of GM is compared with that of the S&P 500 Index over a 5-year period through May 2009; the difference in performance is clearly evident. Ignoring GM's many missteps and failures in hopes the company would turn it around over the long term was simply a lazy investor ignoring the facts and falling asleep at the proverbial wheel.

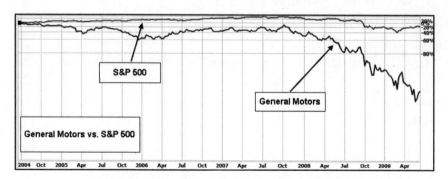

Figure 1.4   General Motors versus S&P 500 Index from 2004 to 2009
SOURCE: TeleChart2007® or StockFinder® chart, courtesy of Worden Brothers, Inc.

Bethlehem Steel and General Motors are not the only two former corporate leaders to fall from grace and wipe out fortunes for the individual investors who bought for the long term. And they will not be the last! You are presented with investment ideas throughout this book that I believe have the potential to outperform its peers over the coming decade. That would be considered a buy-and-hold strategy by many, including myself. However, I by no means am condoning a buy-and-ignore strategy for any investment discussed here. After what occurred in 2008 during the financial crisis, all investors should now realize that buy-and-ignore is a flawed strategy right along with the business model of GM—and we know where that has taken GM.

What better way to analyze the buy-and-ignore approach than to look at a chart of the Dow going back to the early twentieth century. Figure 1.5 is a yearly chart of the Dow Jones Industrial Average over the last 90 years. Buying into the index in 1916 at 80 would have returned an investor over 10,000 percent on her money even after the pullback from the 2007 high. If you were investing in 1916, there is a good chance you are no longer reading books, so even though the number had to be mentioned, investing for 90 years is not realistic.

The buy-and-ignore strategy that results in your investment disappearing is not limited to old industrial companies that have outlived their stay. I can name a long list of technology companies that were

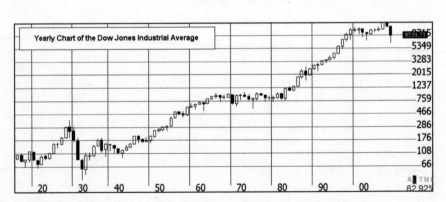

Figure 1.5   Dow Jones Industrial Average: If You Have 90 Years, Simply Buy and Hold

SOURCE: TeleChart2007® or StockFinder® chart, courtesy of Worden Brothers, Inc.

once high flyers only to have their stock certificates worth nothing more than scrap paper. Do you remember Pets.Com and their commercials with the talking dog puppet? Or how about behemoths such as WorldCom, which were destroyed by greed and corruption? Unfortunately, the list is too long for this book, but I think the point is made and you realize that companies in all sectors can result in a final investment value of zero.

Even the financial companies based on Wall Street that are in the middle of the whole game are susceptible to the same tragic ending. If you do not believe me, just ask investors of Bear Stearns or Lehman Brothers. The two behemoths of Wall Street that were household names around the globe succumbed to the recession of 2008 and the end result was shareholders holding nothing more than fancy, but worthless, stock certificates.

To give you a visual of how quickly a stock can go from a darling on Wall Street to a forgotten stock, the charts of both stocks are featured in Figures 1.6 and 1.7.

Simply put, the buy-and-hold (ignore) theme exists because it makes the job of your investment adviser much easier and allows them more

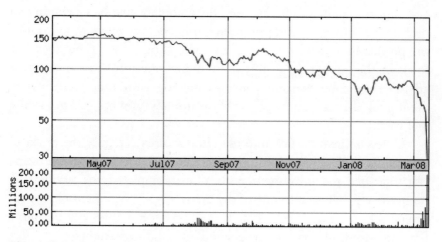

Figure 1.6 Bear Stearns: From Triple Digits to $2 Stock in Months
SOURCE: Yahoo! Finance. Reproduced with permission of Yahoo! Inc. ©2009 by Yahoo! Inc. YAHOO! and the YAHOO! logo are trademarks of Yahoo! Inc.

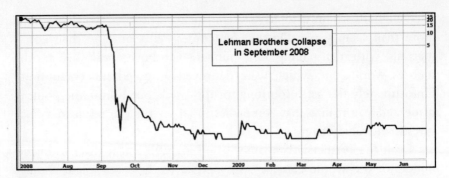

Figure 1.7   Lehman Brothers Collapses to Bankruptcy in September 2008
SOURCE: TeleChart2007® or StockFinder® chart, courtesy of Worden Brothers, Inc.

time on the golf course. Just joking—sorta. In all honesty, the strategy is often used to mask the inability of the majority of advisers to beat the market and the lack of knowledge of the stock market. On an ongoing basis, I am amazed at the lack of general stock market knowledge among advisers who work at major investment firms. You must remember that when you deal with a so-called investment adviser at a company like Edward Jones, or even Ameriprise (sorry for picking on them, but I know from experience), their number one job is to produce for the company.

Unfortunately, producing for the company involves bringing in more assets and generating more income. The key element left out of the producing equation is the client, who should be the number one focus of the adviser. In reality, the number one job of an investment adviser should be assisting you in achieving your long-term investment goals. But as you know, reality is not always what you get in the real world.

Unless an investor falls into the ultra-wealthy category, the protocol is to go through the motions of asking personal questions to determine risk tolerance and investment goals. Once completed, the adviser will lump the new client into one of the prepackaged investment plans with several other clients. If you agree that all investors can be split up into a few categories, all I have to say is good luck and stop reading.

I happen to strongly disagree, and I have built my firm on the premise that each investor is like a snowflake, similar, yet very different.

By taking this route, it would be much easier for me to implement the buy-and-ignore strategy because it would result in a smaller workload. But I also like to sleep at night knowing I am helping my clients reach their ultimate investment goal. I do not offer sure things or strategies that always make money; by offering a hands-on approach that adapts to the changing market environment, however, my clients are one step ahead of their peers.

We take a look in Chapter 2 at the recent recession and how the world ended up in one of the biggest economic slowdowns in decades. Along with a timeline of the 2008–2009 recession, the chapter also delves into several past recessions for a comparison to the most recent recession. I also feel it is imperative to have some knowledge of history when attempting to predict the future in the world of investing. The next chapter is very informative and interesting and it puts the recent slowdown in perspective.

Chapter 2

Recessions that Changed the World

Recessions are a normal event that occurs within a normal economic cycle and are a situation that both investors and consumers must deal with numerous times throughout their lives. The major difference between recessions is the cause—or the event—that triggers the slowdown of the economic cycle and eventually the fall of the stock market. I take a look in this chapter at what sent the United States into its worst recession since the Great Depression as well as analyze and compare the most recent recession with past recessions. The similarities and differences are compelling and will help investors understand that the world is not coming to an end and that doomsday theorists are simply out for good press and headlines.

Contributing Factors of the Recent Recession

The first quarter of negative growth in the United States during the recent recession was the third quarter of 2008, at which time the gross domestic product (GDP) fell by 0.5 percent. The pace of decline increased in the fourth quarter and first quarter of 2009. The stock market hit a high in October 2007. The housing bubble began to burst in 2006. Many financial analysts, however, including myself, conclude that the cause of the recession was in the making years before any of the aforementioned events took place (see Figure 2.1).

There are differing opinions on how exactly the United States ended up in the middle of one of the most devastating recessions in recent history. It's my opinion that there are several contributing factors, including the following:

- Initiatives set forth by Clinton's presidential administration.
- Reckless lending practices.
- The housing bubble.
- Inadequate regulation and oversight by the Federal Reserve.
- Excessive monetary expansion.
- Rising commodity prices.

I discuss each factor in detail in this section before moving on to an in-depth analysis of the weeks and months that made up the recession that began in 2008.

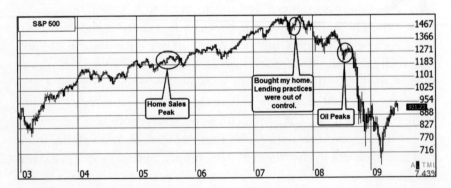

Figure 2.1 How We Got Here
SOURCE: TC2000 Charting Software and Penn Financial Group LLC.

The Clinton Years

Blaming President Bill Clinton for the 2008 recession sounds preposterous, but considering some of his actions while in office it is not a stretch from reality. The Clinton administration was attempting to lock up the lower and middle class vote for the Democratic Party and what better way to do that than to help them achieve the American dream of owning a home. The government began to urge Fannie Mae, the largest underwriter of subprime mortgages at the time, to expand mortgage loan availability among low and moderate income families, the majority of which were not financially ready to own a home, and even others who would never be in a position to buy a home and pay a mortgage.

Homeownership levels increased throughout the mid-to-late 1990s as the government concentrated on making the American dream a reality for more citizens. With the expansion of the American dream was a specific goal for minorities and citizens who were born outside of the United States. This is a great sound bite, and looks good on paper; the reality, however, is that not all U.S. residents can afford to own their own homes, and renters are needed to keep the housing market stable. The availability of loose credit was an added problem that made it easy for the unqualified borrower to receive a loan. While I cannot place 100 percent of the blame on the Clinton administration, they definitely set the wheel in motion for the blowup that occurred in 2008.

Reckless Lending Practices

Because of government pressure and greed by the lenders and borrowers, the lending business moved into a dangerous situation. As long as you had a heartbeat (and sometimes that was optional) there was a mortgage program available for you, and the house of your dreams was only 50 signatures away. I know from experience because I bought a new home in August 2007. Just before the subprime crisis began I was searching for a mortgage on a home in the New York metropolitan area. After finding a perfect home and qualifying for a loan, the mortgage broker made me aware that I could get a house with a few extra bedrooms at twice the cost by borrowing more money. Luckily, I was smart enough to cordially decline and bought the original home. This was not the case for many unsuspecting and greedy home buyers who felt home values would continue to rise. Why not buy as much house as possible was the governing idea.

When the next-door neighbor, a grade school teacher, quit her job to buy and sell homes (referred to as flipping), the real estate bubble was upon us and was about to burst at any time. The situation was not much different from the tech bubble of 2000 when people with solid, high-paying jobs decided to become day traders and lost everything they had. Did you feel sorry for the newbie day traders who had to start over because they lost their money? No, and we should not be sulking for the wannabe real estate moguls who were greedy and took advantage of the reckless lending practices.

The Housing Bubble

In 2005, *The Economist* magazine wrote, "The worldwide rise in house prices is the biggest bubble in history." Homeowners at the time were blinded by the amount of money they could get out of their house with a home equity loan to realize what was taking place. In March 2005, home sales topped out in the United States at 127,000 units (not seasonally adjusted), according to U.S. government census statistics. The original decline was not dramatic, but over the next few years and into 2009, the rate of deceleration increased. In January 2009, the number had fallen to 24,000, the lowest nonseasonally adjusted number since December 1974, which also saw 24,000 units sold. (See Figure 2.2.)

The number of units sold increased in February 2009 to 29,000 units, and in March, the amount rose again to 33,000. April saw a leveling off, as it remained unchanged from March. The good news is that the deceleration has slowed as of June 2009; there is a silver lining for homeowners and anyone affected by home prices, which is, for the most part, everyone.

Inadequate Regulation and Oversight by the Federal Reserve

The lack of adequate regulation can be traced back to former Federal Reserve chairman Alan Greenspan's lack of regulation of certain derivatives, especially the mortgage-backed securities that led to the collapse

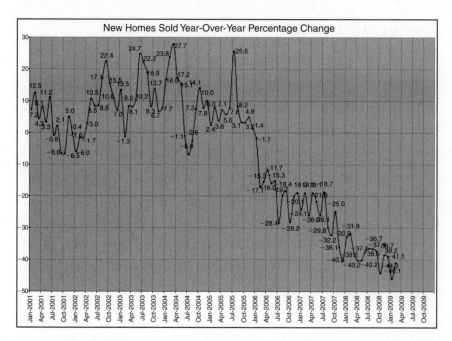

Figure 2.2 The Rise and Fall of Home Sales
SOURCE: U.S. Government Census.

of the financial markets in 2007. The creation of unique and complex financial instruments that were not regulated eventually led to the demise of the derivatives market. Even though I do place some of the blame on Greenspan, he cannot be the scapegoat because there were many others who were guilty of not doing their jobs. Please see the SEC, CTFC, NASD, and a host of other acronyms.

I am not suggesting the government get its hands into the everyday workings of every firm, but if it did do its job correctly, there would have been red flags that should have been investigated. Regulatory agencies in the past have done nothing more than punish those who are following the stringent rules and letting the unethical and, frankly, smarter individuals sidestep the regulations. Again, not to get too down on the agencies, because even the firms that invented the complex credit default swaps and collateralized debt obligations were caught off guard when the environment changed. In hindsight, better regulation going back to the time of Greenspan through the Bernanke years would have helped stave off the recession.

Excessive Monetary Expansion

When the 2000 recession and the tech bubble ripped through the U.S. economy and Wall Street, there was only one move in the mind of Alan Greenspan—lower interest rates. The lowering of rates after the early 2000 recession created an environment for easy money that led to the beginning of the credit bubble that included loans to borrowers who did not deserve the money. Years later, the United States paid for the short-term thinking of Greenspan once again as the former Federal Reserve chairman was too fixated on ending the recession and did not correctly calculate the long-term risks.

Again, it is easy to put blame on others, but all signs points to Alan Greenspan as the conductor of the credit crisis train. Without Uncle Al at the helm, the growth that began after the 2000 recession may not have been as hot, but at the same time the subsequent credit crisis could have been averted.

Rising Commodity Prices

Oil made the headlines in 2008 as it crossed the $100 per barrel mark in February, but the real story was in July when the price nearly hit $150. Along with oil and other energy commodities spiking to highs, there was the rise in agriculture commodities that led to higher food costs at the grocery store. The price of corn spiked to an all-time high in mid-2008, a fourfold increase in less than three years. (See Figure 2.3.) Wheat was in a similar situation, hitting a historic high in early 2008, at a price that was four times greater than it was in 2005.

As prices for agricultural commodities increased, it was passed along to the consumer through higher prices on the shelves. The increase in the price of staples such as pasta and eggs rose at a rate that directly affected the budget of many low- and middle-income families. Combine a 100 percent increase in the cost to fill up the gas tank with higher prices to feed the family, and it was a perfect storm for consumers to slowdown their discretionary spending. Add in one more factor that was just discussed, falling home prices, and it caused consumers to close their wallets and dramatically rein in spending.

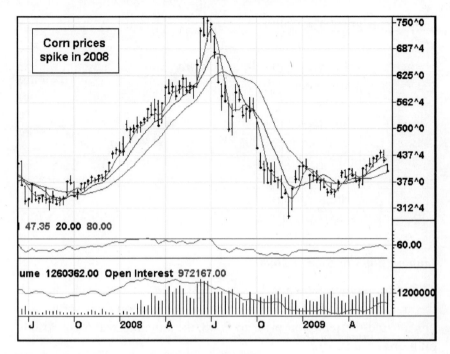

Figure 2.3 Corn Prices Spike in mid-2008
Source: TradingCharts.com.

The list of factors that contributed to the recent recession could go on and on, but no one really knows the true causes and that is not the point of this book. The goal is to help you make money in the Next Bull Market. To learn all we can from the recent recession, I'll break down it down by weeks and months. Consider this a lesson on the anatomy of a recession.

A Timeline of the 2008–2009 Recession

I believe it is important to look back on history as a tool to learn about the future, and not to dwell on what happened. That being said, I would like to take you through the recession, highlighting significant dates and events that helped shape the new global economy. (See Figure 2.4.)

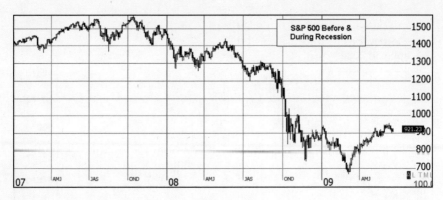

Figure 2.4   Recession Timeline: 2007–2009
SOURCE: TC2000 Charting Software and Penn Financial Group LLC.

January 2008 to August 2008

The chronological timeline begins in 2008 and it takes you through the middle of 2009. Even though there were secondary factors that precipitated the recession prior to 2008, the timeline will focus strictly on more recent events.

January 1, 2008: The market began the year on the defensive as stocks had been falling since October 2007. The Dow Jones Industrial Average, however, was able to finish with a gain of 6 percent in 2007.
January 22, 2008: The Federal Reserve lowered the Fed Funds rate by 75 basis points to 3.50 percent. The move by the Fed helped the market rally from the fresh one-year low it touched earlier in the session. The next 48 hours were bullish as the Dow Jones Industrial Average bounced from a low of 11,634 to close the next day at 12,270. The January low would hold until June.
January 24, 2008: The National Association of Realtors (NAR) announced that 2007 saw the largest drop in existing home sales in 25 years. This was not a big surprise considering the media coverage of the housing bubble that began in 2006.
January 30, 2008: Eight days after its most recent move, the Federal Reserve lowered the Fed Funds rate another 50 basis points to 3.00 percent. At this time, I was concerned the Federal Reserve and, in particular, chairman Ben Bernanke was using too much of the little ammunition left in the arsenal. Unfortunately, my thinking was correct.

February 20, 2008: Oil traded above $100 per barrel for the first time in history.

March 14, 2008: Bear Stearns shares continued to plummet as rumors on the street about a possible bankruptcy and heavy short selling took control. The company got Federal Reserve funding to help curb the falling stock price.

March 16, 2008: In a shocking development, JPMorgan Chase (NYSE: JPM) acquired Bear Stearns for $2 per share in a deal that helped them avoid bankruptcy. The Federal Reserve also threw in $30 billion to back any possible losses from Bear Stearns. The Friday before the takeover the market was down less than 2 percent and the Monday after the announcement, stocks were higher. Surprisingly, a two-month rally ensued after the announcement of Bear Stearns's demise. Many on Wall Street thought this was a one-time event, but as we saw in the months that followed, Bear Stearns was not alone.

March 18, 2008: The Federal Reserve lowered the Fed Funds rate by 75 basis points to 2.25 percent. Stocks cheered the move by Bernanke and his colleagues to the tune of a 3.5 percent gain, or 420 points.

April 30, 2008: The Fed Funds rates were lowered by another 25 basis points to 2.00 percent and the market was fairly muted as the major indexes were unchanged.

July 11, 2008: Oil peaked at $147.30 per barrel and the price for a gallon of gasoline was over $4 around most of the United States. Indymac Bank was placed into receivership of the FDIC and was the fourth-largest bank failure in the history of the United States. The Dow Jones Industrial Average fell 1.1 percent on this historic day.

September 2008

During September 2008, The TED Spread (the difference between interest rates offered on U.S. Treasury bills and Eurodollars), Treasury yields, and the dollar value of gold all set records. Russia falls 10 percent on one day, causing the stock exchange to halt trading. The United Kingdom, Australia, and the United States announced plans to ban short selling on specific financial stocks in some manner. The unemployment rate remained steady at 6.1 percent, the same as August. A total of 284,000 jobs were lost during the month.

September 7, 2008: Investors watch the shares of Fannie Mae (NYSE: FNM) and Freddie Mac (NYSE: FRE) fall over 80 percent in one day as the government guarantees up to $100 billion for each company to keep them out of bankruptcy. In so many words, the two government-linked companies were nationalized. Surprisingly, the S&P 500 rallies 2 percent on the news to close at 1267.

September 14, 2008: Bank of America (NYSE: BAC) bought out struggling Merrill Lynch and Company for $50 billion in what we later found out was a deal somewhat forced by the government. The purchase made Bank of America the largest retail brokerage firm.

September 15, 2008: Lehman Brothers filed for bankruptcy protection; the S&P 500 falls 4.7 percent and the SPDRs Financial ETF (NYSE: XLF) lost 9.7 percent. The filing ended the life of a company that had been in business for 158 years.

September 16, 2008: The two largest ratings agencies, Moody's and Standard and Poor's, downgraded American International Group (NYSE: AIG) credit and sent the stock tumbling. One day later, AIG received $85 billion from the government to avoid bankruptcy. The company completely unraveled in September, as shares of the massive insurer fell from $22.50 to $2 in a matter of weeks.

September 21, 2008: Goldman Sachs (GS) and Morgan Stanley (MS) received approval from the Federal Reserve to reclassify themselves as bank holding companies from investment banks. The move allowed the two firms to access the government's emergency loan fund.

September 25, 2008: Washington Mutual was seized by the Federal Deposit Insurance Corporation (FDIC) and its banking assets were later sold to JPMorgan Chase (NYSE: JPM) for $1.9 billion.

September 29, 2008: FDIC announced Citigroup would acquire the banking operations of Wachovia Bank. The Dow Jones Industrial Average closed the session down 777 points, its biggest one-day point loss in history. I watched the implosion on this historic day from a hotel room at the Four Seasons Hotel in Cairo. Hello, two straight days without sleep. Thank goodness for Egyptian coffee.

October 2008

In October 2008, the Baltic Dry Index, which measures the shipping rate for dry bulk goods around the world, fell by 50 percent in one week.

The unemployment rate rose to 6.5 percent, the highest since early 1994. A total of 240,000 jobs were lost in the month.

October 3, 2008: The House approved the already Senate-approved Emergency Economic Stabilization Act that was responsible for the creation of the infamous $700 billion Troubled Asset Relief Program (TARP). The backbone of the bill was the money that was set aside to purchase the assets of failing banks. To this day, the debate on TARP is alive and well and long after the recession is over, the TARP will be a topic for great discussion.

October 6, 2008: The Dow Jones Industrial Average fell below the psychological level of 10,000 for the first time since 2004. In the stock market, big round numbers are often viewed by investors as turning points. Falling below 10,000 was a breach of a number that many could relate to. At one point, the Dow was down by over 800 points before it rallied back to close lower by 369 points, or 3.6 percent.

October 8, 2008: The Federal Reserve lowered the Fed Funds rate by 50 basis points to 1.50 percent, part of a coordinated rate cut with other central banks around the world. The White House considered taking ownership stakes in private banks as part of the bailout plan. The Dow Jones Industrial Average had little reaction to the move losing only 2 percent.

October 9, 2008: The Dow continued its slide and fell below 9,000, three days after failing to hold at the 10,000 level. The loss of 678 points equated to a 7.3 percent drop for the index.

October 10, 2008: Wells Fargo (NYSE: WFC) won the battle for the assets of Wachovia. The ringing of the closing bell on this Friday also marked the worst week on record for the Dow Jones Industrial Average, losing 22.1 percent. The index was down 40 percent over the last year. Little did we know that the worst was yet to come.

October 14, 2008: The U.S. government announced it would use a portion of the $700 billion TARP funds to help struggling banks, and in turn, the government would take a small ownership stake in the participating companies. The first big whiff of socialism had just rolled into my office.

October 21, 2008: The Federal Reserve announced it would spend $540 billion in an effort to shore up the money market mutual funds that had been under pressure. The money would be used to buy short-term debt from the funds.

October 28, 2008: The Dow enjoyed its second largest point-gain ever, closing the day up 889 points, or 10.9 percent. Amazingly, it looked like a blip on the screen.

November 2008

Job losses for the month of November shot up to 533,000, the highest total since 1974. The unemployment rate also rose to 6.7 percent from a prior reading of 6.5 percent.

November 5, 2008: The day after Barack Obama won the U.S. presidential election, the stock market fell 5 percent from a one-month high set one day earlier. As of mid-June 2009, the index has yet to get back to the pre-election level. Is this a sign of how the market welcomes President Obama or just coincidence? I will let you answer that question so I do not anger any readers this early in the book with personal political views.

November 12, 2008: Treasury Secretary Paulson announced he would not use the remaining $410 billion of the TARP money to buy troubled assets, causing a major uproar from Washington D.C. and taxpayers.

November 13, 2008: The weekly number of new jobless claims soared to a seven-year high and, initially, the stock market did not take kindly to the news. By the end of the trading day, however, the Dow was up 6.7 percent. The rally was short-lived.

November 18, 2008: The heads of the Big Three automakers (General Motors, Ford, and Chrysler) flew to Washington D.C. to plead for bailout money for the struggling auto industry. The three executives flew in on private jets, which caused a major uproar.

November 19, 2008: Another milestone for the Dow Jones Industrial: the average is taken out as the index traded below 8,000 for the first time since 2003.

November 20, 2008: The U.S. stock market formed a short-term bottom as the CBOE Volatility Index (VIX) spiked to one of the highest readings on record, signaling a panic in investors. On the same day, the U.S. Dollar Index closed at its best level in two-and-a-half years. Please remember this inverse correlation between the U.S. dollar and the stock market.

November 23, 2008: The U.S. government secured $306 billion in loans at Citigroup (NYSE: C) and injected $20 billion in capital. The stock opened higher Monday morning and closed the day up 57 percent. (Side note: I bought shares of Citigroup at $4.02 on Friday and sold at $6.00 on Monday morning in anticipation of the government bailout and subsequent rally. It later reached $9.00 before falling back down.)

November 25, 2008: The Federal Reserve announced it would pledge another $800 billion to help stabilize the financial system; $600 billion would be used to buy mortgage bonds.

December 2008

The number of job losses continues to hit new multidecade records and the total hit 681,000 in December.

December 1, 2008: The National Bureau of Economic Research officially declared the U.S. economy had entered into a recession as far back as December 2007. After a five-day rally, the market was greeted by sellers that sent the Dow Jones Industrials lower by 7.7 percent. The five-day rally accounted for a 17 percent rally that temporarily put in a market bottom. According to the definition of a recession (two consecutive quarters of negative growth), a recession did not begin in 2007, but rather it was official after the fourth quarter of 2008. The U.S. GDP declined by 0.5 percent during the third quarter of 2008 and 6.3 percent in the fourth quarter. The first quarter of 2009 also saw negative growth (what an oxymoron) of 5.7 percent.

December 11, 2008: The FBI arrested Bernard Madoff, the man behind the most lucrative Ponzi scheme in the history of Wall Street. The estimates put the Madoff scheme at $50 billion, and since that time the mastermind pleaded guilty and is currently rotting in jail for the rest of his natural life. The Dow Jones Industrial Average was down over 2 percent on the news.

December 18, 2008: The average rate on a 30-year fixed mortgage fell to 5.19 percent, the lowest since April 1971. The drop can be attributed to the Federal Reserve buying into mortgage-backed securities. Over the next few months, the rate would fall below 5 percent before dramatically bouncing back up during the first week of June 2009.

December 19, 2008: The government announced it would help bail out yet another industry—the U.S. automakers. The White House offered $17.4 billion to Chrysler and General Motors in exchange for concessions. In hindsight, that was a great move by the government—not! Both companies would eventually file for bankruptcy protection in 2009.

December 31, 2008: The Dow Jones Industrial Average closed out 2008 as the worst in decades. The 36 percent loss was the worst on record since 1931, during the Great Depression.

January 2009

After a short-term pop to start the new year, stocks continued to move lower, just as they did in 2008. By the end of January, the Dow Jones Industrial Average was lower by 8.9 percent and the unemployment rate had risen to 7.9 percent, further dampening hopes of an economic recovery. A total of 598,000 jobs were lost during the month. Beginning in 2009, five of the seven largest economies in the world were in the midst of a recession, with only China and France surviving the slowdown. A minimal 0.1 percent increase in the third quarter has France on the outside, but will soon join its peers in recession.

January 13, 2009: Citigroup was back in the news, this time merging their brokerage unit with Morgan Stanley's (NYSE: MS) brokerage unit with MS holding a 51 percent stake in the joint venture.

January 28, 2009: The House approved an $819 billion economic stimulus package that President Obama believed would kickstart the economy. The Dow Jones Industrial Average surged 2.5 percent on the news.

January 29, 2009: The weekly jobless claims rose to the highest level since the Labor Department began keeping tabs on the number in 1967.

February 2009 to June 2009

February 4, 2009: Another step toward socialism as President Obama put a cap on the salary a senior executive could earn at a company that accepted TARP money.

February 17, 2009: President Obama signed into effect a $787 billion stimulus package. The Dow Jones Industrial Average fell 3.8 percent and was on the verge of hitting a fresh five-year low.

February 19, 2009: The Dow Jones Industrial Average broke the November low and was trading at the worst level in six years.

February 23, 2009: Both the S&P 500 and Dow Jones Industrial Average closed at the lowest level in a decade. There was still another 8 percent on the downside for stocks before a bottom was created.

March 6, 2009: The Dow Jones Industrial Average hit an intraday low of 6469, the lowest level since May 1997. The index was 55 percent off the October 2007 high. On the same day the S&P 500 hit its infamous low of 666. Surprisingly, the CBOE Volatility Index (VIX) closed at 49, well off the highs of October and November 2008.

March 10, 2009: Two trading days after the March low, the Dow Jones Industrial Average surged 5.8 percent, or 379 points, after Citigroup CEO Vikram Pandit wrote in a memo that the company was profitable through the first two months of 2009. The SPDRs Financial ETF (NYSE: XLF) gained 15 percent and Citigroup was up 38 percent.

March 23, 2009: The Dow Jones Industrial Average closed with a gain of 497 points, or 6.8 percent, and was trading at a fresh one-month high. The rally was led by news that the U.S. Treasury would buy close to a trillion dollars in bad bank assets. This was also the introduction of the "waste of time and effort" Public-Private Investment Program, known as PPIP.

June 12, 2009: The Dow Jones Industrial Average moved back into positive territory for the year after being down as much as 25 percent in early March. The 35 percent rally off the March low in three months had been running out of steam as the milestone was accomplished.

Comparing Past Recessions

History is just that—history. But I find it imperative to look back at history in an effort to better predict the future. Even though each recession is unique in nature, there will be specific patterns and similarities investors can capitalize on. The last five recessions before the most recent economic slowdown will be analyzed from an economic and investment view. The goal is to find recurring patterns that will lead to investment opportunities and better market timing for buying back into the market during a recession.

The 2001 Recession

The early 2000 recession was mild compared to the most recent recession and several others since the early 1970s. From the start of the recession in March 2001 through the official end in November 2001 the S&P 500 lost approximately 15 percent. From the peak of the market in March 2000 through the trough in September 2001 the S&P 500 lost 40 percent.

The unemployment rate hit a high in June 2003 at 6.3 percent, a very modest number for a recession. Because the indicator is often looked at as the lagging indicator, by the time unemployment spikes, the market is well off the lows. From September 2001, when the market bottomed, through June 2003, the S&P 500 gained 4 percent. Along the way, there was the 9/11 terrorist attacks and another major bear market that sent stocks lower before a turnaround occurred in late 2002 and early 2003. The market is typically up drastically from the recession market trough through the unemployment high. The reality is that the economy was close to a double dip recession in 2002, but it officially never registered the required numbers.

The early 2000s were known as the place in time when the bursting of the technology bubble and the end of an 18-year bull market occurred. An investor would have turned a $100,000 investment in 1982 into over $1.5 million by 2000 with a simple investment in the S&P 500 index. Unfortunately, the dart-throwing strategy of investing in the 1990s had to come to an end and it did just that in 2000 when irrational exuberance was responsible for bursting one of the greatest bubbles of all time.

The collapse of a number of once high-flying technology companies led to an increase in unemployment and a contraction in economic activity. Adding to the already fragile economy and stock market was the eruption of corporate scandals that rocked the world. From WorldCom to Enron to Tyco, corporate executives got caught up in the irrational

behavior of the bull market, and this resulted in illegal activity that
ruined both companies and individuals' lives. The lack of confidence in
corporate U.S. and Wall Street was a catalyst for investors to sell stocks
and rethink their investment strategies. An even more horrific event
took place on September 11, 2001, when foreign terrorists attacked the
United States. The attack was an eye-opening incident for Americans,
who now realized that safety at home is no longer guaranteed. The
panic of the attacks on top of the already fledgling stock market and
economy kept the stock market on the defensive for the next few years
until ultimately bottoming in 2002. (See Figure 2.5.)

Two major causes can be attributed for turning around the economy and, ultimately, the stock market. One is lower interest rates
and an accommodating Federal Reserve that helped spur on one of
the greatest real estate markets in history (and, as you already know,
this was also a catalyst for the 2009 recession). The second reason the
United States was able to turn around the economy was the resilience
of the American people. Some refer to it as being naive because of how
quickly U.S. residents can forget about the past and move on. The end
result was the S&P 500 doubling in the five years following the 2002
low before the next bubble burst.

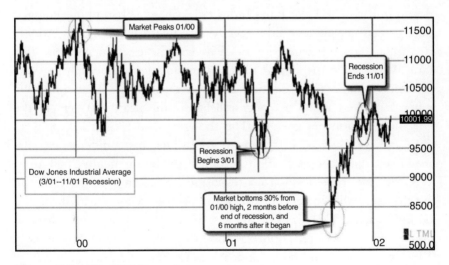

Figure 2.5   The 2001 Recession
SOURCE: TC2000 Charting Software and Penn Financial Group LLC.

The 1990–1991 Recession

The infamous savings and loan scandal rocked the United States in the early 1990s and sent the United States into a recession that lasted from July 1990 through March 1991. During that time the S&P 500 was able to gain 5 percent due to a massive rally that began in the fourth quarter of 1990 and carried on through March. From the peak in July 1990 through October 1990, the S&P 500 declined by 20 percent. The equity pullback was just enough to push the U.S. market into a recession, besting the 20 percent threshold. (See Figure 2.6.)

One year after the trough in the 1990–1991 recession, the S&P 500 was 29 percent higher; two years later, the index was up 38 percent. As a matter of fact the S&P 500 bottomed in 1990 and has not looked back since. The index moved from a low of 295 in 1990 to a high of 1552 10 years later, a return of more than 400 percent. Do you think investors were bullish in 1990 and 1991? No, the savings and loan crisis crushed consumer and investor confidence and buying stocks was not an option for most. Little did many know, but the crisis was the beginning of the next great bull market of the 1990s. Think in a similar fashion today and you will be a very happy and profitable investor a decade from now.

Some economists argue that the early 1990s recession was triggered three years earlier when Black Monday shook Wall Street like no other day in history. The Dow Jones Industrial Average fell an unprecedented 22.6 percent in one day and it took years to get back the losses. Adding to the savings and loan crisis of 1990 was the beginning of the first Gulf War, a spike in oil, and rising unemployment (especially on Wall Street). Unemployment continued to rise through the middle of 1992 when it peaked at 7.8 percent, well below the nearly 10 percent the current recession has risen to. The thoughts of a financial crisis were alive and well just as they were in 2008. The major difference is the media and how they are able to connect to the public. In 2008, most U.S. residents have access to a television or Internet connection and are therefore able to stay abreast of the ever-growing negativity in the business media. This was not the case in 1990, and the panic that has crept into investors in 2008 was subdued. The recession of the early 1990s was shorter and not as dramatic as the recent recession, but there are several similarities.

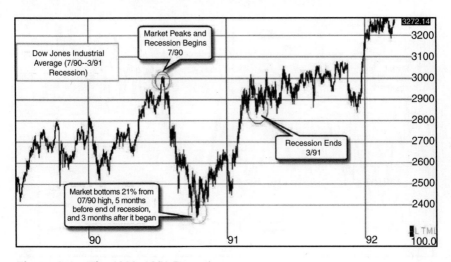

Figure 2.6 The 1990–1991 Recession
Source: TC2000 Charting Software and Penn Financial Group LLC.

The Early 1980s Recessions

There were two recessions in the early 1980s. The first began in January 1980 and lasted six months, through the end of June. The second recession began in July 1981 and lasted 22 months and ended at the beginning of November 1982. The economic slowdown can be attributed to the Iranian Revolution in 1979 and the tight monetary policy in the United States that was attempting to control skyrocketing inflation.

The Six-Month Recession of 1980

During the first recession, the S&P 500 was able to gain 6 percent even though it suffered a dramatic drop during the first quarter. From a high in mid-February 1980 to a low in late March, the S&P fell 22 percent and hit a new one-year low. From the low in March through the high in November 1980, the S&P 500 doubled in value; this move is similar to the one the S&P 500 experienced off the low in March 2009. (See Figure 2.7.) Unfortunately for the bulls, the high in late 1980 did not hold and the next recession was brewing.

In July 1981 the second recession in as many years began and it would not end for another sixteen months. From July 1981 through November 1982, the S&P 500 gained 2 percent even though the index

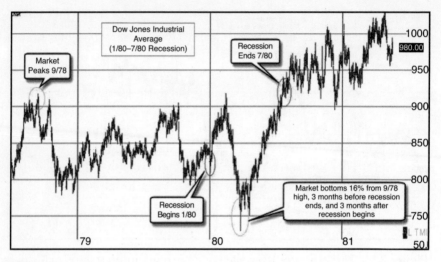

Figure 2.7   The 1980 Recession
SOURCE: TC2000 Charting Software and Penn Financial Group LLC.

fell 25 percent from the 1980 high to the 1982 low. Once again, the movement of the market during the official recession is not nearly as bad as many would believe. The reason for this is the phenomenon that the market bottoms before the end of the recession and the ensuing rallying is enough to wipe out a large part of the losses, if not all the losses. Again, please turn your attention to the bottoming of the stock market in March 2009 and keep in mind that investors are anticipating a market bottom, and this is why the market is rallying in the middle of a recession. By the time the media makes the announcement that the recession is over, it is too late and the first violent move in the next bull market is behind us.

A More Severe Recession: 1981–1982

The second of the early 1980s recession was much more severe and damaging to the economy. (See Figure 2.8.) Until the most recent recession, the 1981–1982 recession was viewed as the worst since the Great Depression. A dangerous mix of high inflation and a contracting monetary policy led to a slowdown in the economy, a banking crisis, and surging interest rates. Inflation in 1979 hit 11.3 percent and rose even higher in 1980, hitting a high of 13.5 percent, and remained in the double digits into the early 1980s.

Unemployment began to increase in the middle of 1981 from a low of 7.2 percent and did not peak until December 1982 when it sat at a high of 10.8 percent. To this day, it is the highest the United States has experienced since the 1980 recession. By the time this book hits your bookshelf the unemployment rate may have already risen above the 1982 high; my belief, however, is that it tops out near 10 percent and will not break it.

Paul Volcker was the Federal Reserve chairman at the time (and, surprisingly, has resurfaced in different circles recently), and his goal was to lower inflation at all costs. To achieve a lower inflation rate, Volcker decided it was prudent to tighten the money supply and raise interest rates. The Federal Funds rate rose from an already high 11 percent in 1979 to 20 percent by June 1981. The prime interest rate got as high as 21.5 percent in June 1982. The high interest rate made it extremely expensive for businesses and individuals to borrow and was a deterrent for the removal of money from saving accounts. This alone was a cause for the economic slowdown. The lack of business borrowing and individuals' hoarding cash caused GDP to move negatively.

A major difference between the 1980s recessions and the current recession is inflation. The most prevalent fear among the government

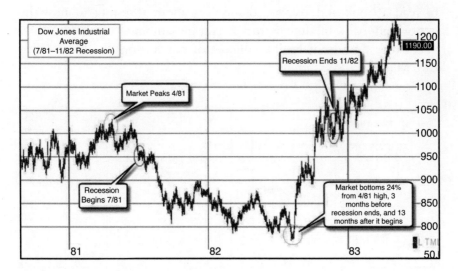

Figure 2.8 The 1981–1982 Recession
SOURCE: TC2000 Charting Software and Penn Financial Group LLC.

and most economists this time around has been deflation, not inflation. As you will find out in Chapter 9, however, inflation is one of my major concerns and if the U.S. government continues to work as a full-time printing press, there is a chance hyperinflation may return in the coming years.

Comparison of the current recession to the early 1980s recession and the Great Depression will not stop and will likely go on for years to come and be a discussion topic in classrooms around the world. I agree there are some similarities to both situations. The number of discrepancies, however, is also staggeringly high. The one similarity to the early 1980s recession that has yet to come to fruition is the case of a new bull market beginning as the recession came to a conclusion in 1982. (See Figure 2.9.) The low in August 1982 of 101 has been the lowest level of the S&P 500 since that date.

If only I had known enough at six years old to buy in August 1982 and hold for the next 18 years. My money would have generated a return of 1,400 percent through 2000 and I would have been one happy 24-year-old in grad school! Chalk this one up to a lessoned learned. That being said, I will not let the next great buying opportunity pass me by, and that is a big reason this book is on bookshelves around the world. I do not want other investors willing to take time to read a book and educate themselves about investing to miss the opportunity of a lifetime, either. If you get anything out of the early 1980s recession, let it be the concept of not missing the Next Great Bull Market.

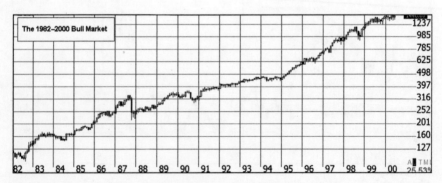

Figure 2.9   The 1982–2000 S&P 500 Bull Market
SOURCE: TC2000 Charting Software and Penn Financial Group LLC.

Mid-1970s Recession

The early-to-mid-1970s was a perfect storm for a recession with the combination of oil prices quadrupling, the costly Vietnam War, and the Watergate scandal rocking the country. The recession officially began in November 1973 and did not end until March 1975, sixteen months later. The stock market had peaked before the recession began, similar to the current recession, in January 1973, when the S&P 500 hit a high of 121, the index's highest level ever. From the peak in 1973 through the trough in October 1974, the index lost 50 percent of its value; again, similar to that of the current recession.

In October 1973, just as the recession was about to begin, OPEC stopped exports to Western nations because of their support for Israel. Within a few months, the price for a gallon of gasoline in the United States quadrupled as it rose from 25 cents to more than one dollar. Sounds eerily similar to the rise in oil that occurred from 2004 through 2008 when the price also quadrupled from below $30 to a high of $140 in 2008. The rise in oil prices during the 2000s does not compare to the oil crisis that occurred in the 1970s. The lines for gas were several blocks long in the 1970s as drivers hoped their gas station still had fuel available when their car arrived at the pump. At one point, one in every five gas stations in the United States was out of fuel, according to the American Automobile Association. The effects of the oil crisis are still felt today and the decade of the 1970s put in motion efforts for the United States to wean ourselves off of our foreign oil dependency. Unfortunately, the reliance on oil is nowhere near where it needs to be and the United States and other developed countries are attempting to introduce new alternative energy sources. I cover specific alternative energy choices in Chapter 6 and how to profit on the green movement.

Without getting off track of the recession discussion, I believe it is important to highlight some of the changes that occurred in the United States after the oil crisis of the 1970s. The most noticeable change was a move toward more fuel-efficient cars, with the establishment of a Corporate Average Fuel Economy (CAFE) standard being set at 27.5 miles per gallon. The CAFE standards have been a hot topic in the mid-2000s as the automobile industry goes through a huge change because of gas prices rising above $4 per gallon in 2008 in the United States. Adding fuel to the CAFE fire (no pun intended) is the bankruptcy of

General Motors (GM), which for 77 years was the largest automobile manufacturer in the world.

Other noticeable changes from the oil crisis include a move toward electric heat in new homes versus heating oil. Speed limits were enforced and fuel efficiency stickers were placed on vehicles. Alternative fuel sources such as coal and natural gas, both prevalent in the United States, rose in popularity. The question now is what will be the major changes due to oil's rise above $140? And considering that I believe oil will surge even higher in the coming decade, what will be the alternative energy sources that will benefit and how can investors profit. There is a more detailed discussion on peak oil in Chapter 11.

One year after the oil embargo began, it was over and so was the pullback in the stock market. The S&P 500 bottomed in October 1974 and nine months later the index was up 60 percent from the low. (See Figure 2.10.) Choppiness occurred for the next five years, but the main trend remained higher for U.S. equities until it ran into the recessions of the early 1980s that were just discussed. A point I want to make again is that by the time the recession is announced as officially over, the stock market is well off the lows. Even more important is that the

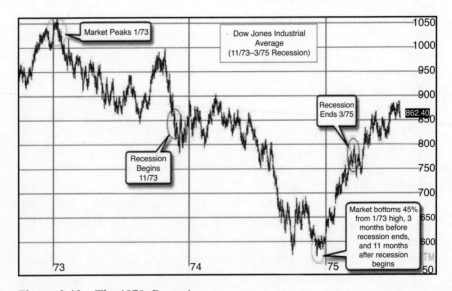

Figure 2.10 The 1970s Recession
SOURCE: TC2000 Charting Software and Penn Financial Group LLC.

low of the stock market hit during the recession is not revisited. This is more of a reason to believe the low in March 2009 is the ultimate low for the early 2008–2009 recession.

The Great Depression: 1929–1938

Arguably, the most severe financial crisis to hit the world in modern times was the Great Depression that began in 1929 and did not officially end until June 1938. (See Figure 2.11.) Everything happened—from a stock market collapse, to a banking crisis, to unemployment numbers hitting unprecedented levels. Unlike the current recession, where consumers are waiting in line to buy the new iPhone, during the Great Depression the lines were for free bread to stave off starvation.

What made the Great Depression so "great" was the length of the economic slowdown and the broad reach it had on all economic and social classes in the United States and abroad. At the height of the Great Depression in 1933 the unemployment rate hit 24.9 percent of the total work force of 11,385,000 people, according to the FDR Library. This unemployment led to a surge in homelessness and the creation of what many referred to as Hoovervilles, or small towns of U.S. residents living in boxes and crates.

By the time Franklin Roosevelt moved in to the White House in 1933, the unemployment number was out of control, the banking system had all but collapsed, and productivity was one-third below the peak level of 1929. Every day, adults and children were dying from starvation and the lack of the necessities needed to live as humans.

The causes of the Great Depression can be debated, but the consensus is that the October fall of the stock market was a major catalyst. On October 14, 1929 the Dow Jones Industrial Average stood at 358, not far from its all-time high of 386 set one month earlier. By September 13, 2009, the stock index had fallen to a low of 195—a drop of 46 percent in a matter of one month. Stock rebounded nicely from the bottom in late 1929 through the first quarter of 1930 and half of the 46 percent drop was recouped.

Unfortunately, the damage caused by the 1929 stock market collapse was enough to send the United States and foreign countries into a spiraling fall that included banks collapsing and unemployment rising.

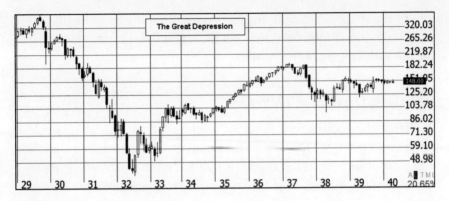

Figure 2.11   The Great Depression
SOURCE: TC2000 Charting Software and Penn Financial Group LLC.

The short-lived rally into 1930 was followed by a two-and-half year bear market that sent the Dow Jones Industrial Average to a low of 40 in July 1932. The fall from peak to trough for the index was a mind-blowing 89 percent. As you can imagine, the stock market collapse of the 1930s was enough to wipe out the wealth of a large portion of the population, forcing a major change in the way Americans live their everyday lives.

When comparisons are made between the recession that began in 2008 and the Great Depression, it not only irritates me, but it is truly a disservice to unknowing Americans. I will agree that the collapse of a number of major financial corporations during 2008 did bring back memories of the Great Depression. There was also a concern for money market funds in 2008 that caused one of the major money market firms to break the buck. But there was not a major run on the banks as there was during the Great Depression. In 2008, a total of 25 FDIC-insured banks failed, and through May 2009 another 36 FDIC banks joined the list. The number may sound high to the unknowing, but consider that there were over 7,000 FDIC-insured banks at the end of the first quarter of 2009 and only 36 failed over the previous 15 months. The amount of FDIC insured banks that have failed is approximately 0.5 percent of all banks.

During the 1920s, there was an average of 70 banks failing annually, more than the current number. The first 10 months of 1930 saw

744 banks fail and the grand total for the 1930s rose to nine thousand! Now take a step back and think about the 35 banks that failed in 2008 and compare it to the thousands that had to shut their doors during the Great Depression. Granted, the comparison is not fair because there were too many banks at the time. That being said, the comparisons between the Great Depression and the current recession are also not fair.

Looking Outside the U.S. Borders

This chapter focused almost exclusively on the United States and the history of recessions that affected the country. In the next chapter, I look at one of the major changes that has occurred over the last decade and that will continue for years to come—the globalization of the stock market.

Chapter 3

Globalization of the Stock Market

I nvesting in stocks that are domiciled outside the United States carried a risky tone to it a decade or two ago. Within the last few years, though, it has become the norm to look for investment opportunities outside U.S. borders. I believe investing in foreign countries, both developed and emerging, will become a mainstay for both aggressive and conservative investors as we move into the next decade. This is one reason I refer to the future as the *New Global Economy*, not the *New U.S. Economy*.

It has been difficult to convince many of my clients and subscribers that investing outside of the United States is no more risky than investing in a U.S.-based blue chip stock. For starters, most U.S. blue chip companies generate a large portion of their sales overseas and are considered multinationals. Some household names in the United States are even more popular internationally, such as McDonald's Corp.

(NYSE: MCD) than they are at home. In 2008, McDonald's generated over 60 percent of its sales outside the United States and sees the biggest growth potential in countries such as China, Japan, and Australia. In essence, Mickey D's is a truly international company that happens to be based in Illinois.

The Next Global Powers

If you believe the United States will be a global power forever, you need to take a look back at history. The only true superpower in the world today is the United States—no other country has the ability to influence events around the world on the same scale as the United States. The term *superpower* truly became mainstream after World War II when the United States and the former Soviet Union were both in the elite group. The United States has cemented its role as the lone superpower over the last couple of decades after the breakup of the Soviet Union.

According to historians, there have been a number of superpowers over the many centuries of recorded time. There was ancient Egypt, the Inca empire, Ottoman empire, Roman empire, British empire, and on and on. The one thing they all have in common is that they are no longer superpowers. The point I am trying to make is that at some point the United States will lose its status as a superpower and another country will take over the role. No one really knows when this will happen, but there is a certainty that it will happen. If I had to take an educated guess regarding the timing, I would say, unfortunately, that the demise of the United States has already begun. Before you look too far into this, please keep in mind that I am not saying the United States is crumbling; its time, however, as the lone superpower is nearing an end.

As investors, we want to try to determine countries around the world that have the potential to be the next superpower. The first country in everyone's mind is China. For a number of reasons, including their population, growth potential, military, and location, China is well positioned. China is one of the four fastest growing emerging markets, known as BRIC countries, explained in the next section.

Not Just another BRIC in the Wall

The BRICs—Brazil, Russia, India, and China—won't be considered emerging markets for long. These countries are on their way to being considered developed countries, and investing in one of these countries comes with a unique set of pros and cons.

Brazil

Where to start with Brazil? A beautiful country that has an abundance of natural resources and beautiful women, how can you go wrong? Another great factor into why I find Brazil to be such an attractive investment opportunity is the political stability it offers compared to its peers in the region and around the globe. That being said, Brazil was not able to avoid the global recession that made its way around the world. Estimates call for GDP in 2009 to fall by 1.5 percent before picking up modestly to 2.7 percent in 2010, according to *The Economist*.[1] The International Monetary Fund (IMF), on their web site, forecasts GDP to be a negative 1.3 percent in 2009 and an increase of 2.2 percent in 2010.

The estimates for both 2009 and 2010 are a major change from the GDP the country was enjoying earlier this decade. President Luiz Inácio Lula da Silva (informally called Lula) was elected in 2002 and in that same year, the country began to turn around economically. From the viewpoint of an investor in the country, he has been great for Brazil and their economy His second term will end in 2010 and there is speculation about who will step up to lead Brazil into the next decade. This is a fairly significant political risk for investors.

Beginning in 2004, GDP growth in Brazil was fairly consistent and impressive, with a gain of 5.7 percent, followed by 3.2 percent in 2005, 4.0 percent in 2006, 5.7 percent in 2007, and strong 5.1 percent in 2008. In 2008, the growth remained high even as GDP fell by 3.6 percent in the fourth quarter. A group of economists polled by the Brazilian government predicted Brazil's GDP would grow by 1.8 percent in 2009, much higher than the other two forecasts mentioned, according to an *Industry Week* magazine article.[2] Even highly intelligent economic forecasters are not certain of what the future holds. Regardless of what the actual GDP is in 2009 and 2010, the odds are it will be better than that of the United States and most developed European nations.

Similar to the United States, Brazil announced in February 2009 that it would increase its investment in infrastructure projects by 142 billion reais ($61.26 billion) through 2010 in an attempt to kickstart a slowing economy. The investment total under President da Silva's second term has grown to 646 billion reais, but the important number is 48 billion reais. The completed public works projects only account for a total of 48 billion reais, or less than 8 percent of the money car marked. With such a large amount of money yet to be spent by the government, it should be a big boost to Brazilian GDP. And even more important to investors, Brazilian infrastructure stocks and the overall market will also benefit.

The possibility of Brazil becoming the next superpower is not very good, but the country does have tools to become a hotbed for foreign investment. The abundance of natural resources in Brazil makes the country an attractive region to other countries seeking to import oil and metals. China has become a major trading partner with Brazil over the last few years, increasing the attractiveness of the country.

When investing in emerging markets, it is imperative to understand the risks as well as the potential rewards. Political risk hangs over nearly every emerging market, including Brazil. Even though President da Silva is the most popular leader in the country's history, he cannot be in office forever, and his second term expires in 2010. The political party he is associated with does not have a clear candidate to replace him, and that could hold back the stock market and slow Brazil's future growth. Regardless of who wins, the chance of violence and disruption is slim, and it will hopefully just be a speed bump.

The second major risk for Brazil involves the developed countries around the world and China. If the recession continues into 2010 and demand for such natural resources as oil and steel decline, it will have a ripple effect on Brazil's economy. One of the reasons I believe Brazil offers the best reward-to-risk of all emerging markets has to do with my belief that the demand for commodities will continue to rise and the election will merely be a short-term situation. The reward potential may not be as high as in other emerging markets, but the risk is much lower.

From the low in 2002 to the all-time high in 2008, the Brazil stock index, the BOVESPA, gained 800 percent as the S&P 500 only doubled in the same time period. In 2008, the BOVESPA slightly underperformed the U.S. markets with a loss of 41 percent. Through May of 2009, however, the index was up 41 percent as the S&P 500 gained only 1 percent. The action of the Brazilian stock market highlights my thoughts on the reward-to-risk of the country. During the worst economic downturn in decades, Brazilian stocks were basically in line with the United States. When times are good, Brazil is able to easily outpace the returns of the United States and other developed countries. The chart of the BOVESPA in Figure 3.1 gives you an idea of where this Brazil has come from and the possibilities of what the future may hold.

The best way to play Brazil with a single investment is through the iShares MSCI Brazil Index ETF (NYSE: EWZ). The ETF is heavily invested in the natural resources sector and has about one-fifth of the allocation in financials. The largest holding, which makes up over 10 percent of the ETF, is Petrobras (NYSE: PBR), one of my favorite energy stocks, and as of mid-2009, a holding for clients. Keep in mind that EWZ does not track the BOVESPA index and will have different returns. For example, in 2008 EWZ lost 57 percent. EWZ gained 57 percent through the first five months of 2009. The numbers show the risk will be higher for EWZ versus the BOVESPA, but so is the reward potential. The reason behind this increased risk and reward is the heavy

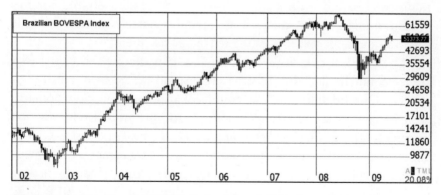

Figure 3.1 Brazilian BOVESPA Index Historic Rise from 2002 to 2008, Before the Global Recession Hits

Source: TeleChart2007® or StockFinder® chart, courtesy of Worden Brothers, Inc.

Figure 3.2   iShares MSCI Brazil Index ETF
SOURCE: TeleChart2007® or StockFinder® chart, courtesy of Worden Brothers, Inc.

concentration on a smaller number of stocks for EWZ versus the index (see Figure 3.2).

Russia

The old Soviet Union was once considered a world superpower before the fall of the empire ended the Cold War. Now the Russian Federation is making a play to become a superpower once again, this time under different circumstances. Instead of battling the United States for world supremacy, Russia will attempt to reach its lofty goal as a friend of the United States (at least that is what former president and current prime minister Vladamir Putin wants you to believe). Politically, the country remains unstable, to say the least, as corruption affects business from the streets to the upper reaches of the federal government.

The political risk of investing in Russia is the highest of the four BRIC countries and this must be understood before investing is considered. On the flip side, the country has a lot of upside potential with its abundance of natural resources, its enormous land mass, and extremely strong military. According to *The Economist*, Russia's GDP is expected to contract by 3.0 percent in 2009 after an impressive increase of 5.6 percent in 2008.[3] A recovery should begin in 2010 with an increase in GDP of 2.0 percent, and over the next three years (2011–2013) GDP is estimated to average an increase of 4.5 percent, all numbers taken from the May 9–15, 2009, issue of *The Economist* magazine.

The contraction of GDP expected in 2009 is due in large part to the decline in prices of energy commodities oil and natural gas. Nearly 80 percent of their exports are energy and metal commodities, and with demand drying up in late 2008 and early 2009, the Russian economy was hit hard. The Market Vectors Russia ETF (NYSE: RSX) fell 74 percent in 2008 and was one of the hardest hit international ETFs traded in the United States. The ETF began a turnaround during the first three months of 2009, gaining 83 percent. By the first of June, the ETF had nearly doubled before pulling back as traders banked profits. Figure 3.3 shows the dramatic fall of RSX in 2008 before rebounding in 2009. The catalyst has been higher energy and metal prices. About two-thirds of the ETF is invested in natural resources stocks, with telecom and finance making up the bulk of the remaining portion. If you agree with my theory about higher commodity prices, Russia stands to be a big winner as long as the country does not run into any political situations that could affect its growth or stability.

Investors that would like to take a much riskier approach to Russia have the option of buying individual companies that trade in the United States. Several Russian companies trade on the NYSE as American depositary receipts (ADRs). I was amazed when doing research for this book at how much the Russian ADRs had fallen during the recession. There were two stocks in particular that caught my attention: Mechel Steel Group OAO and Vimpel Communications.

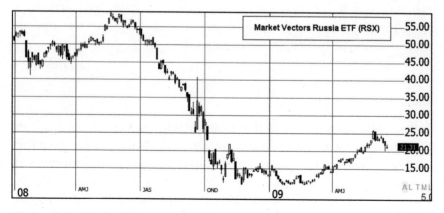

Figure 3.3   Market Vectors Russia ETF
SOURCE: TeleChart2007® or StockFinder® chart, courtesy of Worden Brothers, Inc.

The first is Mechel Steel Group OAO (NYSE: MTL), one of Russia's largest steel producers and mine owners. The company lost over 95 percent of its value during the economic crisis in 2008 from its high in 2008 to its low in January 2009 when the stock bottomed out at $2.56 per share. A combination of nonexistent steel demand, the struggling Russian economy, and too much leveraged debt nearly took the company into bankruptcy. Luckily for shareholders, the debt market and the demand for steel has improved greatly and Mechel has been able to make progress; the stock was up 175 percent through the first five months of 2009. Investing in Mechel is a highly aggressive play, but one that has great upside for a patient investor.

The second Russian stock is a leading mobile phone service provider named Vimpel Communications (NYSE: VIP). The company has more than 50 million mobile subscribers in Russia and surrounding countries such as Ukraine and Kazakhstan. Vimpel took a similar drop to Mechel, losing 90 percent of its value from its high in December 2007 through its low in March 2009. The second-largest mobile phone maker reported a net loss in May 2009 after posting a profit one year earlier. According to the company, the reason for the loss was currency exchange rates. Several countries Vimpel does business in have experienced major drops in their local currency and the bottom line is affected negatively when converted back into rubles. This is an example of another risk with foreign investing: currency risk. Foreign companies have been helped in recent years when converting their local currencies into U.S. dollars because the U.S. dollar has been weak. Vimpel is a high-risk investment with big upside potential for investors that are comfortable with taking above-average risk.

India

If you want to get down to the actual growth numbers, India has been consistently strong. In the fourth quarter of 2008, when most countries were struggling to keep their GDP from contracting, India reported an increase of 5.3 percent. For the entire year of 2008, the country's GDP rose 6 percent, and the most recent estimates have 2009 GDP slowing to 5 percent, mainly due to the global economic situation. Looking ahead at the next four years is what makes India such an attractive investment story. Beginning in 2010, the estimate for GDP growth over the next four years is 6.4, 8.0, 8.1, and 8.0 percent annually. This is amazing growth considering the country boasts the world's fourth-largest economy based on GDP measured on a purchasing power parity basis. Of the G-20 countries, India has the second-fastest growing economy behind the next BRIC country, China.

A major event took place in May 2009 when there was a surprise result in election results that calmed fears about years of political uncertainty. The ruling party, the United Progressive Alliance, solidified its hold on the Indian government and the results should allow stability for at least the next five years. This will allow the government to focus on the growth of the country, which includes both urban and underdeveloped rural areas. Within seconds of opening the following Monday after the election, the Bombay SENSEX Index was up 15 percent. This triggered circuit breakers to halt trading for a few hours and at the end of the day, the index was up 17 percent, its biggest one-day gain in almost two decades (see Figure 3.4). What impressed me even more was the index going up another 2 percent in the two weeks following the one-day surge. The action indicates that there is follow-through and buyers are willing to continue buying, which is a strong long-term technical signal for the country.

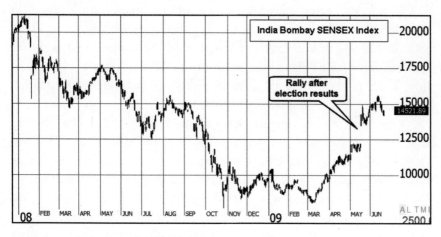

Figure 3.4 Bombay SENSEX Index
SOURCE: TeleChart2007® or StockFinder® chart, courtesy of Worden Brothers, Inc.

There were three major risks specific to India heading into the elections and that has now been lowered to two.

1. Inflation at 9.6 percent in 2008 is a concern for investors; it appears, however, that the number will be dropping in the coming years.
2. Geopolitical risk with long-time nemesis Pakistan has been an issue for years and there is no end in sight. As an investor, you hope for the best, but must realize the risk is present.
3. Political risk has been lowered after the election results were released and they favored a party that is pro-growth and good for the economy.

A minor risk is that of inflation, which could lead to growth coming in below estimates. That being said, *The Economist* (www.economist.com) has inflation falling from 8.3 percent in 2008 to 5.2 percent in 2009 and 4.3 percent in 2010.[4] If that is the case, my inflation concern will be thrown out the window and India is down to one major risk— geopolitical issues. India's neighbor and long-time nemesis, Pakistan, has been volatile recently, to put it nicely. There are rumors Osama Bin Laden is hiding out in the country and that people in the government are siding with the Taliban. In reality, no one knows the truth regarding the situation with the Taliban and Pakistan. The uncertainty is enough to make the rocky relationship with India a risk to investors.

A horrific, coordinated series of bomb attacks took place in November 2008 in Mumbai, India's financial capital. The attacks killed 173 people and it was later confirmed that the group responsible for the murders was a Pakistani military group. This is a grave example of how India is susceptible to terrorist attacks because of its geographic location and relationship with its neighbors.

There are a few options for investors that would like to play the India trade that range from individual stocks to ETFs to closed-end funds. The best play for intermediate-term and long-term investors is often a basket of stocks, and my recommendation, therefore, is the iPath MSCI India Index ETN (NYSE: INP) (see Figure 3.5). The ETN was a laggard in 2008, falling 68 percent, but the chart has improved in 2009 and a long-term buying opportunity remains.

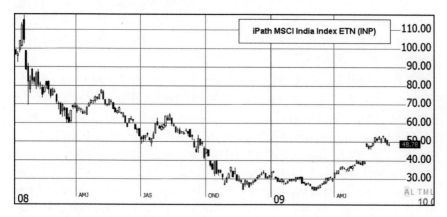

Figure 3.5 Invest in a Basket of Stocks: iPath MSCI India Index ETN
SOURCE: TeleChart2007® or StockFinder® chart, courtesy of Worden Brothers, Inc.

China

One of my favorite investment themes of the next decade is anything and everything to do with China. When a country grows by 9 percent during one of the worst years economically in the world in decades, it is a sign of resilience and potential. During the first quarter of 2009, China's GDP growth slowed to 6.1 percent, the lowest rate in nearly 20 years, according to the Chinese government.[5] I had mixed feelings when the number was released. For starters, I was very pleased with the number, considering how difficult the first quarter was for every country. But, of course, everyone was pessimistic at the time and after reading articles suggesting the China boom was over, I took a step back. I was later reassured of China's growth in July 2009 when the second quarter GDP was reported at a growth of 7.9 percent.[6]

In the end, I decided to concentrate on China being able to grow at a very impressive pace as the world slowed and realized growth would come back as soon as the global economy picked up. Analysts were looking for GDP growth of 6.5 percent in 2009, followed by 7.3 percent in 2010. Even more impressive is the growth estimates from 2011 through 2013—an average of 8.3 percent increase annually.

When analyzing growth in China, investors must realize they are not dealing with the typical emerging market. The country has the second-largest GDP in the world, second only to the United States, when measured on a purchasing power parity basis. If measured on nominal GDP, China comes in third behind the United States and Japan. Over the past 25 years, China has been the fastest-growing major nation, with an annual GDP growth rate above 10 percent. If you are a growth investor, there is no logical explanation as to why you would not have a portion of your portfolio allocated in China-related investments.

As great as the growth was in 2008, the Chinese mainland stock market (Shanghai Index) did its own thing by falling 65 percent. After topping out at 6,124 in October 2007, the index fell as low as 1,664 one year later before finding a bottom. What was so amazing about the 70-plus percent fall in one year is the valuation of the index. In late 2008, the Shanghai Index was trading at a more attractive valuation than the S&P 500. In simple terms, investors were pricing Chinese stocks at a discount to the United States. Add in the growth factor, and the Chinese stocks were a screaming buy versus U.S. stocks. Remember that China grew its GDP in the first quarter of 2009 by 6.4 percent versus a drop of 5.7 percent for the United States in the same period and during the second quarter China increased their growth to 7.9 percent as the U.S. contracted by 1 percent (see Figure 3.6).

Investing in China could be a book on its own and there are already plenty out there already. I will share a few of my favorite China investments throughout this book, however, because many of them are related to the investments themes that are discussed.

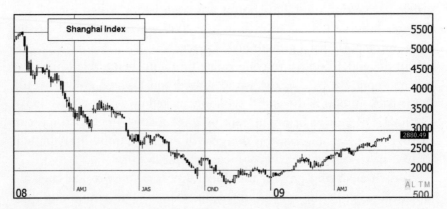

Figure 3.6 Shanghai Index Begins the Long Road Back to the 2008 Highs
Source: TeleChart2007® or StockFinder® chart, courtesy of Worden Brothers, Inc.

Are Foreign Companies Invading the United States?

A political debate that has become a hot spot between Democrats and Republicans is focused on foreign countries' direct investment in U.S.-based companies. As a major supporter of free markets, I do not want to see the United States implement protectionism against foreign investment in U.S. companies. In the same breath, there must be some type of regulation as to who can own what. For example, as a U.S. citizen, would you feel safe if a Middle Eastern country owned one of our seaports?

The port situation was ripped from a 2006 headline that had the U.S. government battling free market representatives. In early 2006, Dubai Ports World, a state-owned company based in the United Arab Emirates (UAE), was planning on purchasing six major U.S. seaports. At the heart of the matter was the security of U.S. ports, which have been suspected to be a port of entry for future terrorists or related weapons. The president at the time, George W. Bush, was in favor of the UAE company owning the ports. The rest of Washington, however, was not on the same page, and on March 8, 2006, a House of Representatives committee voted 62-2 to block the deal. Dubai Ports World eventually pulled out of the deal and a U.S.-based company took over management of the ports.

Whether you agree with the move by the U.S. government to block the purchase of the ports by a foreign country is not the point. What I am trying to get across is that the port situation was not the first and will not be the last time a foreign country or company makes a bid at acquiring a major U.S. company.

Three such situations occurred during the second quarter of 2009 in which foreign money was making its way into prominent U.S.-based companies: Chrysler, Facebook, and the Cleveland Cavaliers basketball team.

The most newsworthy of the three was the merger of Italy's automaker Fiat and U.S.-based automaker Chrysler LLC. In a complicated series of events, Chrysler was forced into bankruptcy protection and at the same time pursued an alliance with Fiat. The so-called merger is more along the lines of Fiat becoming a vulture investor and feeding on the carcass of Chrysler for pennies on the dollar. The merger will allow the Fiat to introduce and produce their small, European cars in the United States. This may result in Fiat hitting the lottery if U.S. drivers continue their move toward smaller, more fuel-efficient cars.

Fiat is known for its small cars that whiz in and out of traffic in Italy. The Fiat brand has also had some issues in the past, and some say Fiat stands for, "Fix It Again, Tony." I am very interested to see how this move changes the landscape for the U.S. auto industry and if Fiat can become a successful vulture. My best guess is that Fiat will sell fairly well in the United States, and over the long term, the alliance will benefit Fiat and its shareholders (see Figure 3.7).

The ever-popular social networking site Facebook announced in May 2009 that it accepted a $200 million investment from Digital Sky Technologies in exchange for a 2 percent equity stake in the private company. What makes this move interesting is that Digital Sky Technologies is a Russian Internet investment group with a main office in Moscow. Granted, the ownership percentage is low, but it displays the pattern of foreign investment in the United States and into a variety of sectors.

Finally, during the same week the Cleveland Cavaliers of the National Basketball Association (NBA), best known as the team where LeBron James plays, sold 15 percent of the franchise to an investment group from China. The move appears on the surface to be a win-win situation for both parties involved. The Chinese firm has the ability to profit from a team that has the sports best player in both the United States and abroad.

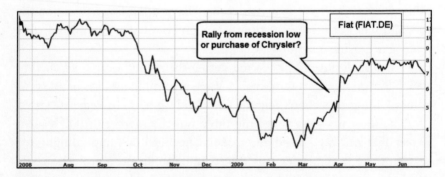

Figure 3.7 Fiat Revving up to Move in to the United States
SOURCE: Yahoo! Finance. Reproduced with permission of Yahoo! Inc. ©2009 by Yahoo! Inc. YAHOO! and the YAHOO! logo are trademarks of Yahoo! Inc.

From the Cavaliers Operating Company's (the entity that owns the team and a 20,000-seat arena) viewpoint the move allows them to take advantage of the Chinese market, where LeBron James is already widely popular. The upside for LeBron and the organization in China is monumental monetarily, and James has been quoted as saying that he wants to become the first billion-dollar athlete. This deal may just help him achieve that.

What all three situations highlight is the movement of foreign money, let's make that large amounts of foreign money, into areas that in the past would have been of no interest to countries such as China and Russia. Possibly even more important, and not touched on yet, is the situation in which foreign countries have the money to spend and are willing to invest it in the United States when the country is at a low point. By investing during the recession, the foreign firms are buying at a discount and making wise decisions with their money that in the long run is another factor behind my thoughts on the new global economy.

Time for You to Make Money

I lay out major investment themes in the next 10 chapters that will lead the Next Great Bull Market and, more importantly, specific investments to profit from the boom. It kicks off in Chapter 4 with a commodity that I believe is poised to be the next oil, as everything associated with it will rise in price. What makes this notion crazy is that we take this commodity for granted and it is a necessity for any human to survive.

Chapter 4

Water: The Next Great Commodity Rally

I t has not been uncommon over the last several centuries for a commodity to be a leading cause of human conflicts, and even wars. The U.S. Gold Rush is just one example, when people fought for land that potentially had massive reserves of gold. Wars over land that house the largest oil reserves in the world have been going on for years and will likely continue as the commodity becomes scarcer. There is currently a mad dash to secure land that has the potential of yielding large amounts of desired commodities such as oil and water. First, as the supply of a commodity begins to diminish, people begin to panic and attempt to horde remaining supplies by placing claims on the land. Another reason for conflict could be the rising price of the commodity, making it lucrative to own the land or the commodity within it.

Over the last decade or two, a commodity that has been at the forefront of a number of serious conflicts has been oil. With the amount of oil coming out of the ground stagnant at best and the future for supply grim, the world powers have been attempting to shore up as much inventory as possible. According to a Worldwatch Institute report, "State of the World 2005," oil production is in decline for 33 of the 48 largest oil-producing countries.[1] As you will read in Chapter 11, peak oil output could be upon us this decade, resulting in falling supplies. With the world demand for oil steadily rising because of growth in the middle class of emerging markets, the end result has been higher prices for oil. I am aware the price of oil has fallen from nearly $150 to the low $30s per barrel, but the long-term trend remains higher and by early summer 2009 the price per barrel was back to $60.

As I mentioned, oil has been at the center of conflicts for years. The question is, what will be the next commodity that people around the world will be fighting over? Water, agua, eau, wasser, or whatever you want to call it. The blue gold, as it is often referred to, will be the next commodity that both developed and emerging countries will be clamoring over.

You may think I am totally off my rocker, and sometimes I feel the same way when I express my thoughts on water and the related investment opportunities. Considering there are two cases of bottled water in my refrigerator as I write this and two bottles on my desk, how can there be a shortage? Well, you need to think outside the box for this investment trend and realize there is more to the world than the neighborhood you live in or even North America.

Why Water?

Right now, there are millions of people around the world who do not have regular access to clean water. Even more people lack clean, running water in their homes. Here in the United States, we consume 408 billion gallons of water per day for uses such as drinking, irrigation, power generations, and so on; this is according to the U.S. Geological Survey.[2] Yes, you and your neighbors have more than enough water, but forget how you live and think about the world outside North America.

It is not only in the underdeveloped parts of the world that water is an issue. In a 2006 Associated Press news story, John Howard, the prime minister of Australia at the time, announced his country was suffering its worst drought in 100 years.[3] The state of California is not only in an economic drought, but also one of its worst water droughts ever, and Governor Arnold Schwarzenegger declared the first drought in the state since 1991. The dry conditions could be attributed to a spring season that left the runoff from the mountains at 41 percent of the average. Critical snowpacks in the Sierra Mountains measured less than two-thirds of their normal levels. How about the Colorado River, which is a major source of water, sitting in the middle of a record-setting eight-year drought? The Midwest is no stranger to droughts either; the region has been hit hard over the last decade with dry weather that directly affects the country's agricultural production.

Here are some amazing statistics that may convince you that the water investment theme is the real deal. The following statistics are from the World Water Council[4] and The Water Project.[5]

- 1.1 billion people live without clean drinking water.
- In developing countries, nearly 80 percent of illnesses are linked to poor water and sanitation conditions.
- 1.8 billion people die every year from diarrheal diseases.
- 3,900 children die every day from water-borne diseases.
- One out of every four deaths under the age of five worldwide is due to water-related disease.
- The EPA estimates water will eventually be the single largest expenditure in the entire U.S. economy.
- According to the World Health Organization, less than 1 percent of the world's fresh water, or 0.007 percent of all the water on Earth, is readily available for human consumption.
- In China, 40 percent of the rivers and 70 percent of the lakes are too polluted to drink. Two-thirds of China's 600 largest cities don't have enough clean water. Half of those also suffer polluted groundwater. In the rest, overpumping has made parts of cities like Shanghai *sink* by as much as two meters.
- Less than 15 percent of China's 1.3 billion people have access to clean water from the tap, and it's costing their economy big time, according to the Chinese Minister of Water Resources.
- 2.6 billion people lack adequate sanitation.

- Daily per capita use of water in residential areas:

  - 350 liters in North America.
  - 200 liters in Europe.
  - 10–20 liters in sub-Saharan Africa.

Three Water Investment Sectors

There are a number of directions you can go when investing in the water industry, and you should ideally have some exposure to all sectors. There are the water utilities that supply the clean water and provide wastewater services around the world to paying customers. The water infrastructure sector includes makers of pipes that transport the water as well as technologies used to repair and install new infrastructure options. Finally, there is a small sector of investments that include companies that own the rights to the watershed land.

Water Infrastructure

The $787 billion stimulus plan signed into action by President Barack Obama in February 2009 should be a major boost to federal and local government projects that have been put on hold because of the recession. An area that has been failing miserably in the United States is water infrastructure, especially in the older urban areas such as New York and Philadelphia. Considering a large amount of the pipes carrying our drinking water or wastewater underneath the streets were originally installed over 50 years ago, it should not be a surprise to read about water main breaks on a regular basis.

The American Society of Civil Engineers (ASCE) 2009 Report Card for America's Infrastructure gave the drinking water category a D–, down from a D in 2001. If our country is going to improve our drinking water, it must begin with the infrastructure. Considering there are currently over 700,000 miles of pipe in the U.S. water infrastructure system, this will take large amounts of time and money. With 408 billion gallons of water running through the U.S. water system daily, it is imperative to have pipes that can handle the demand. Unfortunately, there are pipes transporting water right now that were put into the ground during the nineteenth century. The United States Environmental Protection Agency (EPA) reported that approximately 10 percent of the pipes in the United States are over 80 years old. Many of the pipes, over 80 years old and younger, are past their useful life and need to be replaced. The EPA also reported in 2003 that the total water infrastructure system in the United States will require $277 billion between 2003 and 2022; pipes accounted for 66 percent of that number.[6]

An interesting website to check out is www.watermainbreakclock .com, which tracks water main breaks in the United States and Canada. According to the web site, 700 water main breaks occur every day, on average, in the United States and Canada. Since January 2000, there have been over 2.41 million water main breaks that have cost the two governments a total of $9.67 billion to repair (through June 16, 2009). Stop reading right now and go to www.google.com and type in *water main breaks* and you will find a list of news stories about breaks that have occurred in major metropolitan areas in the last week—guaranteed. Our local and federal governments need to step in and begin replacing the diminishing pipes and take a proactive approach rather than reactive. By tackling the issues before they become major problems will result in more money up front, but a lower amount in the end.

Two stocks, Northwest Pipe Company (NASDAQ: NWPX) and Ameron International (NYSE: AMN), stand to benefit from the federal government supplying the states and municipalities with money to upgrade the water systems. The proactive approach of replacing the old pipes before damage occurs will save the government money in the long run and help increase the bottom line for the pipe companies. The money will also help create jobs and boost the local economies. Because there is a pressure to buy U.S. with the stimulus money, the two stocks discussed here could be well positioned in the coming years even more so than some of their competitors.

Northwest Pipe Company

Northwest Pipe Company (Northwest) might not be the largest company in the sector (market capitalization of $322 million as of June 2009), but they do offer pipes that are in high demand. The company makes welded steel transmission lines that pump water through circulatory systems for government and private water companies. The products range from small ordinary pipes that most would imagine when thinking of residential plumbing. the company also specializes, however, in very large pipes that are wide enough to allow you to walk through them and they are able to carry water that is under extreme pressure.

Looking at the financial numbers, the company reported record sales and earnings during the third quarter of 2008. Sales jumped to $123.4 million from $92.0 million one year earlier. Earnings per share nearly doubled to $1.09 for the third quarter, up from $0.55 in the same quarter in 2007. As the recession worsened in late 2008 and early 2009, Northwest was hurt by slowing sales. According to the company's 2009 first quarter earnings report, it earned 28 cents per share on revenue of $81.4 million. Both numbers were a substantial decrease from one year earlier, but the reaction in the stock price was favorable, as shown in Figure 4.1. The CEO of Northwest, Brian Dunham, states in the earnings release that he expects the next quarter to be challenging before seeing improvement in the second half of the year.[7] The two areas that should continue to carry Northwest are water transmission and energy, as the stimulus spending begins to pick up.[8]

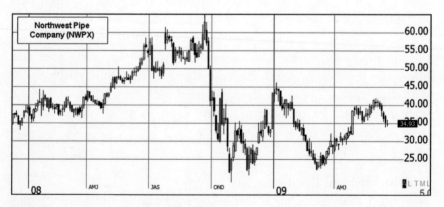

Figure 4.1   Northwest Pipe Company
SOURCE: TeleChart2007® or StockFinder® chart, courtesy of Worden Brothers, Inc.

Ameron International

Ameron offers a variety of different pipes to the water industry and also has an aggregate business—both of which will benefit from the stimulus package. The aggregate division includes ready-mix concrete and other products used by the construction industry. Ameron manufactures steel and fiberglass-composite pipes used mainly in water transmission, sewage projects, and petrochemical plants.

The main difference between Ameron and Northwest is that Ameron offers investors international exposure and the diversification of the aggregates business. The majority of Ameron's plants are located in the western United States, Canada, and Hawaii. The company also has a wholly owned subsidiary that is a major supplier of concrete and steel pipe in several Latin American countries. The company's newest venture involves large-diameter wind towers, an investment that could provide high growth for the company in years to come. The wind power investment opportunity is discussed in further detail in Chapter 6.

Not growing as quickly as Northwest, Ameron was able to report revenue and earnings in 2008 that were slightly higher than 2007 after removing one-time items. On the flip side, the company did note in its earnings statement that the Infrastructure Products and Water Transmission Group were weak. The Water Transmission Group saw sales increase by 13 percent, but a larger income loss than a year earlier. The company believes the division was weak because of the economy and said it has not seen business this slow in a long time. The increase in sales was due to a 42 percent increase in revenue from wind tower sales.[9] I believe once the stimulus money makes its way into the market, the end result will be new projects getting the go-ahead.

The pure play for water infrastructure is Northwest, but both companies should benefit from the improvement and expansion of the U.S. water system. If you want to gain exposure to the piping industry with the possible benefit of international sales and aggregates, Ameron is your stock. The downside risk to Ameron is steel demand worldwide. If the demand for steel does not pick up throughout 2009, it will weigh on Ameron's earnings as it did in the first quarter, which resulted in a sizable fall year over year. Figure 4.2 is a two-year chart of Ameron, and it is clear

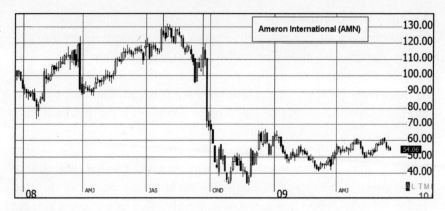

Figure 4.2   Ameron International
SOURCE: TeleChart2007® or StockFinder® chart, courtesy of Worden Brothers, Inc.

that the stock took a big hit in 2008 and has yet to rebound in 2009. The weakness could be the buying opportunity investors look for in a stock.

Water Utilities

The difference between investing in water and investing in other commodities such as oil or soybeans is that everyone on earth demands water. There are alternatives to oil and soybeans, but nothing on this planet has ever been found to replace water. Not only do humans require water, but so do farmers and thousands of other industries we rely on. This is why we turn to the water utility companies that provide us with clean water as investment opportunities. Without the utilities, the ease of access to water would not be possible. I highlight three of the larger U.S.-based water utility companies along with an ETF that invests in a basket of water utility stocks.

Aqua America

The country's largest water utility, Aqua America (NYSE: WTR), provides both water and wastewater services to nearly 3 million customers, with its largest concentration in Pennsylvania. Over the last few years, the company has been on an expansion spree through acquisitions, and it now has a presence in 12 states. In the last five years, Aqua America has completed 90 acquisitions and more than

120 since the early 1990s.[10] As a major player in the industry that always has its eyes out for new acquisitions, Aqua America should remain the leader in the industry. According to Yahoo! Finance, the company currently pays a 3.2 percent annual dividend and has recently been approved for rate hikes on the water they sell to customers. In early February 2009, Aqua America raised its quarterly dividend by 8 percent to $0.135; this is impressive, considering the number of companies cutting dividends.

What really impresses me about Aqua America is how the stock has performed during both bull and bear markets, particularly in bear markets. The S&P 500 topped out on March 24, 2000, before the tech crash of the early twenty-first century. The index fell 26 percent during the following two years and Aqua America rose over 100 percent. In 2008, it also showed great relative strength as the stock was virtually unchanged as the S&P 500 fell 38 percent. The performance I am referring to can be seen in Figure 4.3.

The first quarter earnings report released by the company showed profit increasing by 28 percent in the quarter to 14 cents per share. Revenue jumped by 11 percent to $154.5 million and the company now expects full year profit of 81 cents per share, an increase of 11.5 percent from 2008. These are very impressive numbers considering the economic environment, and even better yet, the stock price has been lagging, offering a buying opportunity.[11]

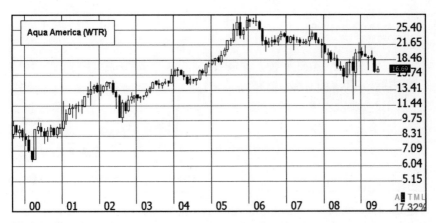

Figure 4.3 Aqua America Long-Term Performance
SOURCE: TeleChart2007® or StockFinder® chart, courtesy of Worden Brothers, Inc.

American Water Works

Similar to Aqua America, American Water Works (NYSE: AWK) is one of the largest water utilities in the United States. The company began trading on the NYSE in April 2008 after it was spun off from German utility company RWE. From the time the stock began trading on April 23, it gained just over 1 percent through the end of the year. This flat return is impressive when compared with the 35 percent fall in the S&P 500, but disappointing when compared with the Dow Jones U.S. Water Utilities Index, which gained 13 percent in the same time frame. With a dividend yield of 4.3 percent and the steady movement of the stock as shown in Figure 4.4, American Water Works would be considered one of the more conservative stocks in the sector. As long as the stock is able to hold above the $16 low as seen in Figure 4.4, the stock remains an attractive long-term investment.

Fundamentally, American Water Works is trading at a more attractive valuation than its competitor, Aqua America. Because of negative earnings for American Water Works, the best comparison is the price-to-sales ratio. American Water Works trades at a reasonable price-to-sales ratio of 1.2 versus 3.5 of Aqua America, according to Yahoo! Finance. Between the two, I consider Aqua America to be the riskier play, but it also has more upside reward potential and the decision to buy one or the other should be based on your risk tolerance.[12]

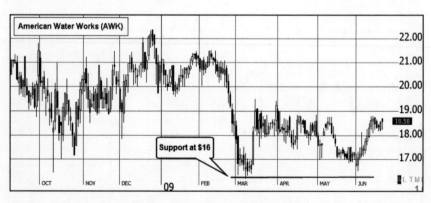

Figure 4.4   Watching Support on American Water Works
SOURCE: TeleChart2007® or StockFinder® chart, courtesy of Worden Brothers, Inc.

California Water Service Group

California Water Service Group (NYSE: CWT), or Cal Water, is the third-largest water utility in the country and the largest west of the Mississippi River, serving 460,000 customers.[13] Of the four subsidiaries that make up California Water Service Group, Cal Water is the dominant force, but is joined by much smaller water companies in Washington, New Mexico, and Hawaii.[14] As the name states, the company generates 95 percent of its revenue from the state of California.

The most recent earnings release (first quarter 2009) saw revenue increase by 19 percent over the previous year as net income shot up to 12 cents per share versus a penny. Considering the state of the economy and the situation that water utility companies are not considered growth investments, the numbers were fantastic. The recent pullback from an all-time high and the 3.3 percent annual dividend make the small-cap company attractive as an individual stock play. Figure 4.5 highlights the all-time high set in early 2009 and the subsequent pullback.

PowerShares Water Resource ETF

There is no true water utility ETF available in the United States, but the PowerShares Water Resource ETF (AMEX: PHO) will give investors exposure to the large-cap utility names. PHO was the first water-related ETF to launch in the United States in December 2005, and I became an instant fan. Not only for the creative symbol: PHO

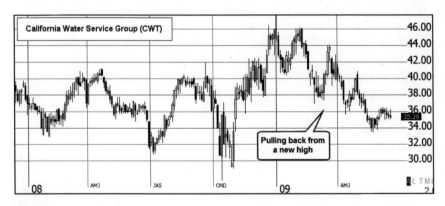

Figure 4.5 California Water Service Group Pulling Back after a New High
Source: TeleChart2007® or StockFinder® chart, courtesy of Worden Brothers, Inc.

and H2O—get it? I was a believer because it was the only way for
investors to gain access to the water industry through an ETF without taking the risk of an individual stock or buying a large number
of water-related companies to create the diversity in the sector that
is needed.

PHO currently has only 11 percent of its assets in the water utilities
sector and the only water utility stock in the top 10 holdings is Veolia
Environment, which is based in France. So, if you are looking for an
ETF to play the water utility sector, PHO is not the best candidate for
your portfolio. That being said, I am an advocate of PHO for the conservative investor who would like exposure to all three water sectors
highlighted in this chapter. The ETF pays a small dividend, 1.1 percent
at the time this chapter was written, and has been tracking the overall
market lately but lagging the water utilities index. Unfortunately, there
is no ETF available when this chapter was written that concentrates
solely on the Dow Jones U.S. Water Utility Index, so PHO is the next-
best choice.

The majority of the top 10 holdings are in the industrial industry,
suggesting they are water infrastructure plays. The largest holding is Tetra
Tech (NASDAQ: TTEK), an industrial company that generates a portion
of its sales from the water infrastructure segment. Of the stocks mentioned in this chapter, here are their weightings in PHO: Northwest Pipe
(2 percent), Ameron (3 percent), Aqua America (1 percent), and American
Water Works (1 percent). Several of the stocks mentioned in this chapter
do not appear in the current PHO allocation model. The PowerShares
Water Resource ETF top five holdings are:

1. Tetra Tech (TTEK)
2. Danaher Corp (DHR)
3. URS Corp (URS)
4. Itron Inc. (ITRI)
5. Valmont Industries (VMMI)

Figure 4.6 is the chart of PHO since it went public in 2005. A rise
in the price in 2009 sent the ETF to a new multimonth high and could
be the start of a new uptrend.

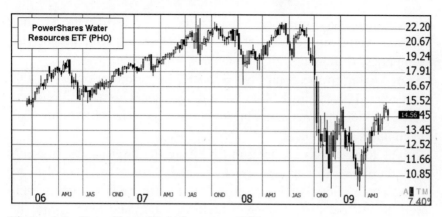

Figure 4.6   PowerShares Water Resources ETF
SOURCE: TeleChart2007® or StockFinder® chart, courtesy of Worden Brothers, Inc.

Watershed Investments

Owning land that was home to gold during the great Gold Rush resulted in large profits. Owning land that is rich in oil has resulted in large profits—just look at the Middle East. Land that is considered a watershed and has an abundance of water will be the next profitable investment. There are water rights transactions taking place right now on the west coast of the United States. According to Ryan Connors of Boenning and Scattergood in an interview with the *Wall Street Journal*, the value of an acre-foot of water (an amount equal to an acre of land covered by one foot of water), has risen from $1,500 in the mid–1990s to $25,000 today. The following two companies are my favorite choices for watershed investments.[15]

PICO Holdings

Through its subsidiary Nevada Land and Resource Company, PICO Holdings (NASDAQ: PICO) is one of the largest landowners in the state of Nevada. PICO also has another subsidiary that is in the water business—Vidler Water Company. Vidler develops, stores, and distributes water in the southwestern United States. The reason PICO made the list of possible investment choices is primarily due to the land subsidiary versus the water company. The water rights that PICO gains through the ownership of thousands of acres of land in Nevada could be very lucrative as water becomes scarcer in the desert state. By filing for water rights on portions of the land they own, PICO will be able to supply new municipalities in northern Nevada with water.

According to the company's web site, the company owns 440,000 acres of land parallel to I-80 in Nevada together with natural resources rights, including mineral, geothermal, and water rights on more than one million acres of land.[16]

The biggest risks investing in PICO are the diversity the company has in businesses that are not directly related to water and the possibility of real estate prices continuing to fall. The stock has been very volatile over the last few years, trading at multiyear highs and lows. Figure 4.7 shows the volatility throughout 2008 and early 2009. The key is to use the volatility in the stock as an opportunity to buy when it experiences wild swings to the downside.

SJW Corp

SJW Corp (NYSE: SJW), also known as San Jose Water, its largest subsidiary, provides water to about one million customers in the Santa Clara County area of California. Another subsidiary that makes SJW not just a run-of-the-mill water utility is SJW Land, which engages in real estate development. But aside from the development, portions of the land they own are home to large quantities of water, giving the company more options with the ability to sell or develop the land.

Figure 4.7   PICO Holdings
SOURCE: TeleChart2007® or StockFinder® chart, courtesy of Worden Brothers, Inc.

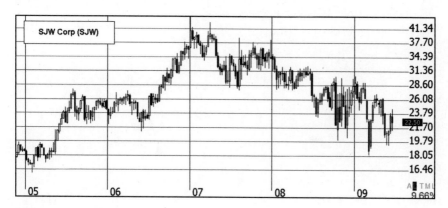

Figure 4.8 SJW Corp
SOURCE: TeleChart2007® or StockFinder® chart, courtesy of Worden Brothers, Inc.

The stock trades in a way similar to the water utility index, but because of its exposure to land, I value it in a different manner. Even though I like that the company operates the land unit, others may disagree or not realize the value of the land. Figure 4.8 is an example of how money has not been flowing into SJW since hitting a high in 2007. That being said, it also offers an opportunity for long-term investors to buy at a discount. Until Wall Street and Big Money realizes the value of land with water in areas that are in desperate need of water—investments such as SJW and PICO will continue to trade on a below-valuation basis. I do believe, however, that in time, both companies will trade at their true valuation.

In Chapter 5 I stick with the theme of upgrading infrastructure in the United States and abroad, as more mind-blowing statistics are revealed along with a slew of investment ideas to take advantage of the new stimulus packages implemented by both the United States and foreign countries.

Chapter 5

Global Infrastructure
Build-Out

D uring the 2008 U.S. presidential election, one of the key topics was infrastructure. The discussions ranged from the need for
new roads and bridges to economic plans that included creating
thousands of jobs in the infrastructure sector. Discussing the deterio-
rating infrastructure in the United States is nothing new to Washington
D.C., but it has unfortunately typically ended with the debates between
dividing parties. If anything were to get done, it included wasted money
on earmarks that include the infamous Alaskan bridge to nowhere and
public works projects that were far from necessary.

The United States is now in a situation in which discussions are no
longer an option when it comes to infrastructure, and action must be
taken immediately. If the government continues to put off the issue, our
nation must be prepared for a major national disaster that will claim the
lives of innocent people.

A small step forward was accomplished in January 2008 when several governors formed a nonpartisan committee to lobby in favor of more spending on U.S. infrastructure. The coalition was named Building America's Future and will act as a not-for-profit organization composed of government officials from the local to national level. Many of the officials in the committee are from the state and local level and are seeking money from the federal government because they are not able to keep up with the demand for infrastructure upgrades in their communities. According to Pennsylvania governor Ed Rendell, it will take $140 billion to repair or replace every deficient bridge in the United States. The governor goes on to say, "There's money when there's a crisis . . . and we have a legitimate crisis here."[1]

Unfortunately, it takes a crisis before the U.S. government is willing to invest money in infrastructure. By taking a reactive versus proactive approach to the infrastructure situation, the government is delaying the cost of upgrades and at the same time increasing the overall end cost. Money is one thing, but when it could lead to the deaths of innocent people, there must be a point at which the government becomes proactive.

With Barack Obama now the U.S. president, it appears that his administration is ready to move forward with the rebuilding of the country's infrastructure. On February 17, 2009, President Obama signed the American Recovery and Reinvestment Act, otherwise known as the stimulus bill, into law. The $787 billion stimulus package is designed to jumpstart the U.S. economy by putting people back to work on shovel-ready projects across the country. Whether you agree with the direction of the stimulus package and the billions that will be spent on pork projects is a debate for another time. The bottom line is that $787 billion is a large amount of money that will be going to companies in the construction, engineering, and materials sectors.

A number that the president himself has thrown out there as early as February 2009 is 3.5 million. Obama was referring to the number of jobs he vows to create in his first two years in office through the stimulus bill. This would be an astonishing feat, but one I am all for. According to a Fox News report, President Obama claimed in early June to have saved as many as 150,000 jobs through the stimulus bill. No one knows for certain how the number was generated, but the real point is that the administration is concentrating on throwing money into stimulus in one way or another, and that is good for the related stocks.[2]

It is a shame that it takes one of the worst economic environments since the Great Depression of the 1930s to bring about spending on infrastructure. But as I have mentioned before, it often takes a crisis for people to change, and that is no more evident than in our U.S. government. I am not alone in believing it is time for the government to finally upgrade the country's infrastructure. In a January 2009 poll by Luntz Maslansky Strategic Research, it found 94 percent of respondents are concerned about the nation's infrastructure. Their top two choices as areas of concern were energy facilities (41 percent) and roads and highways (38 percent); only 15 percent listed bridges. The poll also found that 81 percent of respondents questioned would back an infrastructure program if it included a 1 percent increase in federal taxes. If that does not show the dire need for infrastructure in the minds of Americans, nothing does.

The Bridge to Somewhere

The next tragedy caused by substandard infrastructure will not be the first to claims people's lives. In 2007, a major bridge in Minnesota collapsed as commuters were traveling over the Mississippi River. The I-35 bridge was a major thoroughfare for the Twin Cities and accommodated tens of thousands of cars each day. Many think the bridges in our major cities are safe and the only worry is the rural bridges that do not carry heavy traffic. This cannot be further from the truth. In the end, the tragedy claimed the lives of 13 people and injured 144 who were on or near the bridge at the time of its collapse.

A study by the American Association of State Highway and Transportation Officials (AASHTO) found that U.S. bridges were built to last approximately 50 years. This number sounds reasonable to the pedestrian infrastructure investor. But what makes this number astonishing is that the average age of the country's bridges is 43 years. On top of that, one in five has already eclipsed the 50-year-old milestone. According to the AASHTO, if all the bridges in America were fixed as well as modernized, it would carry a price tag of $140 billion.

While the $140 billion price tag may sound high to simply fix bridges, keep in mind that the number will only rise as the projects are pushed back and the deficiencies worsen. I realize the bridge issue in the United States is not at the top of most people's list of things to do, but, as the AASHTO reported, "Almost one in four bridges, while safe to travel, is either structurally deficient, in need of repair, or . . . too narrow for today's traffic volumes." The same report noted there are five major problems facing the nations nearly 600,000 bridges: age, congestion, soaring construction cost, lack of funds for maintenance, and the staggering costs of new bridges. The age and congestion will only get worse as more drivers are sitting behind the wheel of a vehicle. The cost issue remains, but with the cost of materials going into the bridges (for example, steel) coming down dramatically in the past year, that should alleviate some of the pressure. Lack of funds is the biggest issue because, as our country is in the midst of one of the worst recessions in decades, it is not easy to justify throwing hundreds of billions of dollars at bridges that appear to be just fine.

The wildcard is the stimulus package of President Obama: Will the $787 billion be put to good use, and how much will actually end up at the correct projects. An example of wasted money is the $1 billion FutureGen power plant in the president's home state of Illinois. According to a report issued by Senator Tom Coburn of Oklahoma, the project is outdated and the money could be used better elsewhere. Even the Massachusetts Institute of Technology (MIT) noted in a 2007 report that the FutureGen project was not the best way to go. There is no doubt money will be wasted; the hope is that enough makes it to the right places and the infrastructure issues begin to improve.[3]

When the need comes to fixing the country's bridges, it cannot be overlooked for much longer, and the money will eventually have to be spent on renovations and replacements. I haven't yet mentioned the need for new bridges in areas that are being developed as people expand into rural areas. The question is not a matter of if the bridges will be fixed, but when. My only hope is that it does not take another tragedy to force the government to begin spending money on infrastructure that we rely on every day and assume is safe. As a betting man (well, I am in the stock market every day, which can be thought of as a legal form of gambling), I predict billions of dollars will begin to come out of the government's coffers and into the infrastructure-related investments over the next few years and will last for decades. Repairing and modernizing nearly 600,000 bridges across the United States will not occur overnight and will take years upon years to finish.

Emerging Markets Becoming Infrastructure Giants

As exciting as the U.S. infrastructure plan is to investors, the real money will be spent overseas and, in particular, in the emerging markets. In September 2008, Merrill Lynch raised its forecast on the amount of money that will be spent by the emerging market countries. The estimate was raised to $2.25 trillion annually, for the next three years. To break the number down even further, Merrill Lynch believes that 70 percent of that spending will come from China, Russia, and the Middle East.

I would love to get behind this number, but the continued economic issues that transpired in the fourth quarter of 2008 and early 2009 makes me believe they are on the high end. That being said, even if the number drops to the original number out of Merrill, $1.25 trillion annually, there will be companies that benefit greatly from the money being thrown around. According to the report, China will be the big spender with $725 billion annually going toward infrastructure projects. The next four regions (all above $225 billion each) include the Middle East, Russia, India, and Brazil.

As I mentioned, it would be great if the global economy were in the situation in which both developed and emerging markets were able to spend freely on infrastructure. That is not the case, however, and Russia is a good example. As of early 2009, the country was in a shambles as the price of commodities fell to levels that leave many in the country searching for answers. I assume the infrastructure issue remains important to the Russian government, but it is far from the top of their list. The same can be said for a number of countries that rely on the demand for commodities to boost their economy (for example, the Middle East).

Chinese Stimulus Plan

When discussing emerging markets in any capacity, the main topic must include China, a growth machine. Even though China continues to grow its GDP at a rapid pace, it is no longer in the anticipated double digits it was just one year earlier. The global recession has caused the Chinese government to make unprecedented moves, and in November 2008, they decided to implement their own stimulus package to boost growth back to the double-digit levels. The heart of the plan will involve hundreds of billions of dollars being spent on new infrastructure and upgrades. The plan has the government spending $586 billion over a two-year span—roughly 7 percent of the country's GDP each year.[4] The spending began immediately with $18 billion spent in the fourth quarter of 2008.

According to a USA Today news story, the largest stimulus package in the history of China will focus on 10 areas, including much needed roads, housing, and transportation (rail and airports), as well as rebuilding the Sichuan province region devastated by the 2008 earthquake. The plan includes money going into rural areas that are lacking the basic essentials such as clean, running water and reliable electricity. By installing a water infrastructure system and power grids, the heavily populated rural area of China (where two-thirds of the 1.3 billion people live) can now be able to go out and buy products that require electricity and running water, such as televisions and refrigerators.[5] In the end, the infrastructure stimulus in rural China will lead to more expansion of the middle class and another secondary stimulus.

Keep in mind that infrastructure expansion in China is not a new concept. In the years leading up to the 2008 Beijing Summer Olympics, the government spent hundreds of billions on upgrading everything from the mass transit system to sports stadiums in the urban centers. Going back even further, China used infrastructure spending to boost their economy in the late 1990s during the Asian financial crisis.

Of course, the big question is which companies will benefit the most from the hundreds of billions being spent on infrastructure in the next two years. The situation in China is a bit different from that of the United States because a large portion of the money will be sent to companies that are partially owned or fully owned by the government. The likely winners as far as investing are concerned will be the commodity stocks and, in particular, the steel and concrete sectors. Think about where money will be spent and it is inevitable that steel and concrete will be the foundation of many of the projects, from new building to roads to water infrastructure to mass transit.

Potential Winning Infrastructure Candidates

When choosing the best infrastructure investment for your portfolio, there are several factors to consider. The first factor to be determined is how the company fits into the building process. Is the company an engineer that must be called on in the early stages to propose and eventually plan the project? Or is the company a supplier of the aggregates such as gravel, stone, and cement that are used to build the roads and bridges. The company could be a supplier of construction machinery that will not be called on until the project begins and the supplies are available. Because the process of completing a project can be time consuming, it is important to know when the company you are analyzing will realize the revenue of such projects.

Another factor that is very important is the geographical location of the company and where they generate the majority of their business. A company such as Caterpillar (NYSE: CAT) supplies its construction machinery worldwide and could benefit from infrastructure work in the United States and abroad. There are similar companies that will concentrate on the United States and miss a large portion of the potential overseas business.

Each company needs to be analyzed from a micro view that concentrates on the fundamentals as well as the technicals. Granted, most infrastructure stocks have unattractive charts in 2008–2009, but it must still be considered a factor when choosing a long-term investment. When looking at the fundamentals of infrastructure stocks, the valuations (P/E Ratio, etc.) are not the key figures. Because the stocks in the sector are considered growth plays, the concentration should be on the future growth prospects, not current valuation. Keep in mind that growth stocks often trade at a higher multiple (higher P/E Ratio) than their peers and therefore valuating infrastructure stocks is slightly different.

Finally, there is a little wiggle room when deciding on infrastructure stocks on the basis of specific projects the companies are working on. A personal example of a stock I owned for clients is Enbridge Inc. (NYSE: ENB), an oil and gas pipeline company. The reason for owning ENB was almost solely based on the company being responsible for the building of a pipeline from the Canadian oil sands in Alberta to the Pacific Ocean. The money behind this project was coming from who else but China. At the time, oil was in the middle of a major rally and the stock proved to be one of our firm's big winners before we sold it in 2008. The following stock ideas are explained thoroughly and you will have a good idea as to why they made the list of best long-term infrastructure investments.

Infrastructure Stock Ideas

The four infrastructure stock ideas discussed in this section cover the various stages of the building process. The stocks are my favorite long-term investment choices at the time this chapter was written; keep in mind, however, as new projects are awarded, there could be new investment candidates that arise.

AECOM Technology Corporation

AECOM Technology Corporation (NYSE: ACM) is a global provider of technical and management support services to a broad range of markets, including transportation, facilities, environmental, and energy. Its more than 43,000 employees serve clients in more than 100 countries, which led them to revenue of $5.2 billion in 2008, according to the company's annual report.[6] Some of its projects include the Second Avenue Subway in New York City, Wayang Windu Geothermal Project in Indonesia, the W Hotel in Shanghai, and the 2012 Olympics in London.

In February 2009, the company reported results for its first fiscal quarter of 2009, which ended in December 2008. Net income rose 31 percent to $40.5 million as revenue rose 37 percent to $1.5 billion. The CEO of the company touched on the infrastructure spending around the world as a benefit to the company going forward. He mentioned, in particular, a new university in Abu Dhabi, a major transit expansion in San Francisco, and a number of orders from the U.S. Air Force.

The numbers for the second fiscal quarter of 2009 were not quite as impressive as the first quarter, but the company did report an increase in revenue of 29 percent to $1.5 billion. Net income from continuing operations came in at $43 million, up 20 percent from a year earlier. An important number for infrastructure companies is the backlog, which stood at $9.2 billion at the end of the quarter, up 30 percent from the year before. All the numbers were provided in the company's earnings release.[7]

One of the reasons AECOM is one of my favorites in the sector is due to the diversity the company offers. Not only does AECOM offer international exposure as you can see from the projects mentioned, but also diversification throughout the various types of infrastructure projects—from schools to mass transit to energy facilities. And finally, the number one reason AECOM is my favorite in the sector—relative strength. As the overall global stock market got pummeled in 2008, AECOM closed out the year with a gain of 7 percent.[8] The relative strength is evident in Figure 5.1, which is the chart of AECOM from the time it went public in 2007.

Fluor Corporation

Fluor Corporation (NYSE: FLR) has been around for nearly 100 years and is the world's largest publicly owned engineering, procurement, construction, maintenance, and project management company.[9] The company has a global presence with offices on six continents and in more than 25 countries. The company's web site lists some of Fluor's

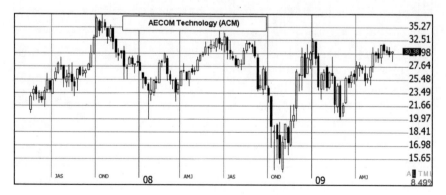

Figure 5.1 AECOM Technology Corporation Displaying Relative Strength
SOURCE: TeleChart2007® or StockFinder® chart, courtesy of Worden Brothers, Inc.

projects as the Trans–Alaska Pipeline, the world's largest polysilicon (used for solar energy) facility in China, an Iraq power plant, and the east span of the Oakland–Bay Bridge, the largest public infrastructure project in the history of California.[10]

In February 2009, it was announced that the United Kingdom gave approval to the construction of 10 wind farm sites off their shores. Fluor and a partner won a bid to build one of the farms, taking the company further into the future of alternative energy. The outlook for Fluor is positive even though it did not do as well in 2008 as AECOM did; the stock fell 38 percent, in line with the S&P 500. I believe the pullback gives investors an opportunity to begin building a position in a strong global leader in a sector that will flourish in the decade ahead. With a forward P/E Ratio below 10 and the PEG Ratio well below 1.0, the valuation model suggests Fluor is a buying opportunity at under $50.

The company reported on Monday, May 11, 2009, that first quarter earnings increased by 50 percent over the prior year. Revenue increased by 21 percent to $5.8 billion. Even though the backlog at Fluor is greater than AECOM, sitting at $29.1 billion, the number declined over a year earlier by 7 percent. The stock initially moved higher on the news and the buying continued into June. Figure 5.2 shows the action in 2008 and 2009 as the stock consolidates and offers a buy opportunity.

Figure 5.2   Fluor Consolidating after Big Sell-off
SOURCE: TeleChart2007® or StockFinder® chart, courtesy of Worden Brothers, Inc.

Granite Construction

Granite Construction (NYSE: GVA) does just what the name says—constructs things. Their forte includes roads, bridges, tunnels, airports, and other related infrastructure projects. Along with the actual building of structures, Granite also supplies the projects with aggregates such as sand, gravel, concrete, ready-mix, and others. Because the company can handle both large and small projects, Granite is poised to benefit from any infrastructure spending in the United States.[11]

Because of Granite's dual exposure to infrastructure spending and its concentration on the transportation aspect of the sector, I believe it is well positioned to win several large contracts. According to the company, it generates nearly 70 percent of its revenue from transportation-related infrastructure such as roads and mass transit. There is also the benefit of being able to supply the aggregates to their own projects as well as others they may not be participating in.

Granite had an outstanding 2008, gaining 21 percent and beating the S&P 500 by 60 percent. A fall in the market and infrastructure stocks in early 2009, however, has seen GVA trade at $30 after hitting $50 in December 2008. I feel an entry anywhere in the $20 to $30 range is too good to pass up on a stock that should continue to do well with or without a stimulus boost. Figure 5.3 is a chart of Granite that shows the pullback in 2009 and the support at the $30 range. Investors should look to that level as a range within which to begin buying.

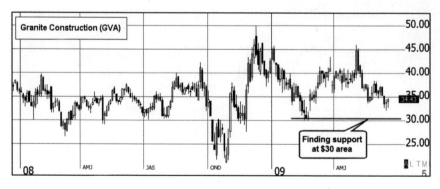

Figure 5.3 Granite Construction Finding Support at $30
SOURCE: TeleChart2007® or StockFinder® chart, courtesy of Worden Brothers, Inc.

URS Corporation

A major global engineering firm that is based in California, URS Corporation (NYSE: URS) works in both the public and private sectors. The firm has three divisions. The URS division is one of the largest providers of engineering, construction, and technical services in the world, with more than 50,000 employees. The EG&G division is one of the top contractors with the U.S. government serving the Department of Defense, NASA, and Homeland Security, as well as other small divisions. With the current state of the world, there is no doubt the government will continue to spend on defense regardless of what President Obama may say in his addresses to the public. The Washington division is also involved in engineering and technical services; it concentrates, however, on infrastructure, mining and power, industrial, and environmental projects. When the government starts to write checks to the infrastructure companies, this division will likely see the biggest boost. The boost from the announcement of the stimulus bill is evident in Figure 5.4, as URS has nearly doubled from the low in March to the high in June.

A few of URS's projects include the 17th Street Bridge in Atlanta, the $1.5 billion nuclear facility in New Mexico, and a mine in Bolivia. The company has a large international exposure and has projects across most industries, similar to AECOM. Unlike AECOM, URS did not have a strong 2008, as the stock prices fell 25 percent during the year. When analyzing the two companies on a fundamental basis, they are

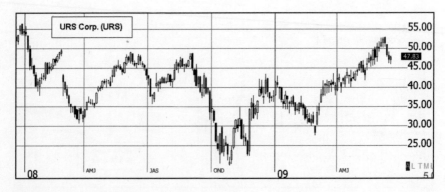

Figure 5.4 URS Corp.
Source: TeleChart2007® or StockFinder® chart, courtesy of Worden Brothers, Inc.

very similar and nearly interchangeable. My suggestion is to take the amount of money you would put into either stock and divide it by two and buy both stocks. For example, if you had $10,000 earmarked for AECOM, the better strategy would be to buy $5,000 of AECOM and $5,000 of URS. This lowers the risk through slight diversification and the reward should not be affected too dramatically, thus offering a higher reward-to-risk opportunity.

Infrastructure Exchange-Traded Funds

Investors in the twenty-first century have become skeptical of individual stocks for a number of reasons that include corruption, lying, and too much company-specific risk. The alternative is sitting out and missing investment opportunities of a lifetime or investing in exchange-traded funds (ETFs). All the information regarding the holdings and specifics for the infrastructure ETFs are taken directly from the ETF's web sites.

SPDR FTSE/Macquarie Global Infrastructure 100 ETF (GII)

SPDR FTSE/Macquarie Global Infrastructure 100 ETF (GII) is a true international ETF, with more than 10 countries represented. However, the nearly 40 percent weighting in the United States and another 13 percent in Japan make the ETF very one-sided. The very small exposure to the emerging markets, which have great potential in the infrastructure area, is a major concern. On top of the lack of country diversification is the 90 percent the ETF has invested in the utilities sector. While the utility stocks can be considered infrastructure investments, from my point of view they would be secondary plays that will not be the major beneficiaries of trillions being spent worldwide. In 2008, the ETF was able to beat the S&P 500, but still lost a hefty 32 percent with the foreign utilities in the top 10 taking the biggest hits. Even though the name sounds like a perfect investment choice for an international infrastructure investment play, I suggest you look elsewhere.[12] Figure 5.5 shows the struggles of GII throughout 2008 and into 2009 even as many infrastructure stocks rallied from the lows.

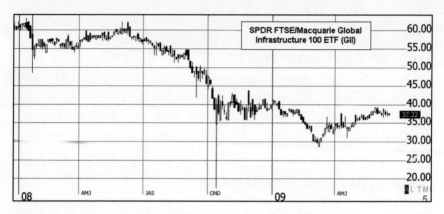

Figure 5.5   GII Lags Its Peers
SOURCE: TeleChart2007® or StockFinder® chart, courtesy of Worden Brothers, Inc.

iShares S&P Global Infrastructure Index ETF

iShares S&P Global Infrastructure Index ETF (IGF) is a slight improvement over GII because its exposure in the utility sector is only 44
percent. The downside is the majority of the top 10 holdings are international utilities that are not the stocks investors want to own to take
advantage of the infrastructure boom in the United States and abroad.
The ETF has 22 percent of its assets in the United States, followed by
three European countries (Germany, France, and Spain), making up a
total of 30 percent. Again, the top countries make up over 50 percent
of the ETF and the exposure to emerging markets is nearly nonexistent. If the goal was to gain exposure to the large-cap foreign utilities
and a small amount of industrials with ties to infrastructure, IGF would
be the perfect candidate. However, the search is for an ETF that will be
the biggest beneficiary from the great infrastructure build-out of the
twenty-first century. In 2008, IGF struggled, losing 41 percent of its
value.[13] The chart of IGF in Figure 5.6 is an example of why investors
are better off looking at alternative ETFs.

PowerShares Emerging Markets Infrastructure ETF

PowerShares Emerging Markets Infrastructure ETF (PXR) is one of
two infrastructure ETFs that concentrates on the emerging markets
(the other is the iShares S&P Emerging Markets Infrastructure ETF
(EMIF)). That being said, after China (16 percent), the United States

Figure 5.6 IGF Struggles to Join Rally
SOURCE: TeleChart2007® or StockFinder® chart, courtesy of Worden Brothers, Inc.

is the country with the second-largest allocation, at 11 percent. The
United States is obviously not an emerging country. There are U.S.-based
companies, though, that will benefit from the infrastructure expansion
in emerging markets. An example would be construction and agricultural equipment maker Caterpillar Inc. (CAT), which is the sixth-largest
holding of PXR. Other countries in the top five are emerging countries, including Indonesia, South Africa, and Brazil. The diversification
throughout continents, even in the top five countries, is impressive.

A major difference between PXR and the first two ETFs is its lack
of exposure to utility stocks. PXR has less than 2 percent in utilities
and concentrates on industrials (56 percent) and materials (41 percent).
When the infrastructure expansion begins, one of the first areas to
benefit will be the material stocks. The bridges and structures must be
made of something—look for the steel, iron, and other material stocks
to see their prices bounce off multiyear lows that were hit in 2008.
The PowerShares ETF is a fairly new vehicle, hitting the market in
October 2008 and was not welcomed with much fanfare. Although
the volume began to increase in early 2009 as the Obama infrastructure plan attracted investors, I expect the ETF to become one of
the few investment choices for both individual investors and money
managers.[14]

Even though PXR only began trading in October 2008, the chart
is very impressive, as shown in Figure 5.7. The ETF is a screaming buy
in the mid-$20s.

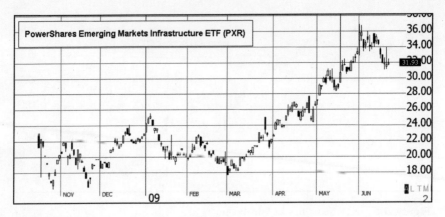

Figure 5.7   PXR Hitting New Highs
SOURCE: TeleChart2007® or StockFinder® chart, courtesy of Worden Brothers, Inc.

PowerShares Dynamic Building and Construction ETF

PowerShares Dynamic Building and Construction ETF (PKB) is a unique infrastructure ETF in that it has zero exposure to the utility sector and has all of its assets invested in U.S.-based stocks. This could be a good or bad thing, depending on what your investment objective may be. If the goal is to gain exposure to the domestic infrastructure upgrades proposed by President Obama, PKB could be the best investment choice.

The ETF has it pros, such as exposure to the U.S. infrastructure plan and large holdings in industrial stocks. On the other side of the coin, the ETF holds stocks that are not directly related to the government infrastructure plan. Examples are Lowe's Co. (LOW) and Home Depot (HD), the two largest home improvement stores in the United States. The last time I checked, Uncle Sam was not walking into your local Home Depot with the government printing press in his pocket. Even with the two home improvement stores in the top holdings, there are plenty of reasons to like PKB as an investment choice. A handful of some of my favorite material and infrastructure stocks are located in the top 10 holdings and therefore make PKB a viable investment choice for investors seeking domestic exposure to the infrastructure boom. Similar to its peers, PKB had a rough 2008, falling 36 percent during the 12-month span.[15] And even though PKB has come off the March 2009 lows, as shown in Figure 5.8, the ETF is struggling to break out in 2009.

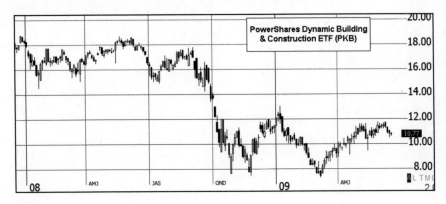

Figure 5.8 PKB Struggles to Break Out
Source: TeleChart2007® or StockFinder® chart, courtesy of Worden Brothers, Inc.

Another area the new administration is concentrating its efforts on with billions of dollars is alternative energy. I highlight my favorite green sectors in the next chapter and list a number of specific stocks and ETFs that investors can profit from.

Chapter 6

The Green Movement: Alternative Energy

W hen oil crossed above \$100 per barrel and former vice president Al Gore was gallivanting around world promoting his movie about global warming, the green movement to alternative energy appeared to be a solid plan. However, one year later with oil below \$40 and Al Gore no longer in the spotlight, the push for alternative fuel sources has been put on the back burner. Against the current economic backdrop, the worst the United States has experienced since the Great Depression, the green movement has a new meaning. The green everyone is concerned about during a recession is cold hard cash; saving the environment is no longer a pressing matter.

While there are a large number of people behind the movement toward alternative energy, there remains a fair share of naysayers. Is global warming really happening or can the recent increase in temperatures be explained by normal cyclical changes in weather patterns?

This is a debate for another time and book because the bottom line is that from an investment point of view there will be opportunities to make big money in alterative energy stocks as governments and the private sector feel the pressure from stakeholders to move to a more green way of doing business.

Depending on which scientist you talk to, global warming and the movement to alternative energy is either necessary or simply a fad. If oil makes its way back to triple digits and the amount of fossil fuels coming out of the ground does not increase, however, the end result will be eco nomically viable alternative energy choices. Another reason alternative energy has become almost a necessary investment for governments is their dependence on foreign oil. The United States, for example, receives a large portion of its oil from countries that, frankly, are not friendly with the United States. If you had to rely on your enemy each day to supply you with the fuel that runs your company, would you feel safe? I sure as heck would not and that is why the United States in particular must begin to wean itself off of its dependence on foreign oil.

You will learn more about peak oil and how rising prices of fossils fuels in the coming decades will force the hand of the United States and other countries around the world to invest heavily in the green movement. The three areas I highlight in the remainder of this chapter are where I believe the most money can be made from an investment point of view. Nuclear power is a sector that has been vilified in the eyes of many because of the safety concerns, but I believe this is overblown and will offer a number of investment opportunities. Solar is the golden child of the green movement, but investors must know where to invest in the sector and I will help decipher the process for you. Finally, wind is my favorite of the three and an array of investment opportunities await you in that sector.

Going Nuclear

The global warming argument for alternative fuels often ends with solar, wind, and other safe and environmentally favorable options. One that often gets overlooked for a number of reasons is nuclear energy.

Because of two extremely serious incidents at nuclear power plants in the last three decades, the case for nuclear energy always begins with safety.

While I am a major proponent of nuclear energy in the United States and abroad, I will be the first to yell NIMBY (Not in My Backyard) if a proposed nuclear power plant were to be erected in my backyard. The incident at Three Mile Island in central Pennsylvania in 1979 was the most significant accident in the history of U.S. nuclear power plants. Even though it was the worst the United States has experienced, there were no reported illnesses from the partial core meltdown.[1] There was also a meltdown that took place at the Chernobyl nuclear power plant facility in the former Soviet Union in 1986. To date, the Chernobyl accident is the worst on record and resulted in 2 immediate deaths, but heavy exposure to radiation has been blamed for many more deaths. The cause of the disaster was blamed on both a flawed design and operator error. In any case, the cause of the Chernobyl meltdown is one that would have likely never occurred in a well-run facility such as those in the United States and other developed countries. Because of these disasters the entire industry is much better run and safety should not be a major concern.

So why are people in the United States in particular so against nuclear energy? The same reason people are scared of anything—the unknown. If they understood the safety precautions that have taken place in the industry since the Three Mile Island accident, there would be many more supporters of the environmentally friendly alternative energy source. Along with emitting very low levels of carbon dioxide (suspected of causing global warming), nuclear energy can generate a high amount of electrical energy in a single plant and the technology is developed and ready to hit the ground running.[2]

Even though the United States has not built a new nuclear power plant in three decades, it does not suggest every country acts in this manner. In May 2008, Italy announced it will resume building nuclear energy plants within five years. This is a major move by a country that two decades ago passed a referendum that banned nuclear energy and deactivated all of its reactors.[3] Italy is not alone. Sweden announced in February 2009 that it would reverse an old government policy that called for all of the country's nuclear power plants to be shut down by 2010. The reason for the reversal is because the country wants to move forward with a long-term, sustainable energy and climate policy.[4] Nuclear power becomes a formidable choice because of the low emissions and the resulting consequence that the country will not have to rely on fossil fuels from unstable regions of the world such as the Middle East and Africa.

A country that has already embraced the benefits of nuclear power is France. According to the World Nuclear Association, as of February 2009, France had 59 nuclear reactors operating and one more under construction. The country generates 77 percent of its energy through its nuclear power plants, the most of any single country. The number one reason behind the focus on nuclear energy is energy security—France does not rely on unstable and often unfriendly nations to supply its people with energy.[5] The United States has more reactors (104) with none under construction, but only generates 20 percent of its power from nuclear energy. There is an amazing upside for stocks that are involved in building nuclear power plants and that mine or supply them with the uranium.

Adding to the upside for stocks in the nuclear energy sector is the emerging markets and, in particular, the BRIC (Brazil, Russia, India, China) countries. China currently generates less than 2 percent of its power from nuclear power plants; Russia is at 16 percent, India 2.5 percent, and Brazil at 2.8 percent. China currently has eleven nuclear power reactors in operation with seven more under construction and an additional 10 about to commence construction. (All of these numbers are provided by the World Nuclear Association.) With the population expanding and, more importantly, the middle class exploding, the demand for energy is increasing at a rapid pace. This has resulted in China doing everything it can to keep up with demand. Along with the pressure from the developed countries to lower carbon emissions, one of the best alternatives is nuclear power.[6]

India does not currently generate a large portion of its power through nuclear power plants, but the ambitions for the coming decades are lofty. By 2050 the country aims to generate 25 percent of its electricity from nuclear power. If this goal is met, it will require the capacity to grow a hundred times that of the 2002 capacity. A report by

KPMG also notes it will cost India $120 to $150 billion in five years, starting in 2008 to upgrade its power infrastructure.[7] I touch on the power grids in more detail in Chapter 5.[8]

Nuclear Energy Investments

The four nuclear energy investments focus on very different aspects of the power generation process. They include the world's largest supplier of uranium, a provider of pure-play nuclear power company, a U.S.-based utility, and an ETF that encompasses all areas. With such a diverse list, you have the option of narrowing your investment objective or you can cover the whole spectrum with the nuclear ETF.

Cameco Corp

Regardless of where the nuclear power plant is located or who runs it, the one main ingredient to producing energy is uranium. Cameco (NYSE: CCJ) is the world's largest producer of uranium, and is based in Saskatchewan, Canada. The company's uranium production accounts for approximately 19 percent of the world supply and it comes from mines in Canada and the United States. Cameco also has rights to uranium-rich land in Canada and Australia that could fuel growth of uranium production in the years to come.

Since topping out in 2007 at a per share price of $56, the stock fell nearly 80 percent in the next 18 months. Figure 6.1 shows the fall of Cameco and the rise off the lows in 2009. The decline was fueled by a fall in commodity prices and, more specifically, the price of uranium. The spot price of uranium fell from a high of $136 in mid-2007 to below $50 in 2008 as the bubble burst on the thinly traded commodity. Figure 6.2 shows the rise and fall of uranium prices that was spurred by the explosion of commodity prices and the worries of a shortage of uranium. Along with falling commodity prices was the recession that ravaged any stock that would be hurt by global growth. The thought process was that global wealth was disappearing and therefore governments and private companies did not have the capital to go ahead with expanding the nuclear power capabilities around the world. While the expansion may have slowed from the pace of the mid-2000s, there is still a big upside for Cameco and the expansion of new nuclear facilities.

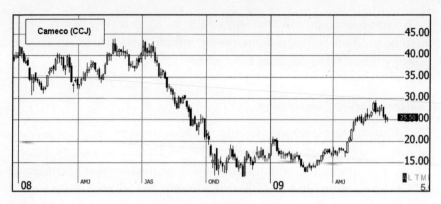

Figure 6.1 CCJ Hurt by Falling Uranium Prices
SOURCE: TeleChart2007® or StockFinder® chart, courtesy of Worden Brothers, Inc.

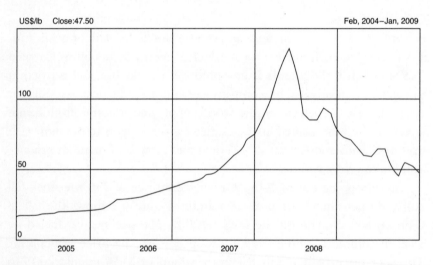

Figure 6.2 Uranium Spot Price
SOURCE: www.cameco.com.

The bottom line for Cameco is that it has to see uranium prices begin to turn around before a sustainable rally in the stock is possible. For uranium to gain in price, any likelihood for such a gain comes down to supply versus demand. If the predictions out of a number of well-respected nuclear power agencies are correct, a sizable amount of new reactors will be coming online in the next two decades. Couple that with the rising demand for energy as the global population increases and the demand for uranium will increase. At the same time, there is likely no major increase in supply hitting the markets, and simple economics tells me that higher prices will be the end result.

Areva

Areva (Paris: CEI) may not be a household name in the United States, but around the world and specifically in Europe, the company is known as the leader of nuclear power generation. The company considers itself a world energy expert that offers its customers technological solutions for nuclear power generation.[9] Based in France, Areva is involved in every step of the nuclear energy process and in my mind is the best pure-play investment in the sector.

The process begins with Areva mining and enriching the uranium that will be used at a nuclear facility they have built and service on a regular basis. Once the fuel is used, it must be recycled, and Areva is available. About a third of the company's revenue comes from its Areva T&D division, which transmits and distributes the nuclear power that is generated by the power plants. And why not make the radiation safety equipment needed by the industry? It is clear that Areva is a rare company that is large enough to cover all the aspects of the niche nuclear power sector.[10]

The price action of Areva is similar to that of many stocks in the nuclear industry and the overall global stock market. After hitting a high in 2008 the bottom was pulled out from under the stock as seen in Figure 6.3. The 50 percent-plus drop from the high of 820 set in 2008 has offered an attractive entry point for investors that have a time horizon of several years and believe that nuclear power will continue to gain market share around the world. The chart in Figure 6.3 shows the fall in early 2009 as well as the rebound off the April low. Entry for Areva below 450 is what investors should be looking for if considering buying.

In January 2009, Areva and the country of Niger announced the terms of a mining agreement that will give Areva access to the Imouraren uranium deposit. When mining begins in 2012, it will create the largest uranium mine in Africa and the second largest in the world, resulting in Niger becoming the second-largest uranium producer. According to reports, the initial startup cost will be approximately $1.6 billion,

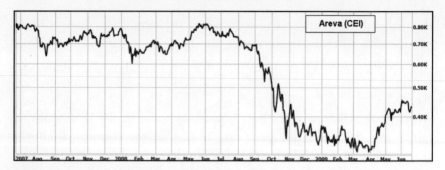

Figure 6.3   Areva—the Nuclear Pure Play
SOURCE: Yahoo! Finance. Reproduced with permission of Yahoo! Inc. ©2009 by Yahoo! Inc. YAHOO! and the YAHOO! logo are trademarks of Yahoo! Inc.

and the mine will operate for 35 years. Beneficiaries of the startup costs will be the mining equipment and engineering firms, many of which Areva can keep in-house through its various divisions.[11]

On June 17, 2009, the U.S. Energy Department announced that it planned to award $18.5 billion in loan guarantees for the construction of new nuclear power plants to four utility companies. There has not been a new nuclear power plant built in the United States in decades and advocates hope this is the first step in a wave of nuclear expansion. Areva is one of those advocates and they are already benefiting from the Energy Department's decision. According to the Washington Post,[12] one of the new power plants will use an Areva design for a Maryland project.

Exelon

Exelon (NYSE: EXC) is one of the largest electric utilities in the United States, with nearly $19 billion in annual revenue and more than five million customers. The company also boasts the largest and most efficient nuclear fleet in the United States and third-largest commercial fleet in the world.[13] The company has 10 stations and 17 reactors that represent approximately 20 percent of all the nuclear energy produced in the United States. According to the company's web site, in 2007 the use of the nuclear power plants versus coal-based generation plants reduced the amount of carbon dioxide emissions by 121 million metric tons. The carbon dioxide emissions avoided by using nuclear power is equivalent to that emitted by 23 million passenger cars—double the amount of cars in Illinois, Pennsylvania, and New Jersey combined.[14]

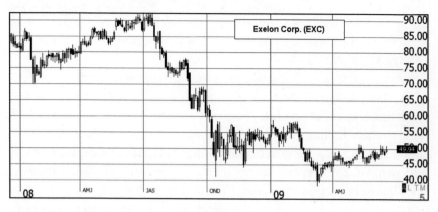

Figure 6.4   Exelon Corp Consolidating Near Low
SOURCE: TeleChart2007® or StockFinder® chart, courtesy of Worden Brothers, Inc.

As an investment opportunity, Exelon will benefit from new approvals of nuclear power plants in the United States. In March 2007, the company became the first nuclear power plant operator to receive an early site permit for possible plant construction. Exelon filed an application for a new nuclear power plant in September 2008 in southeast Texas. Because Exelon is a clear leader in the U.S. nuclear energy industry, it is natural to believe that they will be a beneficiary of a move back into the expansion of the country's nuclear power generation capabilities.[15]

The utility stocks as a whole have struggled through the first few months of 2009, as money has moved into more aggressive sectors. This action has hurt the price of Exelon, as shown in Figure 6.4. The good news is that as long as the stock holds above $40, it will be considered a long-term buying opportunity.

Market Vectors Nuclear Energy ETF

Other than Areva, there are not many pure-play nuclear investment options for investors. Instead of concentrating on a single stock that may offer exposure to the mining of uranium or nuclear infrastructure, there is the route of an exchange-traded fund (ETF). There are currently three ETFs that focus on the nuclear sector, and my favorite is from the Van Eck family of ETFs—the Market Vectors Nuclear Energy ETF (NYSE: NLR). The ETF tracks the DAXglobal Nuclear Energy Index, which is a true global index with a 28 percent weighting in Canada,

22 percent in Japan, 22 percent in the United States, 12 percent in France, and 11 percent in Australia. (These weightings were current as of May 31, 2009.)

As far as sector allocation, uranium mining makes up 40 percent of the ETF, followed by nuclear generation at 24 percent and nuclear plant builders at 22 percent. There are a total of 32 stocks in the ETF, with the top holding mentioned earlier: Cameco. Exelon is the fifth-largest holding, and Areva is the tenth-largest. The annual expense ratio is 0.65 percent, a small price to pay for the diversification offered through the ETF. Keep in mind that an ETF will nearly eliminate the company-specific risk associated with an individual stock, but at the same time, the reward also decreases because of diversification. If you are an investor who believes in the macro theme that nuclear energy will become more of a major player in global power generation and do not want to pick stocks, NLR is the best investment option.[16] Through the first five months of 2009, NLR has been strong because money is flowing into more aggressive sectors, such as nuclear power. Figure 6.5 shows the rebound of NLR off the March low.

Solar Energy

Probably the hottest (no pun intended) alternative energy option in the media and for the general public is solar energy. The solar stocks have seen their stock prices jump to record highs before the recession took them back to earth. When the stock market was hitting new highs in

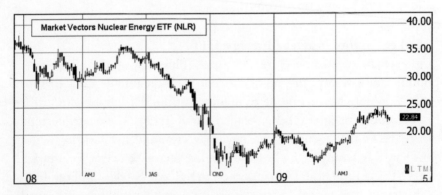

Figure 6.5 NLR Beginning to Move Higher
SOURCE: TeleChart2007® or StockFinder® chart, courtesy of Worden Brothers, Inc.

2007 it was not uncommon to have a solar stock jump 20 percent in a day on news of a new order. The sector became a true growth story as global demand for the alternative energy increased at breakneck speeds.

According to Ardour Capital Investments, revenues for the global solar industry are expected to grow 30 to 35 percent annually in the next three years. This growth will be driven by solar electric output that will likely hit 20 GW in 2011, up from a mere 4 GW in 2007.[17] Worldwide photovoltaic (PV) installations increased by 2,826 MW in 2007, up from 1,744 MW installed in 2006. In 1985, only 21 MW were installed. Over the last 15 years, the demand for solar energy has grown at an approximate rate of 30 percent per annum.[18]

As of 2007, the United States accounted for 8 percent of the world PV market of 2,826 MW. Germany remained the dominant force in the industry, with a 47 percent market share, followed by Spain at 23 percent. Japan was third with 8 percent. These four countries are currently the only major worldwide players. Figure 6.6 shows the breakdown of the PV worldwide market in 2007. The statistics were provided by the research firm Solarbuzz.

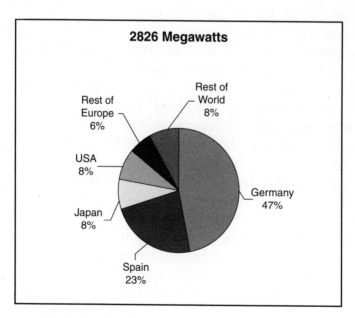

Figure 6.6   World Photovoltaic Market in 2007
Source: Solarbuzz LLC.

Benefits of Solar Energy

The biggest argument from the solar energy advocates has to do with the knowledge that the big, yellow shiny star in the sky can provide clean and efficient energy to our planet. With two billion people in the world without energy, the shining sun is now an alternative to building fossil fuel power plants. Considering that Earth receives more energy from the sun in one hour than the world uses in an entire year, there must be a way to harvest the endless supply of energy. As technologies become more advanced, user friendly, and cost effective, the use of solar energy as a true alternative to fossil fuels will rise. My concern about it, however, is that if oil is below $50 per barrel, the money that was earmarked for spending on solar will be shifted elsewhere. Unfortunately, it will take another spike in the price of oil to create the sense of urgency to move toward alternative fuel sources such as solar.[19]

Other benefits of solar power is its cleanliness and that it is renewable and sustainable. The green movement supporters love solar energy for this exact reason and the news media have definitely jumped on the bandwagon. With zero emissions of carbon dioxide into the atmosphere, solar energy truly is "clean energy."

Similar to other alternative energy sources, solar energy will allow the United States to reduce its dependence on foreign energy, specifically oil. As long as there is sunlight, there is a possibility of implementing a solar energy plan. As the cost of oil and other fossil fuels fall, will solar energy become too expensive an an alternative? Possibly, but that should continue to decrease each year as the technology improves and it becomes less expensive to produce the PV cells. There may be a high initial startup cost to install the solar power capabilities for large-scale projects or even residential setups. But keep in mind that each month the money saved using solar power versus paying the utility costs will result in a breakeven point in the not-so-distant future. Whether you are currently heating your home with natural gas or heating oil, the costs have risen sharply over the past decade and many families struggle to pay their utility bills.

On top of the monthly savings in utility bills, the government is also handing out cash incentives for utilities, corporations, and individuals to make the move toward a solar energy alternative. In the end, money talks and when the price of oil is above $100, the solar alternative is viable. When oil prices are below $50 a barrel, the government must make the conversion to solar worth the taxpayers' money, which it can do through tax incentives.

Solar Energy Investments

The three stocks I chose as my favorites in the solar energy sector are leaders in their respective niche areas. The first stock is the best-known of the solar plays, the second takes us to Europe, and the third is a smaller company that was once a high flyer that has come back down in recent years. All three have their pros and cons and are viable investment options.

First Solar

First Solar Corporation (NASDAQ: FSLR), based in Ohio, makes cadmium telluride thin film photovoltaic cells (PV) that significantly lower electricity costs. If you have ever looked into investing in the solar energy industry or traded momentum stocks, I am sure you have run across FSLR. One of the favorites during the most recent bull market, FSLR began trading in late 2007 at $26 and never looked back. Within one year, the stock was above $250 and topped out in March 2008 at $317 before falling back into the double digits in November 2008. Was the stock overvalued at $317? Yes! Was the stock undervalued at $86? Yes! Investors become irrational at both tops and bottoms and in the case of FSLR there were opportunities to pick up the stock at bargain basement prices. But it is not over.

The stock has a very bright future ahead of it because it is a leader in the manufacture of thin solar modules, and as a matter of fact, is the largest such manufacturer in the world. When the company went public in 2007, its manufacturing capacity was 75 MW; by the end of 2009, the company expects to expand its capacity to over 1 GW, more than 13 times the 2007 number.[20] The expansion allows FSLR to grow in the United States and also overseas. In January 2009, the company inked a deal with Masdar Abu Dhabi Future Energy Co. to become a part of the largest grid-connected PV system in the Middle East.[21] By establishing themselves as a major player in emerging markets around the world, it will only increase the possibilities for FSLR.

One of the arguments against FSLR is the high P/E ratio; a growth stock, however, should fetch a high earnings multiple. In lieu of the P/E ratio, investors should be focusing on the PEG Ratio (price-to-earnings divided by growth) to get a true valuation of a company. According to Yahoo! Finance, in mid-June 2009, the PEG ratio was well below 1.0, suggesting that the growth rate of FSLR is above the P/E ratio. A PEG ratio under one is undervalued and FSLR in the $150-to-$175 range is offering a great long-term opportunity for investors willing to take the risk of an individual stock in the solar energy sector. Figure 6.7 provides a good insight into the ups and downs of First Solar and reinforces the idea that investors should always wait for pullbacks before they buy.

Q-Cells

Q-Cells AG (QCE.DE), based in Germany, is the world's largest independent manufacturer of solar cells. Even the biggest name in the world has not been able to sidestep the economic slowdown. In December 2008, Q-Cells announced lowered expectations for fiscal year 2008 and 2009 after a number of customers canceled orders. The company is now forecasting total production in 2009 to be between 800 MWp

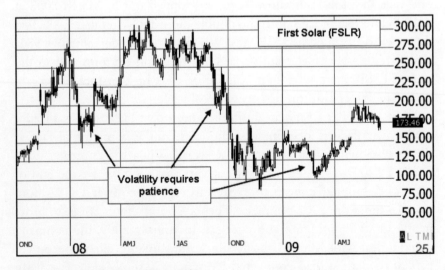

Figure 6.7   Volatility of First Solar
SOURCE: TeleChart2007® or StockFinder® chart, courtesy of Worden Brothers, Inc.

and 1 GWp, lower than the previous forecast. The company lowered its revenue estimates at the same time. If Q-Cells meets its lowered revenue range, it will still result in year-over-year growth of 40 percent. According to the company's web site, it is looking at the second half of 2009 to begin picking up again and that should be fostered by a recovery in the global economy.[22]

The news from the company in December 2008 did not do much for instilling confidence in their investors and the stock continued the fall that began earlier in the year. By March, the stock, which is traded in Germany, fell to a new low, under $10. As you can see in Figure 6.8 the stock has fallen sharply in the past year and investors should not yet be catching the falling knife. Two months after trading below $10, Q-Cells more than doubled and was back above $20 per share. An opportunity to buy Q-Cells below $20 will get the okay from me if you have a long-term horizon. Once the news begins to improve for the solar industry, Q-Cells will be well off the lows and the buying opportunity will have passed.

MEMC Electronic Materials

The company could be considered the building block of the PV solar cell industry. The wafers manufactured by MEMC (NYSE: WFR) become the solar cells that generate solar energy around the world. Sales from the company are global, with three-fourths of revenue coming from outside the United States.[23] MEMC had benefited greatly from rising polysilicon prices that hit a high of $450/kg in the

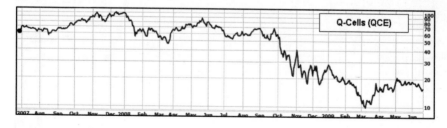

Figure 6.8 Q-Cells
SOURCE: Yahoo! Finance. Reproduced with permission of Yahoo! Inc. ©2009 by Yahoo! Inc. YAHOO! and the YAHOO! logo are trademarks of Yahoo! Inc.

middle of 2008. Just over six months later, the prices fell to $150/kg and several analysts have forecast prices to fall into the double digits. The price of MEMC's stock has gone the way of polysilicon prices and fell over 80 percent in 2008. This is after rising 567 percent during the previous three years.

There are two major reasons the price of polysilicon has fallen so dramatically in 2008 and early 2009. First, the global economic slowdown has lowered demand for solar cells, and thus the wafers. The second reason is the increase of players in the space, thus resulting in supply rising above demand. I can also throw in the situation that the $430/kg price was irrational and for lack of better words—a bubble. Now that the bubble has burst and MEMC is well off the recent highs, there could be an opportunity for investors who are willing to take a chance on a company that is a major player in the solar energy industry. Competition will be fierce, but because of the reputation and diversity MEMC offers in other industries with its other products, I am giving it a green flag.[24] The weekly chart of MEMC in Figure 6.9 shows the runup of the stock price with the rally in polysilicon prices before the recession took down the stock from the highs. The stock was consolidating in 2009, and if it can break out above the $20 range, it could run.

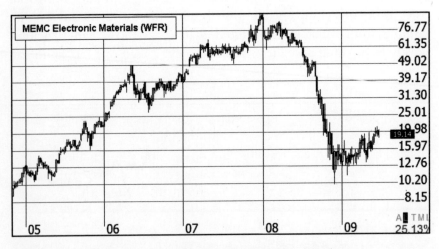

Figure 6.9   MEMC Electronic Materials Looking for a Breakout
SOURCE: TeleChart2007® or StockFinder® chart, courtesy of Worden Brothers, Inc.

Wind Power

Harnessing the energy of the wind sounds like a great idea that makes logical sense to many, including myself. The only problem is that there must be a consistent wind source and even more important, the infrastructure to convert the wind into usable energy must be present. In a 2008 report put together by the U.S. Department of Energy, "20% Wind Energy by 2030: Increasing Wind Energy's Contribution to U.S. Electricity Supply," the government believes it is not out of the question that the United States could be generating one-fifth of its energy from wind farms in nearly every state by 2030.[25]

The wind industry received a major boost when oil tycoon T. Boone Pickens announced in 2008 he was building an enormous wind farm and is a major supporter of the energy source. The Pickens Plan, as it is referred to, calls for wind energy to account for 22 percent of all energy produced in the United States. In the oil tycoon's plan, he backs the expansion of wind farms in the Great Plains and predicts such an expansion would produce 138,000 new jobs in the first year. Over a 10-year period, the number of jobs created by the new wind farms could be more than 3.4 million.

The big push by Pickens has to do with lowering the nation's dependence on foreign oil and I cannot agree with him more. In January 2009, the United States imported 409 million barrels of oil, accounting for 67.4 percent of all oil used in the country. What is even more mind-blowing is the amount of money sent overseas to pay for the foreign oil—$17 billion. If you want to keep track of the rising number, go to the web site www.pickensplan.com, which updates them monthly.[26]

The United States is definitely lagging behind many regions around the world in the field of producing energy from wind. At the end of 2007, the United States was generating less than 1 percent of its electricity through wind power. This is even after growing at an average annual rate of 29 percent from 2002 through 2007. According to the American Wind Energy Association (AWEA), the estimated wind energy potential for the United States is 10,777 billion kWh annually—more than twice the electricity generated in the United States today.[27]

Even though the United States has not been a major player in wind energy in the past, in 2008 it became the world's leader—surpassing Germany. By adding an additional 8,358 MW in 2008, the United States upped its total capacity to 25,170 MW, slightly above the 23,902 MW in Germany. The substantial expansion in wind energy helped push the United States's generating capacity higher by 50 percent in 12 months. The expansion created 35,000 new jobs, bringing the total jobs in the industry to 85,000.

Joining the United States in expanding its wind power capacity by 50 percent was China, who led the Asian regional boom. China now has a capacity of 12,200 MW, up from 5,900 MW one year earlier. "In 2009, new installed capacity is expected to nearly double again, which will be one third or more of the world's total new installed capacity for the year," said Li Junfeng, secretary general of the Chinese Renewable Energy Industry Association (CREIA). The Chinese government has set a goal to reach 30,000 MW of wind power by 2020, but many believe the country will reach that goal by 2010 and will once again double capacity in 2009 to approximately 24,000 MW. Statistics from the Amererican Wind Energy Association in Figure 6.10 show the newly installed capacity in 2008, and it is interesting to see that the United States and China make up over half of all new capacity.[28]

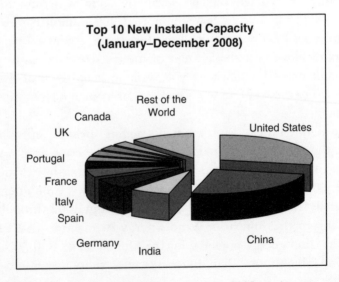

Figure 6.10   New Installed Wind Power Capacity 2008
SOURCE: American Wind Energy Association.

In Europe, where wind power has been more significant for years because of Spain, Germany, and Denmark, the growth of more capacity continues. As more European countries embrace the use of wind power, it is clear that wind is the number one green energy choice in the region. When the growth in the United States, China, and Europe are combined, the end result is tens of billions of dollars being spent in the industry and a number of investing opportunities for investors. The global wind market for turbine installations in 2008 was nearly $50 billion, according to the American Wind Energy Association. My job is to share with you companies I believe will benefit from continued spending in the industry and help you make money.

Issues with Wind Power

Moving the United States closer to the goal of generating 20 percent of its energy from wind is no easy task, and there will be challenges that must be conquered along the way. The country's transmission system that transports the energy harnessed from wind to urban areas is in need of a major upgrade along with the associated power grid. Growth will be needed in the wind-energy workforce and related industries. If the country is to move to 20 percent wind energy in the next two decades, a large workforce will be needed to build the wind turbines and install them around the country and even after they are up and running there will be a need for regular maintenance. Several of the companies that could benefit from growth in demand for wind turbines and related products are discussed next. The U.S. Department of Energy report suggests the wind energy industry could support 500,000 jobs in the United States in the decade preceding the 2030 deadline.

To achieve the 20 percent goal there must be an increase in technology and innovation in the industry. Think back 20 years ago and how technology has changed our lives 10 times over. Nobody can say for certain where wind technology will be in another 20 years, but I can say with certainty that innovation, whether in the United States or abroad, will alter the landscape dramatically, hopefully for the better. Another challenge that is often overlooked is the impact the expansion of wind energy will have on the environment. At first thought, the renewable, green energy is great for the environment.

But consider the land that is needed to house the large wind turbines and the effects it may have on local wildlife. The industry also runs into the same issue the nuclear energy industry has: NIMBY. I cannot blame people for not wanting the monstrous wind turbines in their backyard, and nobody wants to hurt Bambi. But, at the end of the day, no energy source is perfect, and wind will likely be a major player in the United States regardless of what you and I desire.

Investing in Wind

There are several avenues that can be taken when investing in the wind energy sector. There is the maker of the large wind turbines or the maker of the small electronics that run the turbines. Investors can also look at the utility companies that harness wind energy and even look overseas for opportunities. Three stocks and one ETF made the list and what I love about all of them is that they are not household names—yet!

Otter Tail Corp.

The company could be considered a small conglomerate because it has a variety of operations that range from an electric utility to a medical equipment supplier to a manufacturer of PVC pipes. The reason Otter Tail Corp. (NASDAQ: OTTR) is considered an opportunity in the wind energy sector is its ownership of DMI Industries, a major U.S. player in the manufacturing of wind towers. The company has three plants located in the United States and has one of the largest tower manufacturing capabilities in North America.[29] Because OTTR is a conglomerate, from an investment standpoint, the company is not a pure play wind investment, but there is enough exposure to make it a viable choice. Technically, the stock floundered in 2009 after pulling back from an all-time high in mid-2008. The chart is on display in Figure 6.11 and it is evident that the stock is struggling to move higher and that is why I would look for a breakout above $25 for a buy signal.

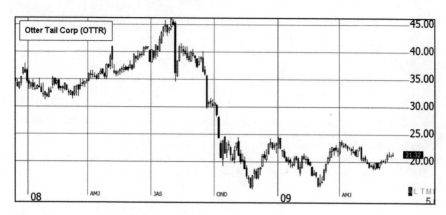

Figure 6.11   Waiting for Otter Tail Corp. to Break Out
SOURCE: TeleChart2007® or StockFinder® chart, courtesy of Worden Brothers, Inc.

Vestas Wind Systems

The Dutch company claims to be the world's leading supplier of wind power solutions and you will not get an argument from me considering Vestas (VWS.DE) has a 23 percent market share and over 38,000 wind turbines installed globally. Not even the worst economic slowdown in decades could stop the growth of Vestas in 2008. The company's annual report shows revenue of 6,035 million euros in 2008, an increase of 24 percent over the 2007 number. The future looks just as bright for Vestas as the company continues its expansion around the world and I am very excited about its growth in both the United States and China. The company expected to deliver its first kW turbines during the second quarter of 2009 from its factory in China. As I pointed out earlier in this chapter, China is well on its way to becoming number two in the world in wind power (behind the United States). Looking out over the next decade, Vestas believes the installed wind power capacity on average will experience an annual growth rate of approximately 20 percent because wind power uses no water and does not emit CO_2.[30]

Technically, the stock found a floor in October 2008, and when the global stock markets hit new lows in March 2009, Vestas did not join them. The relative strength on the chart is shown in Figure 6.12.

Figure 6.12 Vestas Wind Systems Showing Relative Strength
SOURCE: Yahoo! Finance. Reproduced with permission of Yahoo! Inc. ©2009 by Yahoo! Inc.
YAHOO! and the YAHOO! logo are trademarks of Yahoo! Inc.

American Superconductor

So how does a semiconductor company fall into the category of a wind investment? American Superconductor (NASDAQ: AMSC) makes electronic equipment that is used in wind turbines. Their products offers the operators of wind farms the ability to regulate the voltage of the wind turbines. This allows for the elimination of fluctuating voltage that can occur with wind energy. AMSC is definitely not the first name you think of when wind power investing is brought up, but they do have a niche product that is needed and will be one of the areas in which innovation will play a major role. As wind energy evolves, AMSC hopes to be on the cutting edge with harnessing the full power of the wind through innovative electrical systems that will maximize the wind farm. In 2008, AMSC got a boost from a $450 million contract with Sinovel Wind, a Chinese-based company. Based on the growth in China in respect to wind power, AMSC could be positioned well to benefit from the continued expansion.

AMSC bottomed in November 2008 and began a fresh uptrend almost immediately and within six months the stock was up 200 percent. Figure 6.13 illustrates the big rally and at the same time that AMSC has a long way to go to get back to the 2008 high.

First Trust Global Wind Energy ETF

Because of the risk of investing in individual stocks within a sector that I consider risky because of the unknown, one alternate option is an ETF. Another reason an ETF makes sense for the wind energy sector is

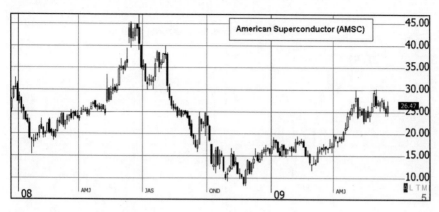

Figure 6.13 American Superconductor Rallies 200 Percent
SOURCE: TeleChart2007® or StockFinder® chart, courtesy of Worden Brothers, Inc.

because it is quite difficult to determine who will be the leader when the technology begins to flourish. There are currently two ETFs in the United States that focus solely on the wind sector. The PowerShares Global Wind Energy ETF (NASDAQ: PWND) was launched in July 2008 and was the second to market. The first to market was the FirstTrust Global Wind Energy ETF (NYSE: FAN), my choice as the better investment option.

The ETF is composed of approximately 56 stocks from around the world, with a heavy concentration in Europe. Spain, Germany, and Denmark make up 50 percent of the allocation and the United States is responsible for 16 percent. Vestas Wind Systems is the number two holding, making up 8 percent of the ETF, while AMSC and OTTR make up less than 1 percent each. The expense ratio is 0.6 percent, an acceptable number considering it is focusing on a niche sector. The ETF began trading in June at $31 per share, and by October it was already down 50 percent because of overall market conditions. The volume and excitement over the ETF and the wind power sector in general has waned, but I believe this is the time you need to begin building a position in the out-of-favor sector.[31] As of June 2009, the ETF had worked its way back into the low teens and has established a bottom at the March low. Figure 6.14 shows the construction action since the low of March 2009 and indicates why I am bullish at a price below $15 per share.

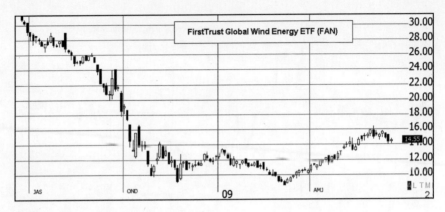

Figure 6.14   FAN is a Buy under $15
SOURCE: TeleChart2007® or StockFinder® chart, courtesy of Worden Brothers, Inc.

Overall, the alternative energy sector offers an array of profitable investment opportunities and at the end of the day it comes down to patience and a little luck with picking the right stock. I have tried to offer both aggressive and conservative options for investors looking for some action in the sector.

I discuss one of my favorite sectors heading into the Next Great Bull Market in the next chapter—commodities. Everything from gold to corn to lithium is discussed, with specific ideas of how to make money as inflation rises, the dollar falls, and the demand for commodities picks up.

Chapter 7

The Long-Term Bull Market for Commodities

The commodity sector was on fire from March 1999 until August 2008. The Dow Jones AIG Commodity Index rose from a low of 74 in 1999 to a high of 238 in 2008; a gain of 222 percent. The S&P 500 lost value during the same time. In Figure 7.1, the Dow Jones AIG Commodity Index shows the rally to new highs and the fall from grace in 2008. The demand for commodities such as wheat and copper exploded along with the growth of emerging markets around the world. As the population grew in the developing countries and more people were moving out of poverty, the demand for such commodities as food and metals surged.

Adding to the increase in the price of commodities was the precipitous fall of the U.S. dollar during the same time. Because the majority of commodities are priced in U.S. dollars, foreign countries are able to get more for their money when the local foreign currency is inflated.

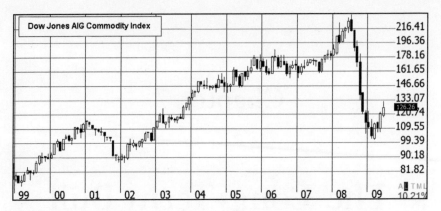

Figure 7.1   Dow Jones AIG Commodity Index over the Last 10 Years
SOURCE: TeleChart2007® or StockFinder® chart, courtesy of Worden Brothers, Inc.

If China were to spend the equivalent of $1 billion on buying wheat, if the U.S. dollar falls 25 percent against the local currency, China can now buy 25 percent more wheat with the same amount of money.

The combination of a weak U.S. dollar and above-average growth in the emerging markets were the main drivers behind the commodity boom, but there were other factors. Supply has been a concern for a number of commodities such as oil. There have not been any new major oil discoveries in the last few years, thus putting a limit on the expansion of supply. Agriculture is another example of commodities that have seen an erratic supply, due to inclement weather around the world. Droughts in Australia and the Midwest have hampered supply in recent years along with hurricanes and other natural forces. Unstable geopolitical landscapes also hurt supply, considering a large amount of commodities come from developing countries.

Each individual commodity has its unique factors that move the price as well. For example, corn was suddenly in high demand the last few years as the United States made a big push toward ethanol. With corn the major ingredient in the ethanol process, the demand surged as did the price of corn. I believe there will be more situations similar to that of corn through the ethanol craze and therefore individual commodities will outperform their peers on a regular basis. I offer my thoughts on all sectors within the commodity industry in this book and list what I believe to be the best investment options in each. The first section discusses precious metals.

Precious Metals

Precious metals, specifically gold, often get a bad rap because the investment vehicle is a favorite of doomsayers around the world. When all else fails, many investors turn to gold to be their safe investment choice. While this is true of what we refer to as goldbugs, there are also numerous other reasons to consider gold and other precious metals as investment options. Three of the main reasons I like gold as an investment for the next few years include higher inflation around the world, the weakening of the U.S. dollar, and geopolitical uncertainty in all parts of the world.

SPDR Gold ETF

Gold has had its time in the sun as a top performing asset and has also been ostracized years later for lagging the market and not offering any real upside. Over the last 10-year period you would have been lucky to have 100 percent of your portfolio in the yellow metal. Gold was trading near $300 per ounce in early 1999 and 10 years later, the metal hit $1,000. During that same time, your investment in the S&P 500 would have lost money. That being said, if you bought gold in January 1995 at $380 per ounce it would have been down over 20 percent in the next four years as the S&P 500 rallied nearly 200 percent.[1]

There are two important points I am trying to get across to you regarding gold. First, buying and ignoring gold for the long term is not the best investment strategy. There must be a price at which you determine is the best price to sell, and greed is a factor that must be limited. Gold is not a buy-and-hold investment, but there are times to be overweight and with the possibility of inflation in the future, now is a time to own gold. There is also my thought process that the market is in the middle of a long-term bull market for commodities and gold will continue to be a big winner in years to come. The second important point is that gold often moves in the inverse direction of the stock market and could be a great diversification tool that will help lower the overall beta of a portfolio.

When investing in gold, there is the option of buying gold bullion and burying it in your backyard, investing in jewelry or coins,

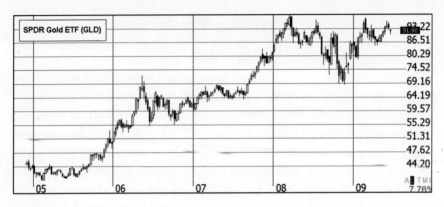

Figure 7.2   SPDR Gold ETF Gold Rush
SOURCE: TeleChart2007® or StockFinder® chart, courtesy of Worden Brothers, Inc.

gold mining stocks, or a gold-tracking ETF. The best way to gain direct exposure to the price of gold is a gold ETF because of the liquidity and ease of buying and selling. The SPDR Gold ETF (NYSE: GLD) is the most heavily traded of the gold ETFs and is an ETF I have owned for several years for myself and clients. As the price of gold moves up and down, so does the price of GLD; the benefit is that instead of taking your gold bullion to a dealer, you are able to buy and sell GLD whenever the NYSE is open for business. The ETF is the best pure play on the price of gold.

Figure 7.2 shows the run gold has had from 2005 to the middle of 2009 as the GLD moved from a low in the $40s to a high of $100 in early 2008. The ETF has been one of my most consistent long-term performing investments for my clients.

iShares Silver ETF

Silver is a metal that is overlooked by many investors because gold is always better than silver; just ask the Olympics or a woman—gold will be their choice. The one major difference besides the price per ounce (gold was at $980 and silver was at $14 per ounce when this chapter was written) is their uses. According to the Silver Institute, silver can be used in batteries, bearings, catalysts, electronics, photography, medical applications, water purification, jewelry, and, of course, coinage, to name a few. Because the precious metal has so many unique features and is much lower in price than some of its peers, the demand for silver has remained steady.

Other than the uses mentioned here, silver is also used by speculators and investors looking to profit from increased demand of the metal. Similar to other precious metals (palladium and platinum), silver will tend to move with the price of gold. However, in 2008, when GLD rose 5 percent, the price of SLV fell 24 percent. The price of GLD and SLV during 2007 through 2008 is compared in Figure 7.3 and it is clear that the price of silver has been lagging that of gold. While owning silver versus gold during that two-year span was not the best strategy, I feel the two metals will revert back to the mean and therefore silver should outperform gold in the coming years. I would not necessarily sell all my gold to buy silver, but I would add some silver to the portfolio to take advantage of what I have determined to be an arbitrage opportunity.

The most liquid silver ETF is the iShares Silver ETF (SLV), which holds actual silver and tracks the movement of the underlying commodity. Similar to GLD, SLV can be bought and sold throughout the trading session in the same manner as a stock. This is much easier than finding a dealer who can give you a good price for your silver coins.

Figure 7.3   SLV versus GLD (2007–2008)
SOURCE: TeleChart2007® or StockFinder® chart, courtesy of Worden Brothers, Inc.

Figure 7.4   iShares Silver ETF Starting to Catch Up to Gold
SOURCE: TeleChart2007® or StockFinder® chart, courtesy of Worden Brothers, Inc.

After lagging in 2008, SLV has begun to move higher in 2009, with a gain of 38 percent through the first five months of the year. Figure 7.4 shows the move in SLV to a new 2009 before pulling back to consolidate. All pullbacks in SLV can be viewed as buying opportunities.

Market Vectors Gold Miners ETF

As goes the price of gold, so goes the gold mining stocks, right? Well, yes and no. Over time, if gold rallies through $1,000 per ounce and continues to make its way higher in the coming years, there is a high probability the gold miners will follow the lead. However, do not expect the gold mining stocks to move hand in hand with the price of gold in the short term. A good example is the July 2008 through February 2009 time frame. In Figure 7.5, GLD is compared with the Market Vectors Gold Miners ETF (NYSE: GDX) and, as you can see, there is a major difference. In July 2008, both ETFs were sitting at a high; in the next seven months, GLD made its way back to the high as GDX remains 26 percent below the old high. The gold mining stocks have clearly lagged the price of gold during that select seven-month span, but it can go both ways.

When investing in GDX, an investor is gaining access to 32 gold stocks that must have a market capitalization of at least $100 million

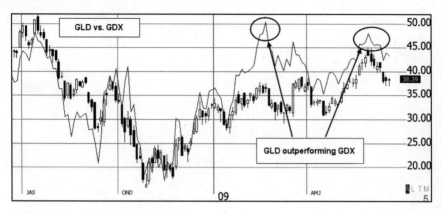

Figure 7.5   GLD vs. GDX
SOURCE: TeleChart2007® or StockFinder® chart, courtesy of Worden Brothers, Inc.

and daily trading volume of 50,000 shares per day on average. The two largest holdings that make up over one-fifth of the ETF are Barrick Gold (NYSE: ABX) and Goldcorp (NYSE: GG), two of the largest gold mine owners in the world. There is an expense ratio of 0.55 percent, which is reasonable considering the diversification GDX gives an investor. The ETF is an overall great investment choice for investors who seek out exposure to gold mining stocks, but do not want to take the risk of a single company. You many not think there is big risk in a gold mine, but think about a mine tragedy or disruption that could halt mining—do you want that risk?[2]

Since bottoming in October 2008, GDX has formed a solid uptrend, with a series of higher highs and higher lows, as shown in Figure 7.6. As of mid-June 2009, the ETF is pulling back and appears to be a buying opportunity. Only time will tell, but if history is correct, GDX should be bought on all pullbacks.

Royal Gold

Royal Gold (Nasdaq: RGLD) is an interesting company because it is a gold stock, yet it is not a gold miner per se. The company owns and manages royalties on precious metal mines and has the right to receive royalty payouts from the production of the mine. By not taking on the cost and high risk of putting money into the mining operations

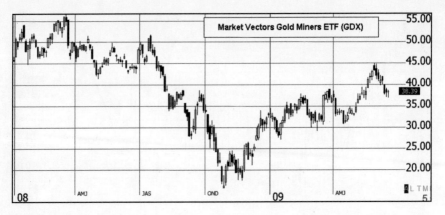

Figure 7.6   Market Vectors Gold Miners ETF in the Middle of a New Uptrend
SOURCE: TeleChart2007® or StockFinder® chart, courtesy of Worden Brothers, Inc.

such as capital and operating expenses, the company lowers the risk to shareholders.

The company is a global play on the metals with exposure to 15 countries, but 64 percent of its gold reserves and 98 percent of its silver reserves are located in North America. With over 100 properties in its portfolio in varying stages of development, Royal Gold is well diversified with mature and exploration-stage mines. Because I like the action in gold over the last year and believe the futures could see $1,500 per ounce in the coming years, Royal Gold is my favorite gold stock. Because I believe Royal Gold will move more closely with the price of gold helped sway my decision. Keep in mind that a large number of gold miners hedge their mining operations if gold continues to rise and they may miss out on a large portion of the prices. Royal Gold will not have the same issue, but may also take a bigger hit if I am wrong and gold falls.[3]

To give you an idea of how Royal Gold has fared versus its peers during the same time as I showed you in Figure 7.6, there is a comparison of Royal Gold versus GLD in Figure 7.7. The outperformance of Royal Gold against a basket of its peers shows why I have chosen it as my only individual gold stock I am recommending. Figure 7.8 is a 10-year chart of the stock going back to a tie when Royal Gold could have been bought for $2 per share.

Figure 7.7   Royal Gold versus GDX
Source: TeleChart2007® or StockFinder® chart, courtesy of Worden Brothers, Inc.

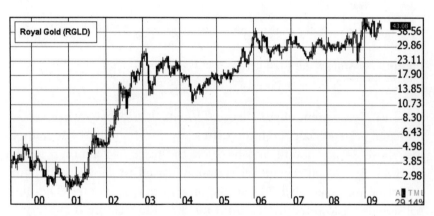

Figure 7.8   Royal Gold, from Speculation to Blue Chip Gold Stock
Source: TeleChart2007® or StockFinder® chart, courtesy of Worden Brothers, Inc.

Industrial Metals

The big three in the world of industrial metals are copper, aluminum, and zinc. Others in the sector include nickel, lead, and iron. All three have their niche uses throughout the world; however, all are tied to the strength of the global economy. This cannot be evidenced any more so than during the last few years as the industrial metals took a wild ride with the global stock market. As countries around the world were growing at a rapid pace, so was the price of the industrial metals.

Figure 7.9   Copper: Ups and Downs over Five Years
SOURCE: www.kitco.com.

Turn your attention to Figure 7.9, which is a five-year chart of the spot price of copper futures. In early 2004, copper was trading just above $1 per pound, and by 2008, the price had gone up nearly fourfold. But when the global recession started to show its strength, the price of copper fell 70 percent in a matter of months. The global slowdown lowered the demand for the industrial metal and warehouse stock levels consequently rose sharply. The supply-and-demand curve states that if supply outstrips demand, the price will fall, and that is what caused the crash in copper prices. In Figure 7.10, the warehouse stock levels of copper are shown and it is clear that they have risen during the recession, but they can quickly drop again as the global economy picks up.

By investing in industrial metals, an investor is betting on the global economy coming out of a recession at some point in the very foreseeable future and that the emerging markets will move back to above-average growth. In Figure 7.11, we can see the direct correlation between the movement of the copper stocks and the emerging markets. During the emerging market rally in the early 2000s, the price of copper rode the wave. When the bubble burst on the developing countries,

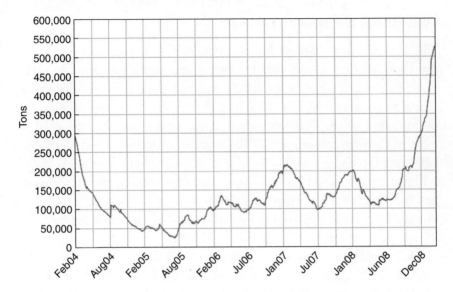

Figure 7.10   Five-Year LME Copper Warehouse Stocks Level
SOURCE: www.kitco.com.

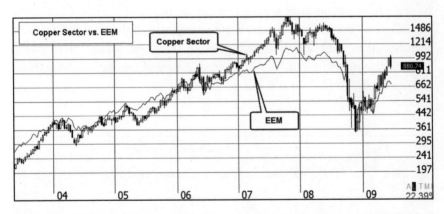

Figure 7.11   Copper Sector versus iShares MSCI Emerging Markets ETF (EEM)
SOURCE: TeleChart2007® or StockFinder® chart, courtesy of Worden Brothers, Inc.

the wind was taken out of the sails of copper and other related industrial metals. Obviously, I believe in the emerging markets as well as the eventual demand for industrial metals such as copper, once the economic slowdown ceases. By the end of 2010, the industrial metals should have found a bottom and the related investment vehicles will once again be high beta options for aggressive investors.

PowerShares DB Base Metals ETF

The PowerShares DB Base Metals ETF (NYSE: DBB) is a vehicle that gives investors equal exposure to copper, aluminum, and zinc. As mentioned before, all three metals have suffered poorly during the global recession. During 2008, the ETF lost 45 percent of its value, lagging the performance of the S&P 500. Even as the major indexes attempted to rally off the November lows, DBB continue to tumble another 15 percent into December 2008. Over the next two months, the ETF traded within a narrow range and held up better than most sectors in the market. In April, the ETF began to slowly move higher, forming a rounding bottom formation, as shown in Figure 7.12, which is consistent with the start of new bull markets.

I began buying shares of DBB for myself and clients in mid-May near $14 and believe it could be a core holding for the Next Great Bull Market. There are three factors that have me giddy with bullishness for DBB. First, inflation is coming and the base metals will benefit from the increase. Second, the U.S. dollar will continue to move lower, another positive for commodities and, in particular, the base metals. Finally, the global economy will come out of the recession and the demand for base metals will increase. Even if only two of the three scenarios play out, DBB will outperform the market, and this is why I feel confident about the future of the ETF in our portfolios.

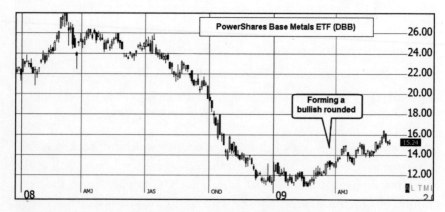

Figure 7.12   PowerShares DB Base Metals ETF Forming Rounded Bottom
SOURCE: TeleChart2007® or StockFinder® chart, courtesy of Worden Brothers, Inc.

Freeport-McMoRan Copper and Gold

Freeport-McMoRan (NYSE: FCX) is the world's largest publicly traded copper company that also mines gold and molybdenum. The company owns the Grasberg mining complex, the largest copper and gold mine in regard to reserves in the world. FCX is also the world's largest producer of molybdenum. Often overlooked is the company's exposure to molybdenum, which is primarily used in the production of steel; 80 percent of the world's demand for the metal is by the steel industry. When the demand for steel rebounds, which it will in time, FXC will be a secondary beneficiary of the rise in prices.

Copper remains the number one product of FCX because it is the world leader. The company currently mines about one-third of its copper equally from three regions around the world: South America, Indonesia, and North America. This diversity, along with reserves in parts of the world that are not as unstable, are two benefits to FCX's portfolio of mines. The price of the stock fell victim to the global recession by dropping over 80 percent from its 2008 high through its 2009 low. This came after a 1200 percent increase from the low in 2000 through the high of 2008.[4] Figure 7.13 shows the price action of FCX over the last decade and it is clear there was a time to make money in the stock and another time to sit it out. I believe the time to sit it out is coming to an end and an entry in the below-$50 range

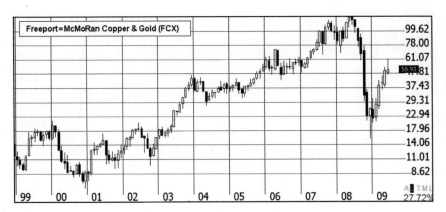

Figure 7.13   The Explosion and Implosion of Freeport-McMoRan
SOURCE: TeleChart2007® or StockFinder® chart, courtesy of Worden Brothers, Inc.

could be a very lucrative long-term investment for investors who can tolerate the expected volatility.

Alcoa

Alcoa (NYSE: AA) is the world's leader in the production of primary aluminum, fabricated aluminum, and alumina facilities. The metal it produces is used in a variety of industries, including aerospace, auto-motive, construction, electronics, industrials, and packaging. The price of copper has taken a beating since hitting a historic high in 2008, but it is not alone. Aluminum fell from a high of nearly $1.50 per pound in July 2008 to $0.56 in February 2009; this represents a fall of over 60 percent. Alcoa, in the meanwhile, has fallen 90 percent from its high in July 2007 to its low in March 2009. The stock traded in late February 2009 below $5 for the first time since 1988.[5] The long-term chart of Alcoa is shown in Figure 7.14. Isn't it amazing how such a steady stock can lose 90 percent of its value in a matter of one year? I do not believe Alcoa will get back to its prerecession levels, but when it is priced below $10 a share, it is hard not to buy.

The Dow Jones Industrial Component has fallen on hard times as prices of aluminum have fallen because of a surge in aluminum stocks. Figure 7.15 shows the eightfold growth in warehouse stock levels as the demand for aluminum has vanished during the recession. Again, Alcoa

Figure 7.14   How Can You Not Buy Alcoa under $10?
Source: TeleChart2007® or StockFinder® chart, courtesy of Worden Brothers, Inc.

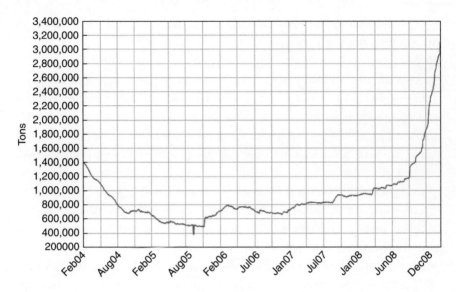

Figure 7.15   Five-Year LME Aluminum Warehouse Stock Levels
SOURCE: www.kitco.com.

is a play only when it is clear the economy is beginning to make its way out of the recession, and as of June 2009, it was all clear to begin buying Alcoa on pullbacks. If you can get Alcoa back in the single digits again it could pay huge dividends in the years to come.

Lithium

The lithium section of this book could have fallen under Chapter 6, a discussion of alternative energy, but at the end of the day, it is a commodity and should be grouped with the other metals. Also, the two stocks I believe offer the best exposure to the lithium market also have ties to other commodities and so the most appropriate part of the book is right here. Many believe, myself included, that lithium-ion batteries will one day replace gasoline as the primary source of energy in automobiles. The one problem is that the technology is still on the cutting edge and costly. Possibly even more problematic is the situation that nearly half of the world's lithium supply lies in just one country—Bolivia.

Foreign companies have already made their way to Bolivia to try to strike deals for the highly sought-after mineral. Oji Baba, an executive in Mitsubishi's Base Metals Unit, said, "If we want to be a force in the next wave of automobiles and the batteries that power them, then we must be here." It is not only the foreign automakers that are clamoring to get their hands on the lithium needed for the next generation of batteries. The now bankrupt General Motors has announced it will build the Volt, a car that will use a lithium-ion battery in combination with a gas-powered engine. And with the U.S. government the new, proud owners of General Motors, President Obama is free to push his green initiative in the auto industry. Regardless of what the consumer may be asking for, there is no doubt in my mind the government will not stop until all vehicles are powered with alternative energy sources, with the big winner being the lithium-ion battery. The auto industry will increase the demand for lithium dramatically. However, they are not the first to use the mineral in batteries. Take off the cover of your Blackberry and you will find a rechargeable lithium-ion battery. Look in the back of your laptop and there is a lithium-ion battery. Lithium has for years has been used in batteries for electronic devices, but the massive, groundbreaking surge will come when automakers begin to produce battery-powered vehicles by the masses.

The concern with Bolivia is that they are not currently on the best of terms with the United States and have been known to nationalize industries in the past. They did this with the natural gas industry in 2006. There are also ties to Venezuela, which in my mind is currently a communist country, under the rule of Hugo Chavez. If Bolivia makes it difficult for the lithium to make its way out of the country by hording it or charge unrealistic prices, there could be a shortage of the mineral for the new batteries. This will be good for companies that have exposure to lithium sources outside of Bolivia. According to the United States Geological Survey, 5.4 million tons of lithium may be in Bolivia; next in line is Chile with 3.0 million tons (see SQM, further on), 1.1 million tons in China, and only 410,000 tons in the United States.[6]

In January 2009, the Department of Energy (DOE) released its 2008 annual progress report for the Energy Storage Research and Development Vehicle Technologies Program. The DOE discusses within the report the viability of lithium-ion batteries and highlighted a number of barriers they must first overcome before they can be con-sidered viable alternatives. Cost and performance appear to be the two biggest issues with the lithium-ion batteries in 2009, which is often true of all new technologies. Do you remember how expensive it was to buy a flat screen television five years ago; today they are in most homes. I believe the lithium-ion batteries will follow a similar path in the next decade.

The United States as of today is not a major player in the manufac-turing of lithium-ion batteries, as Asia dominates the space. I therefore look to companies that supply the lithium to the battery makers as an investment option because they will be the winners regardless of which battery company survives. The two companies that have strong ties to the lithium market and are my favorites to outperform are discussed next.

FMC Corp

FMC Corp (NYSE: FMC) is a global leader in the diversified chemi-cals arena, with exposure to the agricultural and industrial sectors. The company produces chemicals that are used in products that range from batteries to textiles to food and beverages.[7] The lithium division is why FMC is being highlighted in this book; its 5 to 10 percent of the world lithium market it currently holds is enough of a reason to give the company a second look. There is also the situation that FMC has exposure to other chemical sectors that have been hurt during the economic downturn and are now trading at attractive valuations.

On February 4, 2009, FMC announced in its quarterly report that fourth quarter net income came in at $1.02 per share, excluding restructuring and other one-time items. This is well above the $0.59 per share the company reported during the same quarter in 2007. Looking ahead at 2009, in early May, FMC offered full-year earnings guidance of $4.40 to $4.80 per share. Assuming the company is correct and earnings come in at the upper end of the range, FMC is trading at a P/E ratio of approximately 10, with the stock price at $49. It is clear in Figure 7.16 that FMC was directly affected by the global recession, falling over 60 percent in four months during late 2008. Since the dra-matic sell-off, the stock has been outperforming the overall market and looks to have established a solid bottom in the stock price.[8]

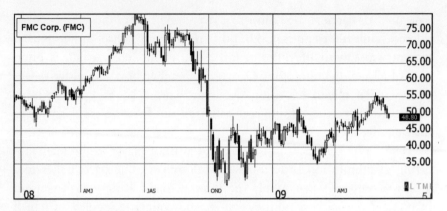

Figure 7.16 FMC Corp Building a Long-Term Base
SOURCE: TeleChart2007® or StockFinder® chart, courtesy of Worden Brothers, Inc.

Chemical and Mining Company of Chile

The Chemical and Mining Company of Chile (NYSE: SQM) is a world leader in its three major business segments: specialty plant nutrition, iodine, and lithium. Of course, the focus for this chapter is the lithium production, in which SQM is the world's largest producer, with approximately 35 percent market share, according to the company's web site. U.S.-based Rockwood Holdings (NYSE: ROC) is number two, with 30 percent, and FMC is third in production of lithium. SQM currently generates 55 percent of its revenue from specialty plant nutrition, 15 percent from iodine, and 11 percent from lithium. Even though the lithium segment remains a relatively small portion of earnings, this leaves enormous upside potential for the company's top line. Keep in mind the number earlier in this chapter that highlighted Chile as the country with the second-largest amount of lithium reserves in the world.

SQM announced in October 2008 earnings for the previous nine months of $381.1 million ($1.45 per share per ADR); an increase of 181 percent versus the same period in 2007. Revenues for the same nine months grew by 56 percent versus one year earlier.[9] The most recent earnings announcement available for discussion in this book, in April 2009, showed an increase of net income by 33 percent over one year earlier, but revenue decreased by 2 percent. Notes in the

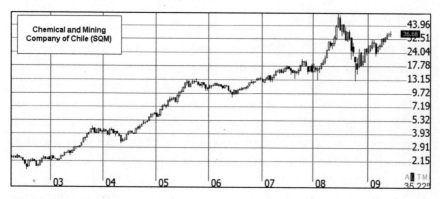

Figure 7.17 Chemical and Mining Company of Chile
SOURCE: TeleChart2007® or StockFinder® chart, courtesy of Worden Brothers, Inc.

company's quarterly report attributed the fall in revenue to the weak global economy.

Even with the slowdown in the first quarter of 2009, it is hard-pressed to find bottom line numbers that are as impressive as SQM anywhere in the world. I believe the growth will be the driver behind SQM becoming a market leader in both the lithium and agricultural chemical industries. Figure 7.17 shows the meteoric rise of the stock price of SQM before falling dramatically with other chemical companies, the agricultural chemical firms, in particular. I believe SQM has the ability to break back through the high of $59 set in June 2008 in the coming years and buying on any weakness is my suggestion.

Coal and Steel

After taking a brutal beating from their high in 2008, both the coal and steel stocks fell to levels that many thought they would never see again. The Market Vectors Steel ETF (NYSE: SLX) fell from a high of $114 in May 2008 to a low of $20 in November 2008. The coal stocks followed a similar path, as many of the major players lost over 80 percent of their value in a matter of months. In hindsight, the November levels were a buying opportunity of a lifetime. But do not fret, there are plenty of opportunities still available for patient, long-term investors in the steel and coal sectors, which are discussed next.

BHP Billiton Limited

BHP Billiton (NYSE: BHP) is the world's largest diversified resources company. With exposure to coal, copper, aluminum, iron ore, uranium, silver, and oil, among others, BHP truly gives investors exposure to a gambit of commodities. During fiscal year 2008, the base metals made up 32 percent of EBIT (earnings before interest and taxes), followed by petroleum at 22 percent and iron ore at 19 percent. The reason it falls under the coal and steel category is because BHP is the world's largest supplier of metallurgical coal that is used with iron ore in the steel-making process. BHP is also one of the largest producers of energy coal used by the power generation industry, according to the company's web site.[10]

Based in Australia, BHP has a unique advantage over many of its competitors because of its proximity to China, which is quickly becoming a commodity hound. Even though expansion has slowed during the last year in China, its growth is still the best in the world and is expected to pick back up after the global recession subsides. Sitting and waiting to take advantage of the increased demand for everything from steel to coal to oil is BHP.

BHP was a core holding at my firm (Penn Financial Group LLC) for years until we decided to take the profit in 2008 when the stock began to break support. The 39 percent fall in 2008 was tough to swallow for investors, but keep in mind that is the same return as the S&P 500, and while the index is at the same level it was in 1997, BHP is up 200 percent. When a long-term view is taken, BHP has been a huge winner for investors who rode out the ups and downs over the last 10 years, and I believe the next 10 will also be very rewarding to shareholders. Since hitting a low of $24 in November 2008, the stock consolidated and began a new move higher throughout the first few months of 2009 as shown in Figure 7.18. Buying BHP in the $50 range is recommended for long-term commodity bulls that believe in a global economic rebound.

Market Vectors Steel ETF

The Market Vectors Steel ETF (NYSE: SLX) tracks the NYSE Arca Steel Index, which is composed of 26 stocks that are involved in the production of steel products or mining and processing of iron ore.

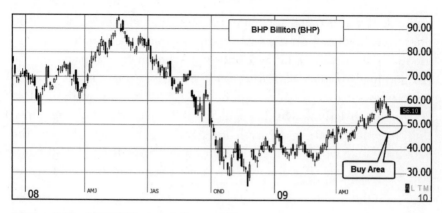

Figure 7.18   BHP Billiton—A Buy at $50
SOURCE: TeleChart2007® or StockFinder® chart, courtesy of Worden Brothers, Inc.

Figure 7.19   Market Vectors Steel ETF
SOURCE: TeleChart2007® or StockFinder® chart, courtesy of Worden Brothers, Inc.

Over half of the stocks are considered large-caps, and 1 percent of them is based in North America. See the list on the following page for the top five holdings that make up SLX. The steel stocks were one of the hardest-hit sectors during the recession because with the slow-down in building, the demand for steel had dropped significantly. In 2008, SLX fell by an astounding 65 percent, and in one six-month span from May to November, the ETF was down 82 percent.[11]

Investing in the steel sector is not for all investors, as shown by the extreme volatility in Figure 7.19. The rallies followed by significant pullbacks are too much for many investors and it is better to pass on the sector. If you are on the fence about buying in steel stocks, my suggestion is to use the ETF as a one-stop solution to company-specific risk and high volatility. Similar to nearly every investment in this chapter, a lot rides on the global recession coming to an end by the end of 2009—which I think will happen. The ETF has been holding above the November 2008 and March lows and a purchase as close to the $20–$30 range would be ideal; realistically, however, the $35–$40 range will be acceptable. The following is a list of the top five holdings of SLX:

1. Vale (VALE)
2. ArceloMittal (MT)
3. Rio Tinto (RTP)
4. Ternium (TX)
5. Mechel Steel Group (MTL)

Agricultural Commodities

What makes the agricultural commodities an attractive investment opportunity is the number of factors that could drive the related stocks higher. An increased demand for food around the world, higher inflation, a weak U.S. dollar, inclement weather patterns, and new technology in the agribusiness sector can all lead to the sector moving higher. On the flip side, the biggest risk is that the global economy does not begin to improve. I like my odds, and will therefore be looking to overweight my clients' portfolios with stock and ETFs in the sector. Two of my favorites are discussed next.

Syngenta

Syngenta (NYSE: SYT), based in Switzerland, is one of the world leaders in agricultural chemical sector. The company may not be a household name, but it did have sales of over $11.5 billion in 2008, the majority of it coming from crop protection. When Syngenta reported its full year 2008 earnings in February 2009, the company increased its sales by 26 percent, and earnings shot up 28 percent, according to the

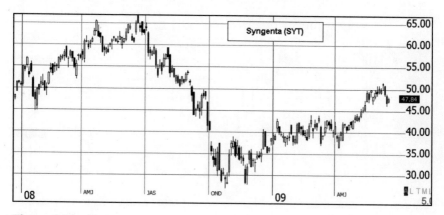

Figure 7.20   Syngenta
SOURCE: TeleChart2007® or StockFinder® chart, courtesy of Worden Brothers, Inc.

company's quarterly report. Despite what was one of the worst years in the past century for the stock market, Syngenta was able to continue growing with record earnings.[12]

The stock fell 23 percent during 2008 even as it was generating record numbers. This is an example of the baby getting thrown out with the bath water: a strong stock falling because weakness in the overall market has caused investors to sell everything and run for the exits. Syngenta finally found a bottom in October 2008 at $27 and has been able to build a solid short-term uptrend over the following eight months, as shown in Figure 7.20. I believe the stock will not revisit the $20s again anytime soon and a pullback into the $30s will therefore be a gift you must accept.

Market Vectors Agribusiness ETF

The Market Vectors Agribusiness ETF (NYSE: MOO) tracks the DAXglobal Agribusiness Index, which is composed of companies in the agriculture business. The index is composed of 44 stocks, half of which are in the United States and are considered large-caps. What makes MOO so attractive to me is its diversity within the agriculture industry: 44 percent agricultural chemicals, 30 percent agribusiness operations, 17 percent agricultural equipment, 7 percent livestock operations, 2 percent ethanol/biodiesel. The expense ratio is 0.65 percent, which is

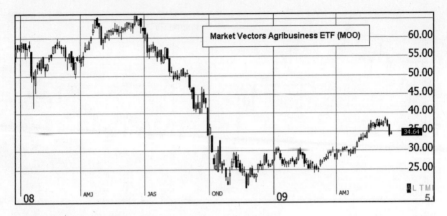

Figure 7.21 Market Vectors Agribusiness ETF
SOURCE: TeleChart2007® or StockFinder® chart, courtesy of Worden Brothers, Inc.

not low, but is reasonable for a niche ETF. All of this information is taken directly from the Market Vectors web site.[13]

Syngenta happens to be the number one holding in the ETF, making up 8 percent of the allocation, followed by fertilizer company Potash (NYSE: POT), also at 8 percent. The number four holding is Monsanto (NYSE: MON), also one of my favorite agricultural chemical stocks, which nearly made its way into the book as a recommendation and at the time this chapter was written is a position for my firm. See the following list for the complete top holdings of MOO. The ETF overall has been one of my favorites for quite some time, but until now has concentrated on individual stocks in the industry. For most individual investors, the risk of owning an individual company is too high, and MOO, therefore, is the best option. Here is a list of the top five holdings for Market Vectors Agribusiness ETF:

1. Syngenta (SYT)
2. Potash Corp (POT)
3. Mosaic Company (MOS)
4. Monsanto (MON)
5. Archer Daniels Midland (ADM)

I move away from the commodity and infrastructure industries in Chapter 8 to concentrate on demographics and, in particular, the emergence of the baby boomers. You will read which investments will flourish when the grayhairs take over.

Chapter 8

Health Care
and the Emergence
of the Baby Boomers

G rayhairs are set to take over the United States. According to the U.S. Census Bureau, the term *baby boomer* refers to U.S. citizens born during the post–World War II baby boom between 1946 and 1964. In total, the U.S. Census Bureau has counted 78 million babies born between 1946 and 1964—an amazing number. As the first wave of boomers move closer to retirement age and are now able to collect Social Security, this country is setting up for a major cultural shift similar to what the boomers brought to the United States over the last few decades.

Preparing for a Population Shift

Depending on whom you listen to, the emergence of the baby boomers into retirement age in the next two decades will either revive or kill the U.S. economy. I definitely do not believe it will kill our economy, but I do not believe it will be the sole factor in reviving it either. A collection of other secular factors, combined with baby boomers enjoying life and willing to part with their disposable money will definitely stimulate certain areas within the U.S. economy. As the boomers gain in age, there will also be a demographic shift that requires the United States to focus on better health care for the aging population. One of the hot topics early on in the Obama administration has been a revamping of the U.S. health care system. Look for more significant developments in the next couple of years as the government attempts to fix the current health care situation.

According to the Centers for Disease Control and Prevention and the Administration on Aging, by 2030, the number of people older than 65 is expected to increase to nearly 20 percent from 12.4 percent. With one-fifth of the population over the retirement age it could cause major changes to the economic landscape. Will all the boomers pull their money out of the stock market at age 65 and become frugal and sit on their cash? Will the boomers put more money into investments because they realize the issue of outliving their money is real? Will boomers continue to enjoy life and shy away from saving and enjoy life by spending on discretionary items?

Honestly, I think the answer could be a mixture of all the scenarios. And the only one that concerns me is the first scenario, which foresees the boomers turning into savers, but without the help of the stock market. Even if the boomers take their money out of stocks and move it into more conservative investments, the money will still be in the market. This shift will benefit companies that offer investment advice and products such as annuities and bond funds. The exact opposite would be to pull the money out of stocks and spending it freely as consumers. While this may sound like a bad situation for stocks, it will help the overall economy because the money being pulled out of the market will go right back into the pockets of the publicly traded companies. In the end, the money is simply being shifted from the pockets of the consumers and into the coffers of the small and large companies supplying the goods and services. As the companies benefit, expect the money to increase wages, employment, and overall, boost the economy.

The following investment themes concentrate on the health care sector because with age comes health issues. With an estimated 71 million people over the age of 65 in 2030, according to the Centers for Disease Control and Prevention report "Healthy Aging," the demand for health care–related services and products will continue its consistent rise. Other than health care, there are a couple of niche investment ideas I want to share with you involving the emergence of the baby boomers. The following specific ideas could help you benefit during the rise of the Next Great Bull Market and the emergence of the baby boomers.

Baby Boomer Investment Themes

Several sectors can be linked to the emergence of the baby boomers, but none more so than health care. It is inevitable that as the years increase, the body begins to do things it has not in the past, which results in more visits to the doctor's office. The aches and pains are a natural part of aging and so are the regular preventative visits to the doctor's office. Along with health care, there the two sectors I believe have the best chance to benefit from the baby boomers are vanity products and money management. The aging process can be cruel, and with the innovations in aesthetics, there will be large amounts of money spent to look good for as long as possible. And the longer life expectancy will result in the need for money managers to handle the baby boomers' assets before and after retirement. All three sectors are delved in to further in the next section.

Health Care

There is one thing I do know in life—each day, we get one day older. With age comes more health issues, some sooner than others, but it is inevitable that the joints begin to hurt a little more each time you go to the gym. Your eyes begin to not focus as well as they did in the past;

when was the last time you had to hold the menu far away to read the prices? If I were able to do my life over, I would be a supplier of $2 reading glasses for the baby boomers; what a business. Does it feel as if you are seeing your doctor more often as the years go by? And suddenly, each week you are heading back to get another preventative exam. Unfortunately, this is part of the joys of aging . . . well, at least, that is what they tell me. I cannot wait to find out!

Long-Term Care Facilities and Home Health Care

Many U.S. residents will at some point have to sit down with their parents and have the discussion about whether it is time to move in to a nursing home. This is not a discussion many of us want to have whether we are the child or the parent, but unfortunately, it is reality. With both the man and woman working most of their lives, it does not leave the spare time needed to take care of an ill parent who requires constant attention. This is when it is time to turn to long-term care facilities or home health care.

The number of baby boomers who will require either a long-term care facility or health care services in their home will steadily rise in the coming decades. The demand for treatment services that range from help with everyday living chores to round-the-clock medical treatment will need to be met by more medical facilities and professionals. The companies that will benefit the most from this trend will be the long-term care facilities that offer a range of services. There is also the niche home health care companies that will make the patient feel at home by providing needed health care at their home. I believe both areas could thrive in the coming decades because it will be inevitable that the number of baby boomers seeking their services will rise.

National HealthCare Corp

By providing 9,772 beds through 76 long-term health care centers, National HealthCare (NYSE: NHC) is a major play in the United States. The company operates 32 homecare programs, 23 assisted living communities, and 7 independent living centers through all of its affiliates. Throughout the facilities, NHC offers services that include pharmacies, hospice, rehabilitation, and Alzheimer's treatment. The company's

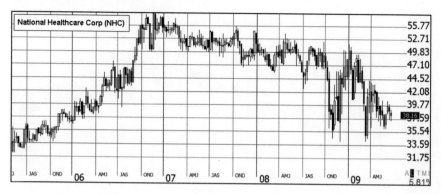

Figure 8.1   Looking for the Downtrend to End for National HealthCare Corp.
SOURCE: TeleChart2007® or StockFinder® chart, courtesy of Worden Brothers, Inc.

exposure to the nursing home business is attractive because it is inevitable that more seniors will require housing alternatives in the coming decades. The other benefit is the diversity between long-term care facilities and home care programs. The needs of patients will vary greatly from full-time care to occasional checkups at the home. NHC has many of these areas covered.[1]

From a technical basis, the company has been much less volatile than the overall market, falling 3 percent in 2008, and trading in a narrow range. That being said, the stock price has been in a steady downtrend since 2006 as shown in Figure 8.1. An attractive entry price for NHC would be in the mid-$30s, where I consider it to be fairly valued. NHC will not be the big winner in your portfolio, but it does add a solid small-cap company in a strong sector to a portfolio.

Amedisys

Amedisys (NASDAQ: AMED) is a leading provider of home health care and hospice services for all ages. The company offers the choice to patients to remain at their home and live comfortably instead of an in-patient facility. This is a trend that has been increasing, as the ill would rather live their lives as normally as possible by staying in their own homes and having the health care providers come to them. The same thought process applies to terminally ill patients who prefer to live their last days surrounded by friends and family in a hospice, and not a typical hospital.

Figure 8.2   Amedisys's Fall from Grace
SOURCE: TeleChart2007® or StockFinder® chart, courtesy of Worden Brothers, Inc.

There is obviously a demand for Amedisys's services because the company reported record numbers during the fourth quarter of 2008. According to the company's quarterly earnings report, net service revenue for 2008 increased by 70 percent to $1.18 billion from $697.9 million one year earlier. Diluted earnings per share during 2008 were $3.22 per share, up 29 percent from 2007.[2] The stock hit an all-time high of $67 in July 2008 before falling to $40 by the end of the year. You would not suspect a home health care company to trade with high volatility, but Amedisys trades in a wide-swinging range. The stock has experienced more weakness in 2009, falling another 20 percent through mid-June. The chart of the stock in Figure 8.2 shows the dramatic fall from the 2008 high, and also the longer-term support in the $20s. Ideally, a buy price below $30 is what investors are waiting for. The long-term outlook remains bullish for the home health care industry as boomers age, but you must expect high volatility from the stock.

Medical Equipment

As the visits to the doctor's office and hospitals increase with age, so does the frustration of long medical procedures and subsequent stays. The insurance companies are also against long stays in the hospital and want to get you back home as soon as possible. You may have experienced this the last time you had a procedure performed. The same surgery that may have landed you in the hospital for several days now only requires one night before you head back to your own bed.

One of the major reasons you are able to get home quicker than ever after surgery has to do with innovative advances in the medical equipment industry. By making the surgery time and, even more important, the recovery time shorter, the medical devices save both the patient and insurance company money at the end of the day and both walk away happy. A phrase often used in the industry is minimally invasive; this refers to the least amount of damage to the healthy body to perform the procedure. For example, instead of using a hole of several inches to perform back surgery, new medical devices allow for very small holes—thus resulting in a much faster recovery period.

What excites me so much about this sector is that investors are getting a combination of so many investment themes all rolled up into one. There is the emergence of the baby boomer, the medical technology innovation angle, and the safety of the health care sector. The biggest risk is the government and any changes they may make to health care reimbursements for surgeries that directly affect the equipment companies. Small risks for individual firms involve a concentration of sales on one product and the situation that if a competitor comes along, that could greatly reduce income.

After weighing the risks and the potential rewards, I have made a small list of my favorite stocks and ETFs in the sector for you to consider.

NuVasive

NuVasive (NASDAQ: NUVA) is a company that falls in line with my investment theme that includes minimally invasive surgical procedures. The company considers itself an innovations-based medical device firm that concentrates on products for the treatment of spinal disorders. *Innovation* is the key word and is why I consider the medical equipment industry a play on technology.

The company is currently focusing on the more than $4.2 billion U.S. spine fusion market. With back pain the number one health care expenditure in the United States, at over $50 billion a year, this will only be expected to grow as the baby boomers start to feel more aches and pains. I know from personal experience the trauma of back pain after watching my baby boomer mother endure serious back surgery.[3] The company's leading product is called the Maximum Access Surgery

(MAS), which is a minimally disruptive surgical platform that includes the software, retraction system, and implants.

In January 2009, the company increased its outlook for 2009 by forecasting revenue for the year to be between $345 and $350 million; this would be approximately an increase of 40 percent from the 2008 number. In April, the company once again boosted full year guidance on their quarterly conference call. The new estimate for 2009 is for revenue of $355 to $360 million. In a year that many believe, myself included, will be difficult for companies in all industries, NuVasive is predicting significant growth increases.[4] What excites me regarding NuVasive is the potential for it to grow as it begins to turn a profit. In 2008, it was the first year this high-growth company was able to generate net income, and now the sky is the limit. The company estimated its earnings per share to be between 11 and 13 cents per share in 2009. Also, just a side note that once the economic landscape improves, look for NuVasive to arise when takeover talks begin again. I would never buy a stock based solely on a takeover potential, but it does sweeten the argument for NuVasive.

NuVasive is a stock that I have owned in the past and sold for a sizable gain at the end of September 2008. In hindsight, the sell was the right move, as the stock continued to fall from its high, as shown in Figure 8.3, down to a multiyear low. Jumping back into NuVasive will require patience and a potential entry near $40.

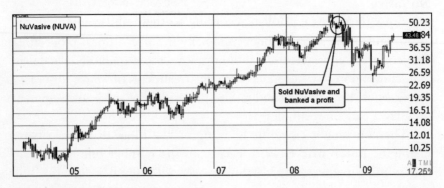

Figure 8.3   NuVasive Sold Just in Time
SOURCE: TeleChart2007® or StockFinder® chart, courtesy of Worden Brothers, Inc.

Stryker

What better company to possibly buy NuVasive down the road than Stryker (NYSE: SYK)? Stryker is one of the largest players in the $28 billion worldwide orthopedic market. The baby boom generation was one that did not sit on the couch, but instead remained active, and many pushed their bodies to the limits. When people are in their 20s and 30s, the human body can take a beating, but over time it wears on the joints and bones. As the baby boomers hit the age when the bones start to creak and the joints do not move smoothly, the only alternative may be surgery and ultimately replacement.

I am betting that everyone reading this book knows someone who has had a knee or hip replaced at some point. There is a good chance it was a Stryker product used during the surgery. Stryker offers an array of products that range from knee replacements to spinal surgery to facial procedures. The diversity gives the company a chance to hold up better during an economic downturn.

When the Stryker reported fourth quarter 2008 earnings in January 2009, revenue rose 3.6 percent to $1.72 billion. In January 2009, the company expected 2009 earnings to be in the range of $3.12 to $3.22; during the April conference call, Stryker lowered its estimate to a range of $2.90 to $3.10. The company is clearly not a growth story similar to NuVasive, but it does carry an impressive array of medical devices and has a well-known name in the industry. Revenue would have been up 3.3 percent year-over-year if it were not for a stronger U.S. dollar, according to the company press release in April 2009.

Technically, the stock had one of the best long-term charts over the last two decades until the recent recession. Figure 8.4 highlights the parabolic move from the mid-1980s through 2008. An investment of $10,000 in Stryker in 1985 would have resulted in $2,452,600 at the end of 2007. Some say we have missed the boat, but I believe the 50 percent pullback from the 2007 high gives investors another opportunity for big gains in the future. A purchase in the $35 to $40 range is a high reward-to-risk opportunity for investors who are patient and have time to let the company turn around its recent earnings troubles.

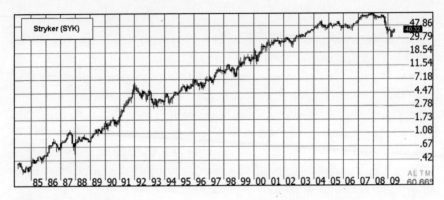

Figure 8.4   Stryker
SOURCE: TeleChart2007® or StockFinder® chart, courtesy of Worden Brothers, Inc.

iShares Dow Jones U.S. Medical Devices ETF

This niche health care ETF focuses on companies that are involved with medical equipment, instruments, and appliances. In all, there are 40 stocks in the ETF, with the top five making up over one-third of all assets. Stryker is the number five holding, making up 6 percent of the ETF, and NuVasive is in the top 20 with an allocation of less than 2 percent. The top five holdings are listed in the following table and all five have their pros and cons, just as any stock in the market. I like iShares Dow Jones U.S. Medical Devices ETF (NYSE: IHI) because it takes away the risk of buying a small-cap company such as NuVasive. However, it also reduces the possibility of an investor getting a big winner similar to Stryker's magnificent rally. IHI is the more conservative play for an investor who would like exposure to the sector without heavy risk. Technically, the ETF has shown great relative strength versus the overall market and its healthcare peers since bottoming in March 2009 (see Figure 8.5). An entry in the vicinity of $40 would be attractive enough for me to call it a buy candidate. In mid-June 2009, a number of my clients owned the ETF.[5] The top five holdings of IHI are:

Stock	Allocation Percentage
Medtronic (MDT)	10%
Thermo Fisher Scientific (TMO)	7%
Boston Scientific (BSX)	6%
St. Jude Medical (STJ)	6%
Stryker (SYK)	6%

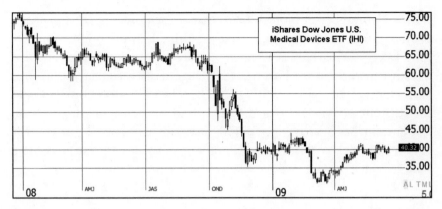

Figure 8.5   iShares Dow Jones U.S. Medical Devices ETF
SOURCE: TeleChart2007® or StockFinder® chart, courtesy of Worden Brothers, Inc.

Biotech Stocks

One of my favorite sectors during the past few years and looking ahead at the next bull market is the biotech stocks. The sector offers two very different opportunities for investors: growth and safety. The growth comes from the fact the stocks are in the business of discovering new technologies in the medical arena and the winners will experience above-average earnings growth. Safety refers to the ability of the sector to outperform during tough economic times. Whether the economy is in the midst of an expansion or contraction, people will still get sick and new drugs and technologies will be needed to treat them. Biotech is the new haven in bear markets and has taken the place of the large pharmaceuticals.

Speaking of large pharmaceutical companies such as Pfizer (NYSE: PFE) and Merck (NYSE: MRK), I believe their best days are behind them. The key to being successful in the drug or biotech industry is the pipeline of drugs and, more important, that one blockbuster that could change the world of medicine. The last few decades saw the large pharmaceutical companies introduce blockbuster drugs for ailments such as high cholesterol and erectile dysfunction, but looking into the future, I see the biotech stocks as the leaders in strong pipelines.

By having strong pipelines and the medical technology and expertise to find the next big drug, the biotech firms have the upper hand. I am not the only person to realize this, and that is why there will be a noticeable number of biotech firms that are acquired by large pharmaceutical firms in search of the next big drug. It is often less expensive for a large pharmaceutical company to buy a biotech company that has already put the money into the early stage trials versus initiating their own clinical trials of a new drug. The benefit to owners of the companies that are acquired is that the price paid is often much higher than the current price of the stock. The takeover premium is just another reason I believe biotech stocks will be one of the leaders in the coming bull market.

Gilead Sciences

Gilead is a growing biotech firm that was founded in 1987 and has since grown to a company that is producing $5 billion in annual revenues. Gilead (NASDAQ: GILD) concentrates on developing medications that help patients who are suffering from life-threatening diseases in what they consider areas of unmet medical need. The company's primary focus includes HIV/AIDS, liver disease, and serious cardiovascular and respiratory conditions.

In late January 2009, the company reported record fourth quarter and full year 2008 financial results. Revenues increased 30 percent in the fourth quarter and 26 percent in 2008 over a year earlier. The company's earnings were affected positively by their continued growth in the HIV/AIDS drug market; Gilead is clearly a major worldwide player in the treatment of the disease. The first quarter earnings report from the company, released in late April 2009, saw net income increase by 21 percent from a year earlier. Once again, the driving factor was sales of the company's two HIV treatments, Truvada and Atripla.

As of now, 70 percent of all treated patients are receiving one of Gilead's products. The Truvada treatment is the most prescribed product in the HIV market and is given to over 34 percent of all patients. An astounding 30 million people suffer from HIV around the world and therefore Gilead will remain a major player for years to come, according to Gilead's web site.[6]

Technically, the stock has one of the prettiest charts since the mid-1990s, when it was trading at a few pennies per share. The recent recession has slowed down the parabolic uptrend, but the stock has held up much better than its peers. Figure 8.6 shows the run Gilead

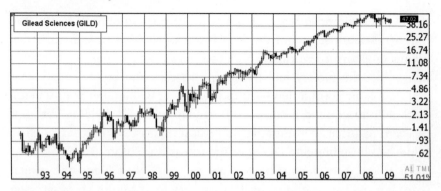

Figure 8.6   Gilead Sciences—From Penny Stock to Giant
SOURCE: TeleChart2007® or StockFinder® chart, courtesy of Worden Brothers, Inc.

made from a penny stock to a worldwide leader in the biotech sector. In 2008, Gilead gained 11 percent as a number of health care stocks plummeted in front of Obama's potentially hurtful new health care plan. There is plenty of volatility in the stock, and investors should use the pullbacks that occur ever few weeks as the opportunity to accumulate shares.

SPDR S&P Biotech ETF

There are certain situations in which ETFs are the better investment versus trying to pick an individual stock. This is no more evident than in the biotech sector, which is why ETFs are so popular. To make my point, I will give you the numbers to back my argument as to why the average investor should consider a biotech ETF versus an individual biotech stock.

Of the 186 biotech stocks I track at my investment firm, Penn Financial Group, only 24 of them closed out 2008 with gains. An investor would have had a 13 percent chance of picking a winning biotech stock in 2008—not very good odds. The odds of picking a biotech stock that lost at least 75 percent, or three-fourths, of its value was 30 percent. To put it another way, nearly one in every three biotech stocks fell 75 percent in 2008. An amazing 9 percent, or 17 biotech stocks, lost 90 percent of their value in 12 months, according to proprietary research done at my firm, Penn Financial Group LLC.

So why would anyone take the risk of owning an individual biotech stock? One word: greed. There is always the chance you pick the next Gilead Sciences at 50 cents and it goes to 50 dollars. But the numbers show that only five biotech stocks doubled in value in 2008, giving investors a less than 3 percent chance of picking the big winner. A lot of investors will be hoping to pick the biotech stock that will double in 2009 to get back to breakeven. Remember than when a stock falls 50 percent, it takes a 100 percent gain (a double) to get back to even. In 2008, 104 biotech stocks lost at least 50 percent of their value—a whopping 56 percent of the sector was cut in half.

The numbers do not lie, and are very similar if I go back several years. It is evident that investors take on very high risk for above-average at best returns with individual biotech stocks. The alternative of a biotech ETF is therefore the best choice for the average individual investor. My favorite is the SPDR S&P Biotech ETF (NYSE: XBI), which held up well in 2008, falling less than 10 percent and easily beating the overall market. Figure 8.7 is the chart of XBI over the previous two years, and it shows the ups and down of the sector. After struggling for the early part of 2009, the ETF is attempting a comeback, and below $50 is a great long-term buying opportunity.

This ETF is composed of 22 biotech stocks, with the largest weighting only 6.5 percent (Myriad Genetics—a stock I discuss further on). The diversity within the ETF and there being not one dominant stock in the allocation along with the 0.35 percent annual expense ratio are two reasons I prefer XBI over other biotech ETFs. Both Genentech

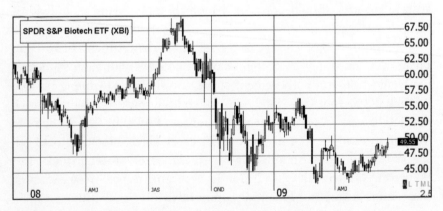

Figure 8.7   XBI Struggles to Establish a New Uptrend
Source: TeleChart2007® or StockFinder® chart, courtesy of Worden Brothers, Inc.

(number 4) and Gilead Sciences (number 10) are in the top 10 hold-ings of the ETF.[7]

Vanity and Prevention

Whether you are a baby boomer or a preteen, you feel good when you look in the mirror and are happy with what you see. You may not agree with this, but it is reality and the direction in which our soci-ety is moving even more in the future. The vanity theme is based on more Americans and foreigners taking care of the parts of themselves they are not happy with through medical treatments. According to the American Society for Aesthetic Plastic Surgery, there were over 10 mil-lion surgical and nonsurgical cosmetic procedures performed in the United States in 2008.

Since 1997, there has been more than a 162 percent increase in the amount of cosmetic procedures; within that number, nonsurgical procedures saw a jump of 233 percent. The top five surgical procedures were: breast augmentation, liposuction, eyelid surgery, rhinoplasty, and abdominoplasty. The top five nonsurgical procedures were: Botox injec-tion, laser hair removal, hyaluronic acid, chemical peel, and laser skin resurfacing. All in all, the total spent on cosmetic procedures in 2008 by Americans was $11.8 billion. All of these numbers were reported by the American Society for Aesthetic Plastic Surgery.[8]

Allergan

As the baby boomers increase in age, gravity will take over and parts of the body that once held up very well will begin to inch closer to the floor. Whether it be wrinkles or breasts, Allergan (NYSE: AGN) has you covered. The company offers products for skin care, eye care, obesity, urologics, and breast augmentation, all areas that tend to need more care as humans age. The company is probably best known to many as the maker of Botox Cosmetic, which is used to firm up the skin and remove unwanted wrinkles. The product is a favorite in Hollywood and therefore is a favorite of anyone attempting to look a few years younger. Because it is a simple outpatient procedure, the product has become popular for people of all ages—from teens to grandparents.

During the fourth quarter of 2008, Allergan was able to report adjusted diluted earnings of 76 cents per share, a 27 percent increase over a year earlier. The sales number was not as impressive, falling 3.2 percent from the fourth quarter of 2007. For 2009, Allergan estimated total product nets sales to come in between $4.1 and $4.3 billion, with the majority of it coming from the specialty pharmaceutical division. The Botox product alone was forecasted to bring in between $1.15 and $1.19 billion in sales in 2009. Adjusted diluted earnings per share are expected to be in a range of $2.69 to $2.75, according to the company, resulting in a forward P/E ratio of approximately 14.0.[9]

The numbers for the first quarter of 2009, however, were not exactly what the company and investors had been hoping for. Allergan reported a 6 percent drop in revenue, down to $1.01 billion and earnings per share of 15 cents after company restructuring and legal fees were included. With the one-time fees removed, the earnings per share was a much more impressive 55 cents. The earnings per share estimate for the year remained unchanged, according to the company's quarterly earnings report. Both sales of Botox and breast implants fell by 6 and 16 percent, respectively, in the quarter. I believe as the economy rebounds and the baby boomers age, it will be inevitable that sales will begin to pick up again.

The price of the stock went the way of the market in 2008, falling 37 percent to its lowest level since 2003 (see Figure 8.8). Maybe it

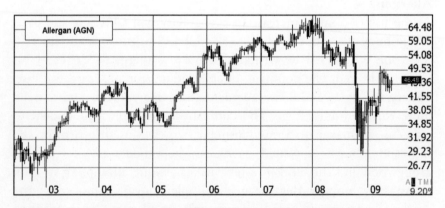

Figure 8.8   Smaller Breasts Equals Smaller Share Price for Allergan
SOURCE: TeleChart2007® or StockFinder® chart, courtesy of Worden Brothers, Inc.

was the circumstance that people cut back from Botox sessions during a recession or simply that the company was slowing its growth. Regardless of the reason, I look at Allergan as a multifaceted play on the vanity that so many baby boomers seek. Even more important is the company's products, which are ranked as the number one surgical and nonsurgical procedures based on the 2008 statistics mentioned earlier—Botox and breast augmentation. The company is positioned well in many areas and the pipeline has new products in clinical trials. Buying Allergan does carry above-average risk, but there is also above-average upside potential, especially from the 2009 lows.

Myriad Genetics

Myriad Genetics (NASDAQ: MYGN) is a unique company in that it has a thriving molecular diagnostics business, but also a drug development pipeline. The company is a leader in the cancer predisposition testing field, which is a test to determine the likelihood of certain cancers. The tests cover some of the most common cancers, such as breast, colon, and melanoma. The company currently offers six different tests, with the best seller focused on breast and ovarian cancer in women. The cost of a test is approximately $3,100 and most insurance policies cover a majority of the cost.

The company reported better than expected earnings for the fourth quarter of 2008 when revenue rose 49 percent to $84.4 million. Net income came in at 43 cents per share, blowing away the 11 cent loss from one year earlier. Myriad attributed the strong growth to its molecular diagnostics business. On the news of the strong results, the stock jumped to a new seven-year high in early February 2009. The CEO was clear in the press release that there is a recession, but that it is not affecting Myriad in the same manner as other companies. Myriad is the type of stock that can do well in a recession and a thriving bull market and could be bought on all 10 to 20 percent pullbacks that occur every few months.[10]

The pullback came after the first quarter earnings results in early May 2009 and the stock fell over 10 percent in one day (see Figure 8.9). The stock fell despite the company reporting an increase of revenue by 42 percent from a year earlier. Analysts had been expecting revenue slightly higher and that is the reason the stock took a big hit after the

Figure 8.9   Earnings Miss Dooms Myriad Genetics
SOURCE: TeleChart2007® or StockFinder® chart, courtesy of Worden Brothers, Inc.

report was released. In the following weeks, the stock has come back, and an entry in the mid-$30s appears to be a price to build a long-term position from.

Money Management

The fall of the stock market has created a new opportunity for money managers to capitalize on the demise of a handful of hedge funds, mutual funds, and advisers that did not make it through the bear market. With unsatisfied investors searching out new advisers, the leaders in the sector stand to benefit from an influx of clients and new assets under management. The stock I discuss next is my favorite in the group.

Affiliated Managers Group

Affiliated Managers Group (NYSE: AMG) is a unique asset management firm that comprises a large group of small, boutique investment companies that offer an array of products and services. At the end of 2008, the company had approximately $174 billion in assets under management through more than 300 products. AMG allows the management team at the individual firms the ability to continue running their operations with AMG's assistance, and for this, AMG shares in the revenue.[11]

By offering everything from individual investment advice to institutional management services to mutual funds, AMG lowers the risk of concentrating on one area of money management. Well-known names owned by AMG include the Third Avenue and Brandywine family of mutual funds. Mutual fund assets have been hit hard during the recession, but the older the investor, the more likely he will move away from individual stocks and into funds—whether I agree or disagree, it is the reality.

During the fourth quarter of 2008, AMG suffered a loss of $1.76 per share versus a gain of $1.53 per share one year earlier. Revenue also suffered a big loss, but the more important figure is the amount of assets under management. At the end of 2007, the company had $275 billion and one year later, it is down to $174 billion. The first quarter of 2009 did not get much better for AMG, according to its quarterly report. Net income fell by 80 percent to 15 cents per share; the silver lining is that it was a pickup from one quarter earlier. The one troubling number is that assets under management continued to fall to $153 billion. Again, the silver lining is that the stock market has rallied significantly since the low in April and a boost in assets under management should be expected next quarter.

Considering the stock market fell nearly 40 percent in 2008 the number is not as ugly as it looks at first glance (see Figure 8.10). The stock actually moved higher for a few weeks after the number because the market had priced in much worse earnings. AMG is a very aggressive purchase, but could be one of the winners of the baby boomers saving as they prepare to live longer than their parents.[12]

Figure 8.10 The Slow Rise from the Bottom for Affiliated Asset Managers
SOURCE: TeleChart2007® or StockFinder® chart, courtesy of Worden Brothers, Inc.

It is a given that the emergence of the baby boomers is upon us. However how it plays out in the economy and stock market is anyone's guess. It is obvious through the last chapter that I believe the boomers will not destroy our economy as some may believe. Rather, I believe they will continue to live life to the fullest as they have over the last few decades and will therefore not crawl into a cave to die. The boomers helped put together one of the greatest stock market rallies in history, and I believe they will not be responsible for the continuation of one of the great bear markets.

A factor that could hinder a global bull market or at the very least help certain sectors outperform is inflation. I get into more detail about the possible causes and resulting effects that inflation could have on your portfolio and how to profit from it in Chapter 9.

Chapter 9

Hyperinflation: The Result of the DC Printing Press

Inflation, not deflation, is the major concern. During recessionary times, it is common for investors, economists, and the government to ignore inflationary concerns. As recently as early 2009, the threat of inflation was being downplayed by economists warning of the possibility of deflation or disinflation. I, on the other hand, look at the 2008–2009 recession as a breeding ground for not only inflation in the coming years, but the very good possibility of hyperinflation. Before I go any further, it is imperative to define these terms so that you understand me throughout the chapter.

Rising or Falling Prices: Which Is It?

Inflation can be defined as the rise in the price of goods and services over a selected period of time. The inflation rate will be the percentage change of an inflation index over time. As investors we often turn to the Consumer Price Index (CPI) or the Producer Price Index (PPI) for our readings on inflation in the United States. The CPI is a measure of the average price of consumer goods and services that the government believes represents a basket purchased by the typical U.S. consumer. The PPI is defined as the average price received by domestic partners for their output. The two sound similar, but they are very different. While the CPI gives us a good look at the cost of living from the viewpoint of the consumer, the PPI focuses on the cost of production of the good. There are times the cost of production does not get passed along to the consumer and vice versa.

Before the recession began in 2008, there was a concern that inflation was too high for the likes of the U.S. Federal Reserve. Both the CPI and PPI were trending above the range the Fed is comfortable with, and Fed Chairman Ben Bernanke made several comments as the stock market was hitting highs. The remarks from the Fed chairman alluded to the assertion that he and the Fed would not let inflation get out of hand and would use monetary policies to see to that. Little did he know that inflation was the least of his concerns.

While inflation is an increase in prices, *deflation* is the exact opposite, a decrease in the general price of goods. This phenomenon occurs when the annual inflation rate falls below zero and, in reality, the real value of money increases. You will hear this referred to as a negative inflation rate as well—somewhat of an oxymoron. The best example of deflation occurred during the Great Depression, and this is why many economists and investment professionals assumed it would be an issue once again during the 2008–2009 recession.

Disinflation is often confused with deflation. While deflation occurs when prices of goods actually drop, disinflation is the slowing of the rate at which prices are rising. An example of disinflation would be the inflation rate falling from 4 percent to 3 percent. The prices are still increasing by a rate of 3 percent, but the rate of increase has fallen. Disinflation occurred during the most recent recession, as it does during most typical recessionary periods. Just to confuse you more I throw in one more term—*stagflation*. Stagflation occurs when the growth rate (as measured by Gross Domestic Product) is falling and prices are increasing. The most prominent period of stagflation occurred in the 1970s when prices were increasing because of higher oil prices and growth was negative. Periods of stagflation are rare and are avoided at all risks by all countries big and small.

History Predicts Inflation

By turning to historical numbers and trying to equate what has happened in the past with the current economic environment, there is no doubt in my mind that inflation will rear its ugly head at some point in the very near future. There is no point in recent history that has been able to sidestep inflation when a government is increasing its money supply at the rate the United States currently is.

During the first 100 days of the Obama administration there was one thing that was certain—the printing presses were working overtime as they continued to pump out more dollar bills. From bailouts to increased pork spending, the U.S. deficit continues to rise, with no end in sight. The only way to pay for the plans the administration is hellbent on pushing through is to print more money or to sell our bonds to any interested investors, in particular the largest foreign purchaser, China. The former is the number one reason I believe inflation is inevitable, and yet the mass media and the government continue to ignore the facts of history.

The Fed and the U.S. government are so concerned about the recession that they have forgotten to include inflation in the equation. Or they are willing to tolerate that some inflation will be needed to get the country out of the recession. I do agree a little inflation is good, but as long as the printing press in Obama's office is running, hyperinflation will become a reality, not just a big word we like to scare people with.

In an attempt to unfreeze the credit markets and get money flowing again, the Federal Reserve announced on March 18, 2009, that it planned to buy $300 billion of long-term Treasuries over the next six months. The Fed said in the same announcement that it will buy an additional $750 billion in mortgage-backed securities in an effort to lower mortgage rates and help create a housing bottom. The news sent stocks higher along with bond prices as yields collapsed.

To gauge what the news meant for the few of us on top of the inflation concern before the masses, all we need to do is turn to the reaction from both gold and Treasury Inflation Protected Securities (TIPS). The SPDR Gold ETF (GLD) was trading near the low of the day ($86.83) when the Fed made its scheduled announcement. The ETF closed the day at $93.09, one of the biggest one-day turnarounds in the trading history of GLD. The 7 percent rally off the intraday low was monumental and a core piece of my inflation thesis. The Market Vector Gold Miners ETF (GDX) gained 15 percent off the intraday low after the news hit the wires.

So, you still are not convinced? The iShares Barclays TIPS Bond ETF (TIP) gained 3.7 percent on March 18, 2009, its biggest one-day move since it began trading in January 2004. Coincidence? I think not! Investors for a day realized that pumping another one trillion dollars into Treasuries and mortgages would eventually lead to inflation, and the numbers discussed here prove that.

On December 16, 2008, the Federal Reserve lowered interest rates to a range between 0 and 25 basis points; in reality, it was a rate cut to zero. It was the day the United States became the Japan of the twenty-first century. The TIP rallied 3 percent after the announcement and a hint by the Federal Reserve that it will consider buying Treasuries, which, of course, is another way to say creating future inflation. The gold ETF, GLD, gained over 2 percent on the same day. If you are noticing a connection between gold, TIPS, and inflation, you are on the right track and will find out later in the chapter how it all comes together.

In Table 9.1, the reaction from historical inflation hedges are shown on days when the Federal Reserve made major announcements regarding buying Treasuries and spending trillions through the creation of a new money supply.

In reality, what the Federal Reserve and the government are saying through their policies is that they are willing to do whatever it takes, and there is no concern regarding how much it will cost. Instead of turning to tax dollars to pay for the bailouts and recessionary programs,

Table 9.1   Inflationary Reaction to Fed Announcements

	December 16, 2008	March 18, 2009
SPDR Gold ETF (GLD)	+2.3%	+3.4%
Market Vectors Gold Miners ETF (GDX)	+6.6%	+10.1%
iShares TIPS ETF (TIP)	+3.0%	+3.7%

the government has decided to print money and flood the money supply. The announcement in March 2009 by the Fed came just hours after the government released the CPI number that showed the biggest spike in prices in eight months.

Inflation had been put on the back burner, with more pressing issues facing the country. The Fed was more concerned with skyrocketing unemployment, falling home prices, a weak consumer, and credit markets that have yet to unfreeze. This is exactly why the Fed said in its statement that it believed inflation would remain "subdued." The Fed went on to say that it "sees some risk that inflation could persist for a time below rates that best foster economic growth and price stability in the longer term." That statement clearly points out that in March 2009, the Fed was more concerned about deflation, and not inflation.

Deflation should have been a concern of the Fed in the near term when it made the announcement, but I believe that Bernanke and his colleagues panicked. The end result will be that the Fed created the bottom in the stock market, but at the same time laid the groundwork for hyperinflation in the future.

Even more evidence of inflation can be found in a TIPS auction that took place during the first quarter of 2009. The TIPS auction saw the U.S. government sell $6 billion in bonds at a yield of 1.59 percent. The yield came in 2 percent higher than higher than expected—a sign of inflation concerns.

Investors can also analyze the difference between rates on 10-year government notes and similar TIPS. The difference can be used to show the outlook among traders for consumer prices, also known as inflation. The spread widened to 1.35 percentage points during the first quarter of 2009 from a reading of nearly zero at the end of 2008. The average over the last five years has been 2.26 percentage points. The numbers do not suggest that inflation is here today, but what they are is an early indicator that inflation is beginning to creep into the minds of traders. The trend is just beginning and now is the time to prepare your portfolio for the upcoming surge in prices.

As consumers, we will likely feel inflation the most in two ways, the grocery store and fuel. Commodity prices have fallen during the recession on the basis of decreased demand for goods and supplies either remaining steady or increasing in certain situations. To try to combat falling prices, a large number of commodity companies lowered their output, thus resulting in lower supply. Why would the copper miner or natural gas producer continue to pull commodities out of the ground when the demand was not there?

My biggest fear is that when the recession ends and the Next Great Bull Market begins, it will lead to a new economic growth period. While I truly do want this to happen, the fact that I am concentrating on inflation as I write this has me a bit nervous. I can give you examples that range from oil to wheat. The supply levels have fallen and when the world economy begins to expand again, the commodity suppliers will not be ready, and supply will therefore remain flat as demand increases. Simple economics suggests the end result will be higher commodity prices and, put a different way, inflation.

To take this one step further, what about the trillions of new currency being printed by not only the United States, but other countries around the world. The combination of stagnant supply, increased demand, and more money to fuel the demand will result in hyperinflation. Do not be surprised when you are paying $5 per gallon to fill your vehicle. Do not be surprised when the price of bread and rice and milk continue to rise. And finally, do not blame the speculators as we did the last time. This time there is only one entity to blame—your government. So to lessen the blow to your portfolio and your wallet, keep reading for a list of investments that will help you hedge against inflation and even make some money as prices skyrocket.

Finally, please do not put your faith in the media when it comes to determining when inflation is now a concern. By the time CNBC or any other outlet begins producing special segments on inflation and how investors can profit from inflation, you know it is too late. I want you to take a look at the price of gold when that occurs and there is a great chance it will already be above $1,000 per ounce. Before the rally occurs you will have an opportunity to buy gold in the $800s and you should take advantage of the discounted price.

Preparing for Hyperinflation

Whether prices are rising or falling, there will be specific investment classes that outperform during the varying inflationary periods. Because the odds are that the United States is moving into a high inflation environment in the years ahead, the discussion about where to put your money in regard to inflation will focus on investments that outperform when inflation is rising. I give you in these pages a wide variety of investment options if you agree with me in reference to inflation and want to allocate your portfolio accordingly.

iShares Barclays TIPS Bond ETF

The iShares Barclays Treasury Inflation-Protected Securities Bond ETF (NYSE: TIP) tracks an index of fixed-income securities that represent the inflation-protected sector of the U.S. Treasury market. The securities that make up the basket are Treasury notes that are inflation-protected and linked to the CPI numbers (discussed earlier in this chapter). The principal of a TIPS increases with inflation and decreases with deflation as measured by the CPI. A government-issued TIPS pays interest twice per year at a fixed rate. Because the principal will be fluctuating with inflation and deflation, so will the semi-annual interest payments. As inflation rises, so do the interest payments, and on the flip side, if deflation occurs, the interest payments may decrease. When a TIPS matures, the investor will either be paid the adjusted principal or the original principal, whichever is greater. There is no risk the investor will receive less than the original amount invested in the TIPS.

Because TIPS is actually composed of a basket of TIPS, the ETF will pay out dividends, not interest, on a monthly basis as income is passed through to the investor. During 2008 and early 2009, the TIPS dividend payments have been inconsistent and sporadic. The yield for TIPS is difficult to determine because of the unknown dividend payments

Figure 9.1   iShares Barclays TIPS Bond ETF—A Conservative Inflation Hedge
SOURCE: TeleChart2007® or StockFinder® chart, courtesy of Worden Brothers, Inc.

from the ETF. However, if inflation does become a reality in the years to come, I would expect the yield to be in the high single digits. On top of the dividend yield, there is the potential for capital appreciation of the ETF as the principal amount invested in the individual TIPS increases with inflation.

Investing in TIPS directly or in the ETF will not make you rich overnight or over time, but what it will do is offer diversity to a portfolio that will likely be adversely affected by a rise in inflation. A TIPS purchase would not be a short-term investment, but rather an asset that is considered a long-term income-producing, hedging investment (see Figure 9.1).

SPDR Gold ETF

The precious yellow metal that has been used as currency for centuries tends to become more prominent when times are tough. Considering that the world has suffered through one of the worst global recessions in decades, it should be no surprise that the price of gold has risen. In March 2008, an ounce of gold rose above $1,000 per ounce for the first time ever. In the following three months gold prices fell about 30 percent down to $700. As the global recession accelerated into the first quarter of 2009, the price of gold once again hit the $1,000 mark. The two instances in which it hit $1,000, the precious metal quickly fell in price as the psychological level drove investors to take profits.

The major reason gold rallied to $1,000 in February 2009 was the stigma that gold will always be worth something, unlike a stock certificate, which could become a mere piece of scrap paper at the end of the day. Over the last few decades, gold has been the preferred safe investment for investors attempting to put their money somewhere that will not be affected by the outside economic forces. Whether this is absolutely true or not is not important, the historical experience is that demand for gold increases during times of uncertainty and that increased demand ultimately results in higher prices per ounce.

An example of gold's lure of safety was apparent the week after the September 11, 2001, terrorist attacks on the World Trade Center. The price of gold shot up 9 percent as the stock market fell 12 percent. The inclusion of gold in a portfolio before the terrorist attacks would have helped soften the blow that all portfolios took at the time. This is one reason I almost always have some type of exposure to gold through the SPDR Gold Trust (NYSE: GLD) or gold stocks. As much as I wish it was, this world is not safe from terrorists or other political uncertainties, and this makes gold a hedge against such instances.

Even though what I have discussed about gold so far makes it an attractive hedging tool for any portfolio, this chapter is about inflation. Historically, gold has also been a great hedge for inflation because as inflation rises, the value of your dollar decreases. However, the value of gold does not, and investors therefore move their assets into gold to avoid the future loss of the value of money.

During the late 1970s and early 1980s, the United States faced double-digit inflation that ate away at historically high interest investors were receiving on their money. If investors would have chosen to invest in gold in lieu of interest-bearing accounts, the end result would have been precious (no pun intended). In June 1977, an investor could have purchased an ounce of gold for $137. By January 1980, that same ounce of gold was selling for nearly $900 per ounce. During the same time frame the S&P 500 was up approximately 10 percent (see Figure 9.2).

Clearly, the best place for your money during the hyperinflation period of the late 1970s was gold. So, if you agree with my thought

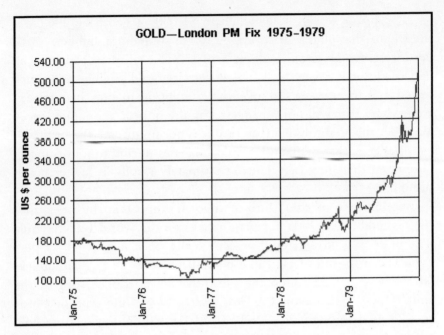

Figure 9.2 Gold Futures Rally from 1975 to 1980 During Inflationary Period
SOURCE: www.kitco.com.

process on inflation and that the DC printing presses will eventually spur on a devaluation of the U.S. dollar, you must consider gold as a hedge. Even if you do not agree with me about inflation, there are geopolitical risks forever hanging over the world that make gold one of the only true havens (see Figure 9.3).

PowerShares DB Base Metals ETF

The PowerShares DB Base Metals ETF (NYSE: DBB) is composed of three industrial metals: aluminum, copper, and zinc. As inflation increases, most investors turn naturally to gold as the investment of choice in the metals sector. However, the base metals will also see an increase in price with inflation on the rise. The three metals that make up DBB have the distinct ability to increase with inflation and will also outperform when the economy is increasing because of their ties to global expansion.

For example, copper is used in everything from wiring in home appliances to telecom networks to new buildings. When the global economy is

Figure 9.3   SPDR Gold ETF Rising from 2005 Low
Source: TeleChart2007® or StockFinder® chart, courtesy of Worden Brothers, Inc.

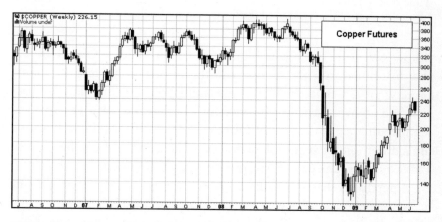

Figure 9.4   Copper Futures Attempting to Rally Back to $4 Per Pound
Source: www.stockcharts.com.

slow, the demand for copper will fall as the need for it slows down. But inflation should be able to prop up the price in the event the economy does slow in the coming years because inflation should be here, regardless. Assuming both growth and inflation are present in the coming years, a more likely scenario, a metal such as copper will thrive and the old high of $4 per pound will be taken out (see Figure 9.4).

The ETF is rebalanced each November and the allocation is reset back to one-third of the assets in all three commodities. Throughout the year, depending on when you check the allocation, the weightings may be dramatically different. In mid-June 2009, zinc had risen to

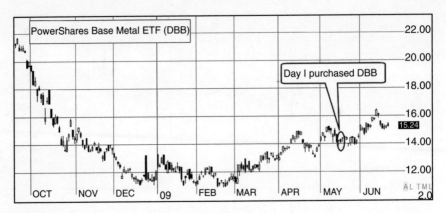

Figure 9.5   PowerShares DB Base Metals ETF Experiences Heavy Volume at
Time of Purchase
SOURCE: TeleChart2007® or StockFinder® chart, courtesy of Worden Brothers, Inc.

40 percent of the ETF, with aluminum falling to 23 percent. This was
due to outperformance of zinc and the underperformance of aluminum. What differentiates ETFs from mutual funds is that they are passive, and at any given time an investor can find out what exactly they
are investing in. In the case of DBB, we know the portfolio will not be
altered but once a year, and at that time the allocation will be reset to
the original parameters of one-third into each commodity.

I purchased shares of DBB on May 18, 2009, for myself and clients
at approximately $14.33, with a realistic target of a 50 percent gain in the
next two years and a more lofty goal of a double in the same time frame.
(See Figure 9.5.) The reasoning for the purchase of DBB in May was
based on the attractive price of the metal along with a trifecta of potential
outcomes that included higher inflation, a weak U.S. dollar, and an
increase in demand for base metals, especially in the emerging markets.
My thought process of the trifecta has been shared through several media
outlets and I feel very confident in the decision to purchase under $15.

Freeport–McMoRan Copper and Gold

Investing in the physical commodities has its advantages, but there are also
benefits to putting money in the companies that are in the business of
mining and selling the metals. While the commodity futures will often
be less volatile and more attractive to investors during times of inflation,

the big gains can be found in the commodity stocks. For example, from 2005 through 2008, the Dow Jones AIG Commodity Index gained 27 percent, and during the same time frame, the multinational mining company BHP Billiton (NYSE: BHP) increased by 190 percent. The company I am about to highlight, Freeport-McMoRan Copper and Gold (NYSE: FCX), gained 168 percent during the same three-year span.

Keep in mind that with higher reward, there often comes higher risk, and that is the case in this situation. Short-term swings in the price of the futures contracts could move a commodity ETF 10 to 15 percent in a few weeks. It is not uncommon in this environment, however, for a commodity stock to move 15 percent in one trading session. That being said, if you are willing to take on more risk for the potential rewards—keep reading.

FCX is an interesting company because it gives investors exposure to two very different metals that both benefit from inflationary environments—gold and copper. Gold is a precious metal that is viewed as a safe investment and a currency. Copper is also used as currency, but is more of an industrial metal that is in demand around the world. Coming in as the number two copper producer in the world (Codelco is number one), FCX has the leverage to benefit from a rise in copper prices. The company is also the world's largest producer of molybdenum, a metal that is unique in that it is light and very strong.

The fate of FCX relies on the price of copper and this goes back to the demand factor and, specifically, China. The announcement of a Chinese stimulus plan in early 2009 was a boost for copper prices, as it was evident that the Chinese government did not want its growth to slow any further. The stimulus packages implemented by the U.S. government and others around the world have also helped copper rally during the first quarter of 2009. If my thinking is correct and the recession will be in the rearview mirror by the end of 2009, a low in copper prices and, therefore, the price of FCX, will have been made.

As much as FCX is a play on inflation, it is also counting on an economic turnaround and the Next Great Bull Market to begin sooner rather than later. But it does have a wild card up its sleeve—molybdenum. Even though you may never have heard of molybdenum before this book, the world of mining sure has. The demand for the metal over the last decade has increased dramatically, sending the price higher and

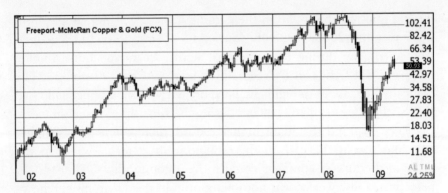

Figure 9.6   Freeport-McMoRan Copper and Gold
SOURCE: TeleChart2007® or StockFinder® chart, courtesy of Worden Brothers, Inc.

making it the best performing of the major base metals since 2000. Molybdenum is used in a number of diverse areas, including nuclear power, aerospace and defense, the water industry, chemicals, and building materials. When comparing apples to apples, I look for the companies that have a slight advantage over their competitors and FCX's exposure to molybdenum gives it an edge over its peers and is my favorite copper play for the Next Great Bull Market (see Figure 9.6).

PowerShares DB Agriculture ETF

One group of commodities that will always be needed around the world regardless of the economic situation is found in agriculture. The billions of people that call Earth home need commodities such as wheat and soybeans to continue living a healthy life. On top of demand that will never cease to exist, agricultural commodities are also an inflation hedge perfect for most portfolios.

The PowerShares DB Agriculture ETF (NYSE: DBA) invests in four agricultural commodities equally—corn, soybeans, sugar, and wheat. The ETF began trading in early 2007 and enjoyed a great run into early 2008, nearly doubling in price (see Figure 9.7). Both corn and wheat hit all-time highs in 2008 as demand was surging along and supply was suffering from droughts and other market factors. In 2008, DBA fell 21 percent, much better than the S&P 500's other commodities.

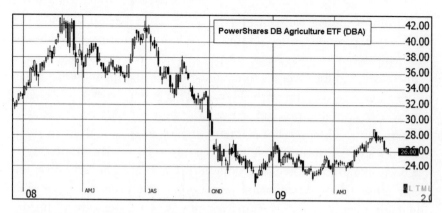

Figure 9.7   PowerShares DB Agriculture ETF
SOURCE: TeleChart2007® or StockFinder® chart, courtesy of Worden Brothers, Inc.

While prices fell fairly dramatically in 2008 off the highs, the one benefit the agricultural commodities have over their peers is that they have an artificial price floor. What I mean by that is that they can fall only so much because, as I mentioned earlier, we all must eat, and until food producers come up with artificial wheat, corn, or soybeans that can feed the world (think *Soylent Green*), the price floor will be evident. Even in the toughest times, food remains a necessity for all humans. In comparison, copper will also always have some demand, but new construction can be put on hold for a couple of years—eating cannot.

There are several fundamental reasons agricultural commodities are a solid long-term play for the next bull market, and I discuss these next: expansion of the middle class, which results in a higher demand for food; China; and production concerns.

For starters, more wealth is created in a bull market, and therefore more people around the world will be moving out of poverty and into the middle class. One of the first ways they will spend their newfound wealth will be on more and better food. This results in higher demand for the commodities.

Number two is a follow-on to number one: China. With approximately 1.3 billion mouths to feed in China, and the population growing along with their wealth, the country must stockpile food for its citizens. China is the world's top importer of soybeans, importing

37.8 million metric tons during the 2007–2008 period. During the 2004–2005 period, China imported 25.8 million tons of soybeans. That equates to an increase of 47 percent in three years. I expect the Chinese demand for soybeans to continue to rise and question the ability of the supply to keep up with the pace. This is why soybeans is one of my favorite commodities and at the same time a hedge on food inflation. As the stock market was attempting to form a bottom in April 2009, the soybean futures were breaking out to a fresh six-month high.

Reason number three is production. There are concerns that the credit crunch has caused many commodity producers to either shut down completely or to lower their output. When demand picks up, the producers will not be prepared to get back online immediately or at all. Considering credit will remain tight for the foreseeable future, a surge in food prices is not out of the question in the next two years.

The fourth major catalyst is the unknowns such as weather. A big reason wheat hit an all-time high in 2008 was a major drought in Australia that was the worst in decades. Droughts in the midwestern United States have also caused major challenges during the last few years. When all is said and done, the agricultural commodities may be a play on inflation for some investors, but the more I think about it, there is substantial upside potential for the growth investor as well (see Figure 9.7).

With inflation almost guaranteed in the coming years, it will be imperative that investors prepare their portfolio with investments that will also perform well during the Next Great Bull Market. The investment options listed in this chapter encompass the characteristics sought after. There is a heavy concentration on commodities, and I am okay with that because I believe the sector will be a leader of the next rally.

Commodities play an important role in developed countries, but they are the base of the economy for most emerging and frontier countries. I focus in Chapter 10 on the frontier markets, which are small-growth countries that have yet to fully discover their investment potential. Countries such as Vietnam and the United Arab Emirates are two that are highlighted in the next chapter.

Chapter 10

Finding the Next Brazil: Investing in Frontier Markets

I nvestors who were lucky enough to invest in the BRIC countries (Brazil, Russia, India, China) in the 1990s made enough money that they are not as affected by the recent global recession. Consider that in 1993, the Brazilian BOVESPA Stock Index was trading at 23 and in 2008 it hit 73,000; the numbers do not seem fathomable to investors who concentrate only on U.S. equities. There may not be many comparisons to the 15-year rally in Brazil, but other emerging markets have gone through similar economic booms.

When the rally began for the BRIC countries in the 1990s, they were not yet considered to be emerging markets. The high risk and instability associated with the countries put them into the frontier markets category. As the political situation and economy improved along with the local stock market, the countries were upgraded to the category of emerging markets. Even after they became known as emerging market countries, their respective stock markets continued to move higher into the mid-2000s. That is until the global recession hit all markets, from emerging to developed.

While there was plenty of money to be made after the BRIC countries became popular investment options as emerging markets, the big money was made when they were still infants known as frontier markets. To put the concept into a layperson's terms, think of the frontier markets as preteens, the emerging markets as teenagers, and the developed markets as fully grown adults. The developed market adults are somewhat stable, and do not have the same volatility as their younger brethren. The emerging market teenagers have lots of upside as they go through puberty on the way to adulthood, but there will be more volatility and could be wild mood swings. The preteens have the most upside, as they are about to enter their teen years before moving on to adulthood. That being said, some of the preteens will have trouble in their teens, go down the wrong path, and not end up as successful adults. This is the risk you take with a frontier market country; there is the risk that the country never gets off the ground because of any number of factors. The end result could involve an insolvent stock market and an economy that folds. With such enormous risk, there must be a similar upside reward potential to make it enticing for investors. I highlight in this chapter the potential rewards and risks associated with specific frontier markets around the world.

Risks Facing Frontier Markets

Every investment has a risk because nothing in the financial markets is ever guaranteed. Investments offered by the U. S. government are guaranteed by the full faith and credit of the United States, but if something were to happen to the country, it could default on its promise. The possibility of the United States defaulting is almost nonexistent in the foreseeable future, but other countries are not as stable. Investing in frontier markets carries a number of risks that make the strategy aggressive and not the best choice for conservative investors. The four risks that plague frontier market investors include political risk, liquidity risk, currency risk, and concentration risk. Each risk will be looked into further in the following section.

Political Risk

When investing in underdeveloped countries, the most predominant risk will be political risk. As a country begins to engage in growth and move away from the thinking of itself as a third-world country, the political landscape will change dramatically. The move into the frontier markets category involves more money for the country and the government must be able to handle the increased fiscal responsibility. Because many frontier market countries were very poor in the near past, it is not uncommon for politicians to be unethical in their business practices. Outside of the government, there is a great difference in how a developed nation does business versus a business deal in a country such as Nigeria. Whether you agree or disagree with either way of doing business, it is reality, and as an investor in frontier markets, you must be comfortable with the situation.

There are endless examples of specific political risks around the world in emerging and frontier markets. Venezuela is an example that many are familiar with because its dictator is often in the news—Hugo Chavez. Over the last few years, he has moved to nationalize several of the country's largest industries. He has burned bridges with several major countries along the way, including the United States, and has aligned the country with terrorist countries such as Iran. The risk with investing in Venezuela is that your investment could be fine one day and nationalized the next because the dictator made that decision. There are also risks of civil war, which occurs often in African countries, trade embargos, terrorism, social uprisings, and many more. The issue with political risk is that even though you can prepare for certain situations, there are too many factors to consider when investing in frontier markets. An investor must realize it comes with investing in frontier markets.

That being said, there is also heightened political risk within the developed countries of the world. The United States, which many consider the most developed nation in the world, has undergone several major changes politically and economically. President Obama and his administration have moved closer to socialism and are taking away parts of the free market that the country was built on. This is viewed as a negative by investors and the U.S. stock market paid a major price in the early months of 2009. To an extent there is political risk in every country, an investor must decide if the risk is worth the potential reward.

Liquidity Risk

When an investor would like to buy or sell an asset and cannot do so in a timely manner, there is liquidity risk present. This type of risk arises when investor A wants to initiate a trade with an investment but cannot locate an investor B. Most developed markets will not carry liquidity risk, but even the United States has liquidity issues with thinly traded securities. Look at the issue with some of the complex derivatives that helped create the credit crisis; many of the derivatives no longer had a market, and buyers and sellers could therefore not be matched together, the end result being liquidity risk in the rare derivatives market in the most developed country in the world.

With frontier markets, the issue will be the lack of development of their stock market infrastructure. Many of the stock exchanges have been around for only a decade or so and are therefore in the infancy stages of the business cycle. Mistakes and bad decisions are to be expected in their early years. One way around the liquidity issue is to buy only frontier market companies that are traded on a major exchange in either the United States or another developed country. American Depositary Receipts (ADRs) are foreign companies that are traded on a major U.S. stock exchange and available for U.S. investors to purchase in the same manner as a U.S.-based stock. While liquidity risk can be dangerous, it can be nearly eliminated before an investment decision is made.

Currency Risk

Currency risk is the type of risk that arises when there is movement in one currency versus another that will affect your investment. For example, investors who put their money into frontier and emerging markets before the global recession saw a bump in their gains because the local currencies gained ground versus the U.S. dollar. Assume the Brazilian real gains 10 percent against the U.S. dollar in one year; your investment in a Brazilian company will experience extraordinary gains when the local currency (real) is converted into U.S. dollars. The real is now able to buy more U.S. dollars, and you thus have more U.S. dollars in your pocket.

The exact opposite could occur if you invest in a country that has a currency that is losing value against the U.S. dollar. A sizable drop could cause a gain in an investment to disappear after the currency conversion back to U.S. dollars. The second aspect of the currency risk involves a government that will attempt to devalue its currency in order to make its exports less expensive to buy in other countries. In late 2008 and early 2009, the valuation of many Eastern European countries' currencies fell as much as 25 percent against the U.S. dollar. As a matter of fact, Kazakhstan was forced to devalue its currency to make its exports prices competitive with neighboring countries such as the Ukraine, Russia, and Hungary.[1] As the local currency falls 25 percent, it will take a major toll on the value in U.S. dollars and therefore greatly depreciate the frontier market investment.

Concentration Risk

The risk of having too many of your assets in one investment is a broad definition of concentration risk. The probability of a large loss or gain is increased as a greater percentage of an investment is concentrated in a narrow sector of the market. Investing in frontier markets involves concentration risk, because as you read in the next section, many of the countries rely on a single large export. The Middle Eastern countries are a great example of a region that is overly reliant on the price and demand for oil. When times are good in the energy sector, the countries flourish, but when the tides change, as they did in 2008, they will tend to struggle.

To help combat concentration risk, an investor can consider a frontier market ETF that has exposure to countries in various regions that do not rely on a single sector of the market. There is a list of specific frontier market investments for you to consider later in this chapter.

What Are the Frontier Markets?

The MSCI Frontier Markets Index includes local stocks from 22 countries in four continents. The highest concentration comes from central and eastern Europe, where many of the old Soviet-occupied areas are now individual frontier countries. Even though the region has the most countries represented in the index the allocation is most heavily weighted to the Middle Eastern countries. The following is a breakdown of the 22 countries.

Africa

The large continent of Africa is represented by four countries: Nigeria, Kenya, Tunisia, and Mauritius. Nigeria is the second-largest allocation in the index, accounting for 12 percent. The remaining three African countries make up less than 4 percent of the total index.

Of the four African countries, the most intriguing is Nigeria because of its size and resources. Nigeria is the most populous country in Africa and the eighth-most populous in the world, with more than 140 million people. The International Monetary Fund (IMF) predicted the Nigerian economy would grow at 8.1 percent in 2009, making it one of the fastest-growing economies in the world. *The Economist* magazine took a different stance on Nigeria's expected GDP in 2009, forecasting growth of only 3.5 percent and 4.8 percent in 2010. Even at the lower end of the range, the numbers are much better than growth you will find in most developed countries.

In 2008, the country grew at 6.8 percent,[2] an amazingly strong number considering the global landscape and the fall in oil prices, according to preliminary numbers from the Central Bank of Nigeria.[3] Since 2005, the GDP has grown by at least 6 percent and even more important, inflation has fallen from 17.8 percent in 2005 to an estimated 7.3 percent in 2008, according to the IMF.[4]

Nigeria is widely considered a country that relies on the demand for its oil for its livelihood. This may be true, but according to the IMF, growth in the nonoil sector is expected to reach 9 percent in 2008. The fall in oil prices in 2008 and 2009 has taken a toll on Nigerian growth and the stocks in the region. However, when the bull market takes off, so will the demand for oil, and the country should be back on its feet and ready to continue its above-average growth. Even though the country is attempting to lower its reliability on oil in the future, it will take time, and the possibility of oil demand not coming back is the biggest risk to investing in this African country. The good news is that oil prices have more than doubled off the early 2009 low, and this has given the country's stock market a boost. A given is that the political environment in the region is not the most stable, and at any point, a civil war could break out in the region that would affect the country's economy. A chart of the Nigerian stock market can be seen in Figure 10.1.

Asia

Only two Asian countries are represented in the index: Vietnam and Sri Lanka. Vietnam makes up 1.5 percent and Sri Lanka a mere 0.3 percent. Neither of the countries will have a noticeable affect on the movement of the index, and if exposure to either country is the

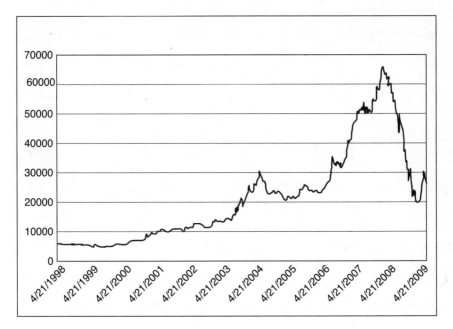

Figure 10.1   Nigerian Stock Exchange

goal, an alternative approach must be taken. Many of the Asian countries have graduated from the frontier markets asset class and are now considered emerging markets. Of the two, only Vietnam is intriguing to me as an investment choice. Before the global recession hit, Vietnam was quickly becoming one of the most sought-after frontier markets for investors. The stock market in Vietnam was on a tear the last few years and suddenly hit a wall before collapsing during the global bear market for equities (see Figure 10.2).

The IMF pegged GDP in Vietnam grew by 8.2 percent and 8.5 percent annually during 2006 and 2007, respectively.[5] With all economies slowing around the world, Vietnam's growth fell to 6.2 percent in 2008, and estimates are as low as 3 percent in 2009 before picking back up to 4 percent in 2010, according to *The Economist* magazine.[6] Inflation was a major concern for the country in 2008 with the average increase in prices a whopping 23 percent; this is up from 8.9 percent in 2007. *The Economist* forecasts, however, for inflation to drop substantially to 5.1 percent and 3.6 percent in 2009 and 2010, respectively. The biggest risk with investing in Vietnam is the current political situation

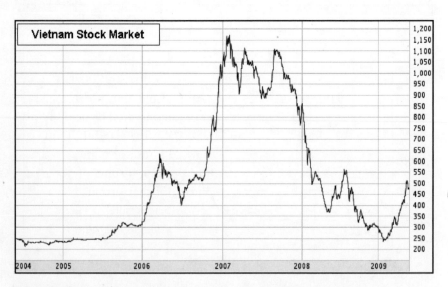

Figure 10.2   Vietnam Stock Market Bouncing Off the 2005 Low Is a Bullish Signal
SOURCE: www.vietnammarkets.com.

and the governing Communist party. The government has been known to monitor the news media (newspapers, Internet, etc.), and until it begins to take a turn in the direction of democracy, there is always the risk of a political uprising or a version of nationalization. One similarity between Vietnam and Nigeria is that both are major exporters of oil. Vietnam also has a strong clothing and textile export pipeline, however, that adds diversity. The slowdown, unfortunately, has hurt both industries and Vietnam's GDP has paid for it.

Central and Eastern Europe

Nine of the 22 countries in the frontier market index are located in Central or Eastern Europe. The country with the largest asset allocation in the region is Kazakhstan, with 3.5 percent; all nine, however, make up only a total of 9.5 percent of the index. The region is an interesting place for investors because of its proximity to emerging market Russia, developed countries in Western Europe, and the unstable region of the Middle East. There are both positives and negatives to the location, but overall, the growth potential is high with the right government initiatives.

I focus on Kazakhstan because it has the largest weighting in the region and is an interesting play on energy. Growth was very strong in 2006 when the GDP came in at 10.7 percent, but over the last few years the growth has been slowing for the country. In 2007, GDP fell to 8.9 percent, and estimates for 2008 are 2.8 percent. The forecast for 2009 is even worse, with *The Economist* predicting a GDP below 1 percent.[7] One silver lining is that the 2010 GDP is expected to jump back above 3 percent as oil prices move higher. Because of higher oil prices in early 2008, the country was able to record a surplus of $6 billion, which is approximately 4 percent of GDP. But that surplus is expected to disappear in 2009 as oil exports slow and prices fall.[8]

Investing directly in a country such as Kazakhstan is next to impossible and not a strategy I would recommend because of the extremely high political risk and reliance on oil and mineral exports. There are also the ties to Russia, which is an emerging market country with a questionable political situation. In the end, the risk outweighs the potential reward and I suggest turning your head to Kazakhstan. That being said,

Figure 10.3   Central Europe & Russia Fund (CEE) Mounting a Comeback
SOURCE: TeleChart2007® or StockFinder® chart, courtesy of Worden Brothers, Inc.

there is a potential for the region to come back with the Next Great
Bull Market and the 10 percent exposure gained through the index is
welcomed.

The Central Europe & Russia Fund (NYSE: CEE) is a closed-
end fund that invests in Russia and other Eastern European countries.
The chart in Figure 10.3 is a good illustration of the stock markets
in the region. After bottoming in 2001, the closed-end fund rallied
through the middle of 2008 before crashing with the global recession.
A dramatic rally from the 2009 lows has recouped some of the losses
for the region, but there is much more upside potential for the frontier countries.

Middle East

The Middle East is represented by seven countries in the index and
is the region with the largest exposure by far. The country of Kuwait
makes up 40 percent of the index and is joined by the United Arab
Emirates (UAE), Qatar, Oman, Jordan, Bahrain, and Lebanon. Even
Lebanon, which carries the lowest weighting in the region, comprises
2.5 percent. The index could be called the Middle East Frontier Index,
considering 71 percent of the assets are based in the region.[9]

The first thing that comes to mind when the Middle East is mentioned is oil and the second is most likely war. With the majority of the world's oil coming out of the Middle East and the region being at war for a large portion of the past two decades it should not be a surprise that that is how people think of the region. Stability in the region has improved, attracting large amounts of money, and with the price of oil skyrocketing in the 2000s, it was the root of a new group of wealthy individuals. As the price of oil has fallen, the result has been a drop in the local Middle Eastern stock markets. Investments into infrastructure have fallen from record levels as investors from in and out of the region tighten their wallets until the economic storm passes. Once the global economy turns around and the Next Great Bull Market begins, the region will be a beneficiary as the demand for oil increases.

Anytime an index with over 20 components has a 40 percent weighting in one, it is a cause for concern and brings into question the diversity of the index. With that the case in the frontier markets index, it is imperative to delve further into the country of Kuwait.

The GDP in Kuwait was 6.3 percent in 2006, 4.6 percent in 2007, and 8.5 percent in 2008. The steady growth can be attributed to the increase in demand for oil throughout the world. Looking at 2009, the expectations for growth drop substantially to 2.7 percent based on the assumption that oil demand will remain lower for most of the year. Growth was expected to return in 2010 as the global economy improved and oil demand picked back up; forecasted estimates called for an increase in GDP of 4.8 percent.[10]

The proximity to Iraq and other unstable countries makes investing in Kuwait risky. Add in that 95 percent of their exports are oil and the risk increases even more. The bonus is, however, that the country has the United States on its side (just look at the 1991 Gulf War) in the event any geopolitical situations arise. While the United States on their side is a good attribute, investors are clearly focused on the price of oil when it comes to Kuwaiti stocks. After rallying nearly fourfold from 2004 through 2007, the Kuwait Stock Exchange Index fell over 60 percent from its high in 2007 through the end of 2008 as the price of oil tumbled. In Figure 10.4, the rise and fall of the Kuwait Index is illustrated.[11]

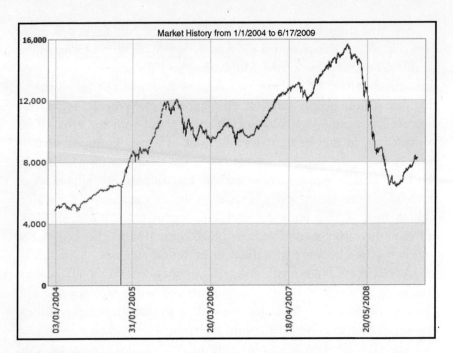

Figure 10.4   Kuwait Stock Exchange Index Falls 60 Percent from the 2008
High in Nine Months
SOURCE: www.kuwaitse.com.

Not far from Kuwait is the number two holding in the index, the
United Arab Emirates (UAE). The country is one of the most stable in
the region and has been the focus of the national media because of the
country's extravagant lifestyles of the rich and famous. The cities of Dubai
and Abu Dhabi are now household names after breathtaking buildings and
outlandish construction has taken place with petroleum dollars. The
surge in oil prices overnight made the small Middle Eastern country a
wealth-and-growth machine.[12] The GDP grew 9.6 percent in 2006 and
7.4 percent in 2007, but was expected to fall all the way down to less
than 2 percent in 2009 because of falling oil demand and prices. Similar
to Kuwait, growth should begin to pick up again in 2010 back to the 4
percent level.[13] A chart of the meteoric rise of the Dubai Stock Market is
highlighted in Figure 10.5. After exploding from the 1000 level to nearly
9000 in less than two years, the index has come all the way back down to
1000. Was this a bubble that burst and marks the end of the opportunity,
or is this the opportunity of a lifetime for investors? I side with the latter.

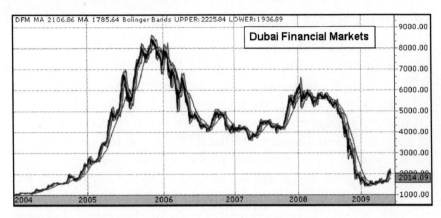

DFM MA 2106.86 MA 1785.64 Bolinger Bands UPPER:2225.84 LOWER:1936.89

Dubai Financial Markets

Figure 10.5   The Rise and Fall of the Dubai Stock Market
SOURCE: www.asmainfo.com.

I could go into greater detail about Qatar and Oman, but it would be a waste of time and effort because, from an investment point of view, all four countries are very similar. Also, I do not recommend investing in one single Middle Eastern country, but rather in a basket, similar to the frontier index or an ETF that is focused on the region. I highlight a few frontier market ETFs in the next section that investors could consider when investing in the potentially rewarding, yet risky regions of the world.

Frontier Market Investment Options

The investment options traded on major U.S. stock exchanges for the frontier markets are limited to a small number of companies and ETFs. I concentrate on four ETFs that provide exposure to the frontier markets for investors with a wide variety of risk tolerances. The first two ETFs invest in several regions of the world and concentrate specifically on frontier markets. The third ETF option invests only in Africa in both frontier and emerging markets. The last investment choice is an ETF that gives investors exposure to emerging and frontier markets mainly in Eastern Europe. All four have their pros and cons and more specifics can be found by reading on.

PowerShares MENA Frontier Countries ETF

The PowerShares MENA Frontier Countries ETF (NASDAQ: PMNA) is based on the NASDAQ OMX Middle East North Africa Index. The ETF is composed of stocks from eight countries, with the top two located in Africa and not in the frontier index discussed earlier: Morocco (21 percent) and Egypt (17 percent). Kuwait, Jordan, the UAE, and Qatar all make up at least 12 percent of the ETF and will have an impact on the movement of the investment vehicle. Investors looking for exposure to the Middle East as well as North Africa by the way of Egypt and Morocco should consider PMNA to be the best ETF choice.[14]

Even though the region depends heavily on the price and demand for petroleum products, over half of the allocation of 50 stocks in the ETF is financials. For a frontier market to take the step to emerging market status, one of the keys is the financing of expansion. The money often comes from outside sources, typically developed countries wanting a stake in the growth, but the local banks play an important and essential role. Exposure to financials located in a frontier market is therefore one avenue of playing the potential growth. With PMNA, an investor is taking significant risk because the ETF focuses on a niche sector within a small and unstable region of the world. The upside, though, over the next few years is substantial, and the only question is whether an investor can tolerate the risk and has patience. The chart of PMNA in Figure 10.6 is similar to

Figure 10.6   PowerShares MENA Frontier Countries ETF (PMNA) Forms a Bullish Saucer Bottom
SOURCE: TeleChart2007® or StockFinder® chart, courtesy of Worden Brothers, Inc.

many frontier and emerging markets in that it fell dramatically at the end of 2008 before forming a bullish saucer pattern in early 2009.

Claymore/Bank of NY Mellon Frontier Market ETF

The Claymore/Bank of NY Mellon Frontier Markets ETF (NYSE: FRN) began trading in June 2008 just as the global stock markets were about to take a nosedive. The ETF fell 60 percent over the next eight months as every stock market in the world was hit by the global recession. Many of the countries FRN invests in were 70 percent off their highs and are were sitting at or near their bottoms and, more importantly, a great long-term valuation. Figure 10.7 shows the fall and rebound of FRN, which hit a new multimonth high in June 2009. The one difference between FRN and the focus of this chapter so far is that FRN has heavy exposure outside of the Middle East. The country with the number one weighting is Chile (26 percent), followed by Poland (22 percent), Egypt (15 percent), and Columbia (9 percent).[15]

The sector breakdown is also a bit different because it does not have as high of a concentration in financial stocks. The sector is still the most heavily weighted, but makes up only about one-third of the ETF. Telecom and energy make up about 15 percent each, with utilities and materials both coming in at 12 percent. Investors in search of a frontier market ETF that also has some exposure to the lesser-followed emerging

Figure 10.7   Claymore/Bank of NY Frontier Market ETF Hitting a New Multimonth High
Source: TeleChart2007® or StockFinder® chart, courtesy of Worden Brothers, Inc.

markets at a reasonable cost (annual expense ratio of 0.65 percent) should look to FRN as the best current option.

Market Vectors Africa ETF

When the Van Eck family of ETFs launched the Market Vectors Africa ETF (NYSE: AFK) in July 2008, it was the first of its kind for investors. Similar to FRN, the launch date could not have been much worse for the Africa ETF. In the seven months following the launch, the ETF fell over 50 percent to a new low. After finding a low in February, AFK, as shown in Figure 10.8, rallied with the rest of the world, and by the middle of June 2009, the ETF was up over 25 percent. The ETF takes a fairly concentrated approach by investing in 50 stocks that are either based in Africa or generated the majority of their revenues in the continent, considered offshore holdings, according to Van Eck.

The ETF is made up of about 28 percent offshore companies with the remainder based in Africa. Three countries discussed already, Nigeria, Morocco, and Egypt, compose 44 percent of the allocation. The country with the largest exposure is South Africa, with 27 percent. South Africa is considered an emerging market and is probably on the verge of moving to developed status in the coming decade. The ETF is therefore not a true frontier market ETF, but it does give investors exposure to the North Africa region similar to PMNA. If I had

Figure 10.8 Van Eck Africa ETF Rebounding from the 2009 Low
SOURCE: TeleChart2007® or StockFinder® chart, courtesy of Worden Brothers, Inc.

to make a choice between AFK and PMNA, I would prefer the latter because of its additional exposure to the Middle East region.[16]

SPDR S&P Emerging Europe ETF

Another region that has a high concentration of frontier market countries is Eastern Europe. Gaining exposure to the region of small countries is difficult because there is not a specific ETF that concentrates on it without also including Russia. Of the possibilities, my favorite at this time is the SPDR S&P Emerging Europe ETF (NYSE: GUR). Even though Russia accounts for 65 percent of the ETF, there is good exposure to Turkey (13 percent) and Poland (11 percent). The Czech Republic and Hungary also combine for 11 percent of the allocation.[17]

This is a situation in which you must look at the top holdings because after further review, two Russian companies (Gazprom and Lukoil Oil Company) make up 32 percent of the ETF. With both companies operating in the energy sector, the concentration in energy stocks is half of the ETF. As the prices of oil and natural gas have fallen during the global recession, GUR lost two-thirds of its value in 2008 (see Figure 10.9). A turnaround in energy commodity prices is a must for this ETF to find traction—something I see occurring in the Next Great Bull Market. There is one large asterisk next to this ETF, however—political

Figure 10.9   SPDR S&P Emerging Europe ETF More than Doubles Off the February Low as the Russian Stock Market Rebounds
SOURCE: TeleChart2007® or StockFinder® chart, courtesy of Worden Brothers, Inc.

corruption and instability in Russia. In the end, GUR could be a big winner as energy commodity prices rise, but the risk is too high for most investors.

While on the topic of energy and oil, this makes for a great segue into the next chapter, which discusses the potential of peak oil and how this will affect both commodity and stock prices in the coming years. Keep reading to find out how to profit from a surge in oil prices as demand picks back up and supply tightens.

Chapter 11

Peak Oil: Making Money with Oil at $100

I rrational pricing often offers new investment opportunities. Forecasts for oil to hit $100 per barrel in 2007 were greeted with great skepticism as most on Wall Street laughed at the idea of triple-digit oil prices. Within one year, the price of oil not only broke through the century mark, but nearly pierced the $150 level. From the beginning of 2008 through mid-July 2008, the price of oil surged over 50 percent and it appeared the rally was never going to end. The forecasts for $200 and then $250 per barrel began to become the norm and everyone from the professional trader to the weekend warrior was trying to figure out a way to profit from the surge in oil.

With oil nearing the $150 mark, the hysteria was running wild as every media outlet from the *Wall Street Journal* to the local news was leading off with the price of oil each day. It was important, of course, because it meant the price of gasoline was also rising. But the oil craze became a hysteria and eventually led to the bubble bursting in July 2008. As a contrarian, I should have known that when the noninvestor asks me how to buy oil, the bubble was about to explode, and I mean *really* explode. I will admit that I am human and got caught up in the hysteria as well and was positioning my portfolio for a rise in oil to $200, if not higher.

The first pullback in oil occurred mid-July as the price fell approximately 20 percent. At the time, the sell-off felt like a normal, healthy pullback during a long-term uptrend, and most oil bulls used the weakness as a new buying opportunity. By mid-August, the price of oil was back to the 200-day moving average and forming a base. Figure 11.1 shows the movement of oil in 2008 and highlights the pullback in August, which, according to all the technicals, was a buying opportunity. As the chart shows, the price of oil fell a few weeks later through the 200-day moving average and was eventually back into double digits.

So the question everyone wants answered revolves around two things: where oil will be a few years from now, and if $150 oil was an anomaly or a true value of the commodity. I will tackle the latter first. In hindsight, when oil was trading at $150 in 2008, the price was irrational, just as all prices are before a bubble bursts. The price at the time does not appear to be irrational, as investors see dollar signs, and in this case, barrels of oil, when they throw more money at the rising price. The irrational exuberance, as Alan Greenspan once put it, was in full force with the rising price of oil in 2008. That same irrational behavior

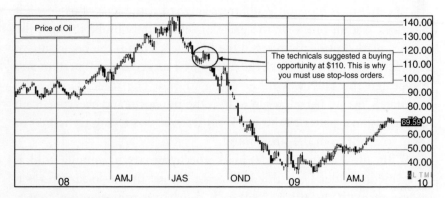

Figure 11.1   Oil in 2008
SOURCE: TeleChart2007® or StockFinder® chart, courtesy of Worden Brothers, Inc.

is also evident at market bottoms—a topic that is covered further on along with the answer to the first question of where oil will be trading in the future.

Defining Peak Oil

Before getting into price targets for oil, the topic of peak oil must be covered to lay the groundwork for my argument of higher oil in the future. According to Investopedia, peak oil is defined as a hypothetical date referring to the world's peak crude oil production, after which production rates begin to decrease. According to the International Energy Agency (IEA), global oil output could peak in 2020, a mere decade in the future. The IEA partly attributes this to understanding that investment in new oil exploration and infrastructure has been hurt by the global recession. The credit needed to fund the new rigs is not available and the end result will be stagnant supply, if not a fall in supply, in the coming years. In early 2009, the IEA's chief economist Fatih Birol said that conventional crude output could plateau in 2020 and called the development "not good news" for a world that is still heavily dependent on crude oil products.

Because the IEA is not known for their peak oil predictions, I find it intriguing that just one month before the 2020 prediction, the IEA had pegged peak oil at 2030. It is amazing how one month can change the number by an entire decade, even though the credit crisis has had a major effect on oil production and exploration. Honestly, no one really knows when peak oil will occur, but with a highly respected IEA looking for production to peak in the next decade, we ought to have something of a concern. In 2008, the IEA also updated its prediction on the rate of decline of oil in the world's existing oil fields. The 2007 forecast that was included in the 2007 World Energy Outlook called for a rate of decline of 3.7 percent; 12 months later, the same agency upped the number to 6.7 percent.

The IEA is not alone in the dire forecasts for peak oil in the near future. The vice president of Toyota Motor Sales USA made a statement in early 2009 alluding to peak oil in the near future. He said in reference to $4 gasoline in 2008, "It was a brief glimpse of our future.

We must address the inevitability of peak oil by developing vehicles powered by alternatives to liquid-oil fuel." Toyota is not the only major automaker moving toward mass production of electric vehicles. General Motors has plans to roll out the Volt, an all-electric car, in 2012. That is, if they are still in business then.

Factors Driving Oil Back to Triple Digits

Oil back above $100 will be a reality sooner rather than later, in my opinion. Heck, by the time you read this book, the cost of a barrel of crude could be in the triple digits. There are three major factors that I believe will lead the move higher, led by an increase in global demand after the recession. The underinvestment in exploration and production during the economic slowdown will lend a hand to the third factor, stagnant supply. Ultimately, increased demand coupled with flat to decreasing supply will result in higher oil prices.

Global Demand

Demand for oil and petroleum-related products fell sharply during the 2008–2009 global recession, and this was evident in the price of oil falling over $100 per barrel. The IEA announced in January 2009 that oil demand would fall by nearly 1 million barrels per day during 2009. However, they also predicted the demand would increase by 1 million barrels per day in 2010, taking the per day number back to where it was before 2009. The IEA's forecast is based on an expected economic recovery.

A global economic recovery is crucial to the price of oil moving back to the triple-digit level. The slowdown from the United States to China has taken a toll on demand, but once manufacturing begins to ramp up again, the emerging, high-growth countries such as China and India will begin demanding large amounts of oil. There is no alternative to oil at this point for emerging nations that are looking to expand their infrastructure and, by extension, their middle class. Do you really believe that a family in China that has lived in poverty for generations will hold out for a solar panel when they can afford to heat their home with fossil fuel now? Absolutely not. And this is what most American investors do not comprehend: There is life outside the United States, and most of the growth in this world is outside our borders.

Underinvestment

As mentioned before, the global recession caused by the credit crisis spread its web into the energy field in several ways. One was the lack of credit for exploration and drilling companies to expand the search for new oil reserves and tap the reserves they have already discovered. This lack of funding caused several projects around the world to be delayed or postponed indefinitely. Because it is not as easy as turning on a spigot to get the oil flowing, any delay in drilling could push back the actual oil extraction by a few years. If the global recession ends by 2010, as I believe it will, the demand for oil will once again increase and the supply will not be available. This leads to the next factor that will lead oil back to triple digits.

Stagnant Supply

My biggest argument for higher oil prices over the last five years has been stagnant supply. Even if demand does not increase at a rapid pace, if supply remains stagnant, the supply and demand curve predicts higher prices for oil. Simple economics states that as supply decreases, or demand increases, the price for the product will increase, and vice versa. This equation also explains why oil has fallen in 2008 through 2009; supply remained flat as demand dropped off significantly because of the global recession.

An example of a supply issue is the Cantarell oil field in Mexico, owned by the state-run oil company, Pemex. In January 2009, Mexican oil production fell by 9.2 percent to the lowest level since 1995, due in large part to the dwindling output of the aging Cantarell oil field. Cantarell has been Mexico's largest oil field for years, that is until January 2009 when it fell to number two behind the Ku Maloob Zaap oil complex, according to Pemex. The Canarell oil field pumped out 772,000 barrels of oil per day in January, down from 811,000 barrels per day in December 2008, and off an eye-catching 38 percent from one year earlier.

Mexico and the Cantarell oil field are not alone in the falling production dilemma. Aging oil fields around the world have hit their personal peak oil production numbers and are now on the way down each year. Granted, there are new oil fields coming online, but will they be able to keep up with the decline caused by the aging oil fields? If the amount of money being put into the exploration and drilling of new wells continues to be absent, there is no way the new fields will be able to fill the void of production left behind by the current, aging oil fields.

In January 2009, the IEA noted that supply from producing oil fields will decline dramatically, and to offset the fall by 2030, the world will need "45 million barrels per day of new capacity, or the equivalent of four Saudi Arabias." Regardless of whether the IEA is correct, the thought of needing more Saudi Arabias within the next 20 years is frightening and by itself is enough to convince me that oil at $40 per barrel is a bargain and may never see those levels again.

Profiting from Rising Oil Prices

There are several areas investors can focus on to make money within the oil sector and achieve conversification for their portfolio. *Conversification* is a term I use to describe a mix of the traditional *concentration* and *diversification* investment strategies, and explain it in more detail in Chapter 14. The major oil companies such as ExxonMobil and Chevron are typically staple holdings for many investors through either direct ownership or indirectly through mutual funds or ETFs. A niche area is the Canadian oil sands stocks that focus on turning the sand found in northwest Canada into oil through a rigorous process. As supply continues to fall and aging oil fields are in need of repair, the oil infrastructure arena will be major beneficiaries of money going back into the buildup and repair business. An area not explored very much in this book is natural gas, which is very abundant in the United States. Natural gas stocks suffered major sell-offs during the global recession and I believe there is opportunity for willing investors. The four investable areas are discussed next along with specific investment ideas.

Canadian Oil Sands

Oil from sand—what an amazing concept. Fortunately for all of us, it is one that has come to fruition in the tar sands of Northwest Canada. In the late 1960s, Suncor Energy pioneered the commercial development of the Athabasca oil sands located in Alberta, Canada. The area is considered to be one of the largest resource basins for petroleum products in the world, with Saudi Arabia the only region ahead of it.

There are a few issues facing the Canadian Oil Sands going forward. Oil has fallen more than $100 from its high, and the nontraditional process of producing oil from oil sands is not as viable as it is when oil is trading at more than $100 a barrel. There is a wide range of estimates as to the price at which oil sands production becomes practical. I believe it lies somewhere between $65 and $80 per barrel. During the first quarter of 2009, oil averaged about $45 a barrel and the related stocks consequently had a tough time getting out of the way of themselves. The sector began to improve as 2009 moved along, however, and some investors predicted that oil would move higher once again by the end of 2009 and beyond.

Suncor Energy

On March 23, 2009, Suncor (NYSE: SU) announced a $14 billion acquisition of Petro-Canada (NYSE: PCZ), which sent shares of both companies higher on the day it was released. The combination of the two major Canadian oil sands players was greeted with open arms by the investment community because the merger was considered synergistic. The newly formed, much larger company will be well positioned when the price of oil begins to climb back to the $100 per barrel level in the years to come. As mentioned before, getting oil out of the tar sands is not cheap. The combination of the two firms, however, creates a situation in which costs can be lowered and output increased—a perfect scenario.

As mentioned earlier, Suncor was the first company to successfully develop the Canadian oil sands into a viable oil-producing region. While the oil sands segment of the company is the reason Suncor has made the list, I must let you know they are also involved in natural gas production, refining, and have now moved into biodiesel and wind power. As you know already, wind power is an energy source for which I believe the opportunities are limitless. According to the company, Suncor currently has four wind farms in operation and other projects in the planning stages.[1] The company is well known for its Sunoco subsidiary that refines and distributes petroleum products through the Sunoco brand name.[2]

The addition of Petro-Canada brings on a 12 percent stake in Syncrude Canada, 100 percent ownership of MacKay River, and a 60 percent ownership of the proposed Fort Hills oil sands project.[3] Not only will the combined company be a major player in the oil sands, but it will also expand its operations in the refining and marketing and distribution activities. There is suddenly a new major player in the game going after the dominance of Imperial Oil (NYSE: IMO). In Figure 11.2, the long-term chart of Suncor shows its rise from the late 1990s low to its high in 2008 before the oil bubble burst. The stock is now over 100 percent off the 2008 low.

Imperial Oil

Imperial Oil (AMEX: IMO) is Canada's largest oil company and can be compared to ExxonMobil in the United States. As a side note, ExxonMobil owns about 70 percent of Imperial. The company is the largest refiner in the country and a leader in the production of crude

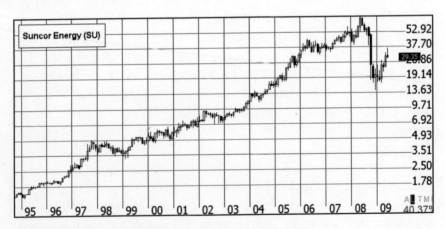

Figure 11.2   Suncor Energy Following the Price of Oil
SOURCE: TeleChart2007® or StockFinder® chart, courtesy of Worden Brothers, Inc.

oil and natural gas. Imperial accounts for approximately 6 percent of the total energy output in the country of Canada.[4] The company is also involved in the petrochemical industry and operates the Esso brand retail gasoline stations, according to the company's web site.[5]

The majority of the company's production takes place in the Northwest of Canada in the province of Alberta. Along with the traditional forms of energy production, Imperial is also a leader in the Canadian oil sands. It is a 25 percent owner of Syncrude Canada, a conglomerate of several companies that operates the largest oil sands project in the world. In addition to Syncrude Canada, Imperial owns the Cold Lake development, which has nearly 4,000 active wells and is developing (in conjunction with ExxonMobil Canada) a new oil sands site north of Syncrude Canada, called the Kearl oil sands project.[6]

Imperial Oil had a rough 2008, along with the majority of oil companies, as the price of crude fell from $150 down to $30. After hitting a low during the fourth quarter of 2008, however, the company began to find a bottom, and over the next six months started to move higher again (see Figure 11.3). As long as oil continues to move higher over the next few years, as I believe it will, the outlook for Imperial and its array of operations looks promising. What makes Imperial unique is its exposure to the oil sands, as well as being the largest refiner in Canada. The mix creates a diversified investment opportunity for investors looking to branch out from a pure 100 percent oil sands play.

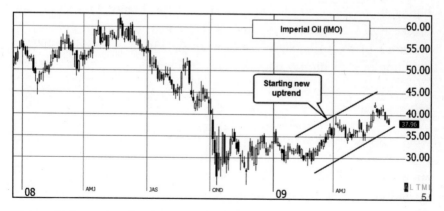

Figure 11.3 Imperial Oil Benefiting from Higher Oil Prices
SOURCE: TeleChart2007® or StockFinder® chart, courtesy of Worden Brothers, Inc.

Canadian Natural Resources Limited

Another one of Canada's largest energy companies, Canadian Natural Resources (NYSE: CNQ), is now a major player in oil sands and natural gas. The company's exposure to the oil sands is through its Horizon Oil Sands project, which is located in Alberta. In March 2009, the company announced that Horizon Oil Sands commenced its first shipment of synthetic crude to the pipeline. This was good news, that the company was now shipping oil from the area and could be poised to increase the production as the price of oil begins to rise.[7]

In March 2009, when the company reported its 2008 fourth quarter earnings, the net income from continuing operations surged 28 percent from one year earlier. For the year, adjusted net earnings grew 45 percent and revenues before royalties increased by 29 percent in the face of falling oil and natural gas prices. With my forecast of oil and natural gas both moving higher in the coming years, CNQ is well positioned to benefit from increased production at its Horizon Oil Sands project along with the large exposure to natural gas. In early April 2009, the price of natural gas was closing in on $3.50, a multiyear low, and the stock price of CNQ was trading at $40, well off the low of November 2008. A rally in natural gas back to a respectable $5-to-$6 range would be a huge boost to the bottom line for CNQ, which suggests that the stock will be valued back at 2008 prices.[8]

By June 2009, the price of natural gas continued to struggle with breaking above the $4 level, but the stock of CNQ has been moving higher in anticipation of a rally in natural gas. Figure 11.4 shows the breakout of CNQ above resistance at $50 and a subsequent pullback in the stock price. An entry in CNQ near the $50 level could result in a doubling of your money over the next two years.

The Majors

The "majors," as they are called in the energy sector, are the big names most investors are familiar with, such as ExxonMobil and Chevron, among others. Almost all the major energy companies have integrated operations that span from oil to natural gas to refining to alternative energy divisions. The upside to the major oil companies is the instant diversity within the energy sector. If the refining business is booming,

Figure 11.4   Canadian Natural Resources: A Very Attractive Buy at $50
SOURCE: TeleChart2007® or StockFinder® chart, courtesy of Worden Brothers, Inc.

but oil prices are down, the majors will not be affected as greatly as a more concentrated energy company. The other benefit to a major is the pricing power it has due to its lower cost of oil and gas production. This benefit is synonymous with most large companies in a variety of sectors.

The downside to a major is that they can oftentimes be overly diverse and, if I am correct about oil moving back to $100, the majors may not enjoy the big gains of the smaller companies. But it comes down to risk versus reward. Many of the majors have less risk and pay healthy dividends, but at the same time the reward will be limited compared with the small-cap plays.

ExxonMobil

The granddaddy of them all, ExxonMobil (NYSE: XOM), is the largest company in the United States, based on market capitalization, and the largest publicly traded oil and gas stock in the world. Exxon is a diverse company with operations in the following areas: exploration, development, production, refining, marketing, chemicals, and lubricants. We all know Exxon as the oil and gas producer and gas station owner, but they are also the world leader in synthetic motor oil and a powerhouse in the petrochemical sector.[9]

At the end of 2008, Exxon reported record profits of $45.2 billion and was sitting on $31 billion in cash. Keep in mind this is after one of the worst years in the world economy in decades and included a six-month span that saw the price of oil fall more $100. The fact that Exxon was able to continue increasing revenue at a solid pace in such a hostile environment is a sign that when the economy does turn around and the demand for oil once again picks up, Exxon will be there to capitalize. Even with the strong earnings in 2008, the stock lost 15 percent. But this was much better than the 38 percent loss of the S&P 500. Add in the dividend yield of more than 2 percent and this is why Exxon has been a core holding in many of our portfolios.[10]

The short-term action in Exxon is nothing that will get you to the edge of your seat, but the long-term chart is impressive (see Figure 11.5). After a couple of years of moving lower, Exxon is now sitting in the range of $60 to $70, which is an attractive buying opportunity for long-term investors interested in owning an oil blue chip stock.

Petrobras

According to the company's Vision 2020 document, Petrobras (NYSE: PBR) is striving to be one of the top five largest integrated energy companies in the world, and I believe they will attain that lofty goal. Most analysts may not consider Petrobras a major oil company in 2009, but because this book looks at how to make money in the future, I place Petrobras in the major category. Based in Brazil, Petrobras is involved in the exploration, production, refining, marketing, and transportation of

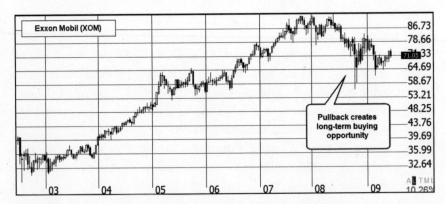

Figure 11.5 ExxonMobil 2-Year Pullback a Buying Opportunity
Source: TeleChart2007® or StockFinder® chart, courtesy of Worden Brothers, Inc.

petroleum products in Brazil and abroad. The company has more than 100 production platforms, 16 refineries, and 6,000 gas stations.[11]

Petrobras is one of my favorite stocks across all sectors not just because oil will once again see triple digits, but also because it is based in Brazil. The number one reason, though, is that its exploration division has found large reserves of both oil and gas in recent years, which puts it in line to be a major supplier in the years to come. Granted, it takes time to set up rigs and begin getting the oil and gas out of the ground, but having the reserve potential alone is similar to owning land with gold in it.

In November 2007, Petrobras announced the Tupi discovery, a deep underwater field that could contain up to 80 billion barrels of oil equivalent. The company was not able to extract its first crude oil until May 2009. The amount of crude coming out of the field will only be about 15,000 barrels per day to start, but is expected to ramp up to 100,000 per day by 2010. Petrobras also announced a major natural gas discovery in January 2009 in the Santos Basin, a shallow water area off the coast. The company believes the discovery is of great importance and will add to its gas reserves.[12]

The company is not stopping there. In early 2009, Petrobras announced it will invest nearly $175 billion into exploration and production. This is on top of $10 billion lent to Petrobras by a Chinese bank to finance deepwater oil exploration. The agreement is just the tip of the iceberg for Brazilian (Petrobras) and Chinese energy relations. China is smarter than many think; it realizes the need for energy will continue to increase around the world and is positioning itself in Brazil to be the major buyer of petroleum products from the South American country. The scenario works perfectly for Petrobras, which is in the driver's seat for supplying China with energy for decades into the future.[13] From a technical point of view, the Petrobras chart was a thing of beauty until the price of oil collapsed in 2008. Figure 11.6 shows the rise and fall of Petrobras and also the nearly 200 percent rally from the November 2008 low through the middle of 2009. At the time this chapter was written, I owned shares of Petrobras for myself and clients and it is one of my favorite commodity stocks for the Next Great Bull Market.

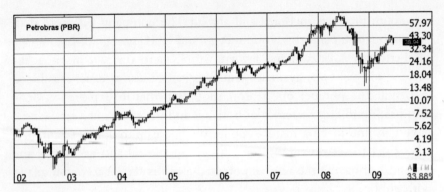

Figure 11.6 Petrobras Is a Favorite Commodity Play near $40
SOURCE: TeleChart2007® or StockFinder® chart, courtesy of Worden Brothers, Inc.

Natural Gas in the United States

Investors who have been sitting with money in natural gas have not been smiling since the 2008 recession began. After hitting a high of nearly $14 per million BTU in mid-2008, the price of natural gas fell to a low of $3.25 in May 2009. During that time, the Natural Gas Index, a basket of natural gas stocks, also took a major swoon, falling 60 percent from its 2008 high to its low in March 2009. The factors behind the dramatic fall in the price of natural gas are many, but the main reason was the difference between supply and demand. As storage inventories have swelled (up 29 percent over last year and 35 percent versus the five-year average), the demand has not been available to pick up the extra slack lying around. The waning demand has been driven by faltering industrial demand, lower power demand, and normal weather.

As the country moves away from its dependence on foreign oil, one of the big names in the industry, T. Boone Pickens, has been pushing for the use of natural gas as an alternative. Other big names in the industry are also behind the cleaner-burning and more domestic abundant energy source, but the idea has yet to take off and affect prices. Because the United States has large amounts of reserves of natural gas on our own soil, it makes the move to natural gas a viable option. The one problem is cost and persuading the power industry to do the same. The key will be getting the government behind the move and offering incentives for the conversion to natural gas as an alternative to crude. I do believe this will eventually take place here in the United States and possibly other countries. The chance to buy natural gas below $4 is tough to turn down because the possibility of $10 natural gas in the next five years is highly likely.

I decided on April 22, 2009, that it was time for a potential rally from the lows and time to begin investing in natural gas. The United States Natural Gas ETF (NYSE: UNG) was purchased for clients and myself as our play on a potential double in natural gas in the next one to two years. I believe very confidently in the investment because UNG could be back in the $30s, if not higher, by the end of 2011. From our entry price of $14.11, this would represent more than a 100 percent gain. Figure 11.7 shows the chart of the natural gas futures and how they fell from their high in 2008 to their low in May 2009. The time I began to buy UNG is circled, so you can see how we do in the coming months and years with this investment.

Range Resources

Range Resources (NYSE: RRC) is an independent oil and gas company that operates in the United States, mainly in the Southwest, Northeast, and Gulf Region. The company tends to target areas that have shale and coal bed methane. It has over 11,000 proven drilling projects and its leasehold is more than 3.4 million acres. With the

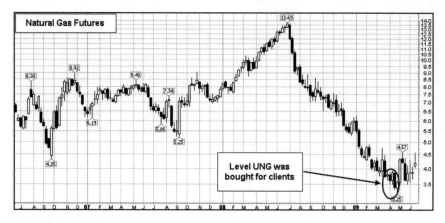

Figure 11.7 Natural Gas Futures Attempt to Find a Bottom in 2009
Source: www.stockcharts.com.

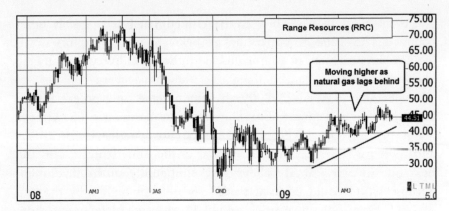

Figure 11.8   Range Resources Outperforming Natural Gas in 2009
SOURCE: TeleChart2007® or StockFinder® chart, courtesy of Worden Brothers, Inc.

majority of its sales coming from natural gas, it should not be a surprise that the stock has fallen well off its 2008 high, but the stock began to turn around in late 2008 as the price of natural gas kept falling. This divergence shown in Figure 11.8 is one of the reasons it is an attractive investment opportunity.

When Range Resources reported its 2008 earnings in February 2009, the numbers were once again at record levels. Revenue rose 53 percent in 2008 to $1.32 billion and GAAP net income increased by 50 percent from one year earlier. Even in the light of a global recession, Range Resources was able to expand its portfolio by adding another 400,000 acres of land, with the majority in the Marcellus Shale. I have a personal stake in the Marcellus Shale and know the potential sitting underneath the old farmland in Pennsylvania. The hunt for land in the area and drilling slowed dramatically as natural gas and oil prices plummeted, but I was confident it would pick back up by the end of 2009. A combination of higher natural gas prices and the opening of the credit markets to fund the expansion will be a key to Range Resources or any other natural gas play.

In the Saturday June 13, 2009, issue of *Barron's* magazine, Range Resources' CEO, John Pinkerton, was quoted as saying, "Our company will be ten times bigger than it is" if the Marcellus Shale proves to be as big as some are predicting. All in all, the company controls some 900,000 acres of land in the Marcellus Shale and, in essence, Range Resources is a bet on the extraction of natural gas from the area.[14]

Energy Commodity ETFs

As an alternative to investing in stocks in the oil industry, many investors would prefer to invest directly in the actual energy commodity.
Until recently, investing in energy commodities such as oil futures
required a futures trading account. As with nearly every investable area
in the world, ETFs have opened the door to investing in the energy
futures market. Even though the price of the underlying commodity
and related stocks will likely move over time in the same direction, the
short-term trends can often diverge.

In Figure 11.9, the chart shows the short-term divergence between
the price of oil and the CBOE Oil Index. As the price of oil continued
to hit highs in mid-2008, the CBOE Oil Index, which is a basket of
oil-related stocks, began its decline two months early. The addition of an
energy commodity ETF also adds to the goal of achieving diversification
within the portfolio.

United States 12-Month Oil ETF

The United States 12-Month Oil ETF (NYSE: USL) is designed to
track the movements of West Texas Intermediate light sweet crude oil.
The ETF differs from its peer, the United States Oil Fund (NYSE:
USO), in that it takes the average of the front month contract and
the next 11 months. USO and most oil ETFs invest in only the front

Figure 11.9   Price of Oil versus CBOE Oil Index
SOURCE: TeleChart2007® or StockFinder® chart, courtesy of Worden Brothers, Inc.

month contract and are forced to *roll out* the contract to the next month when the monthly contracts expire.

The oil futures will either trade in contango or backwardation. *Contango* is an upward sloping curve in which the contracts further away from the current month are trading at a higher price. When a contract expires and a typical oil ETF has to buy in to the new front month, it could result in paying a higher price on the basis of the contango situation. *Backwardation* is the exact opposite of contango and occurs when the future contract prices are less than the current price. Because USL does not have to take 100 percent of its assets and roll out every month, it allows for less price volatility in the ETF and is why we prefer USL to its peers. The ETF has lagged oil prices slightly, but has still been able to rally well off the lows hit in February 2009 (see Figure 11.10). An entry in the mid-$30s would be ideal for a long-term investor.

United States Gasoline ETF

The United States Gasoline ETF (NYSE: UGA) is managed by the same company as USL, but instead of oil, UGA tracks the movement of gasoline prices. The ETF tracks the price of the unleaded gasoline futures contracts on the New York Mercantile Exchange. Unlike USL, which uses contracts that span one year, UGA invests in the front month contracts and will be forced to roll out when the contracts expire each month.

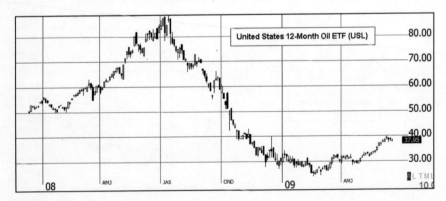

Figure 11.10 Looking for an Entry in the $30s for United States 12-Month Oil ETF (USL)
SOURCE: TeleChart2007® or StockFinder® chart, courtesy of Worden Brothers, Inc.

When gasoline was above $4 per gallon in 2008, it was not uncommon for me to receive several calls a week from investors asking how they could profit from gasoline prices spiking. The reason for the calls was twofold. For starters, the investors wanted to make money from rising gasoline prices. Second, they also wanted to hedge the higher expenses they were incurring every time they filled up their gas tank. The best answer I had was UGA; unfortunately for callers, that was about the time gasoline topped out and from a high of $67 in July 2008, UGA fell all the way down to $16 by the end of the year (see Figure 11.11). Since hitting a low in December 2008, the price of unleaded gasoline has been slowly climbing higher. We must all realize that $4 gasoline will once again be a reality and the most direct way to play this is through UGA, which has already doubled off the December 2008 low.

PowerShares DB Energy ETF

Most readers might be turned off or a little too risk averse to take on a position such as USL or UGA, with which you are betting on one specific commodity to move higher. To help lower the concentration risk, I recommend you consider the PowerShares DB Energy ETF (NYSE: DBE), which invests in a basket of five energy commodities. The base allocation for the ETF is light sweet crude (22.5 percent), brent crude (22.5 percent), heating oil (22.5 percent), RBOB gasoline (22.5 percent), and natural gas

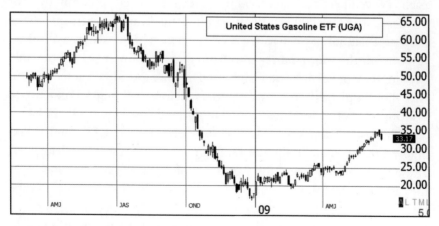

Figure 11.11 United States Gasoline ETF—A Play on Rising Prices at the Pump
SOURCE: TeleChart2007® or StockFinder® chart, courtesy of Worden Brothers, Inc.

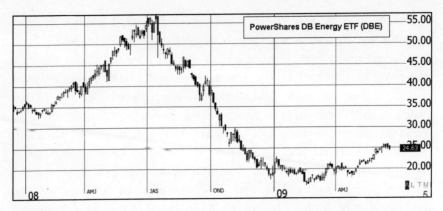

Figure 11.12   PowerShares DB Energy ETF Hitting 2009 High and
Building a Base
Source: TeleChart2007® or StockFinder® chart, courtesy of Worden Brothers, Inc.

(10 percent). The ETF is clearly heavily weighted to the price of oil, but at
the same time, an investor gains exposure to heating oil, gasoline, and natural gas, all with one purchase.

One must share my opinion that oil will move higher to consider
DBE, and that for the most part, all five energy commodities will move
in tandem over time. That being said, there will be times when one
or two will lag and the benefit of this ETF is that you will lower that
commodity-specific risk with the purchase of DBE. Keep in mind
that the weightings mentioned earlier are the base allocation and that
each November the commodities are rebalanced accordingly. For
example, in April 2009, RBOB gasoline made up 26 percent of the
ETF and natural gas had fallen to 7 percent. The rebalance will likely
involve putting more money into natural gas at a lower price, hopefully
becoming beneficial.[15] The chart of DBE is almost identical to USL, in
that they both hit bottom in February before building a constructive
bottom and a new intermediate-term uptrend (see Figure 11.12).

The last section was dedicated to energy-related ETFs, and if you
enjoyed that, you are in for a real treat in the next chapter. In Chapter 12,
I discuss in greater detail the explosion of exchange-traded funds over
the last few years and how they are changing the investment landscape
forever. Whether you are already a user of ETFs or getting your first
taste of them in this book, the next chapter will prove to be useful in
expanding your knowledge of the subject.

Chapter 12

The ETF Explosion

When the introduction of exchange-traded funds (ETFs) hit the market in the 1990s, many believed it was simply a fad that would go the way of so many other Wall Street products. Twenty years after the SPDR S&P 500 ETF (AMEX: SPY) began trading, it is one of the most popular trading and investing vehicles on the street. At the end of 2008, there were approximately 845 ETFs or ETNs traded on U.S. exchanges. If you think the number is high, there another 500 currently in registration with the SEC and the total by the end of 2009 could soar to close to 1,500.[1]

Before I go any further, it is necessary to give a simple, yet correct description of what an ETF really is. An exchange-traded fund is a hybrid between a stock and a mutual fund that offers some of the best characteristics of both investment vehicles. The ETF is similar to a mutual fund because it is composed of a basket of stocks that track an underlying index. Over the last few years, the introduction of commodity and currency ETFs have changed the landscape of the industry, and instead of just stocks that make up the ETFs, there are now alternative investments in the allocation of ETFs. The specifics of ETFs and their advantages over stocks and mutual funds are highlighted further on.

If you are wondering what an ETN is, I am sure you are not alone. An exchange-traded note, otherwise known as an ETN, is a debt security of the issuing company that is designed to track an underlying index. For example, the iPath Dow Jones-AIG Commodity Index ETN (NYSE: DJP) is an unsecured debt offering from Barclays, which runs the iPath ETNs. Through the ETN, Barclays will provide the investor with the exact performance of the underlying index minus fees, which are typically 50 basis points (0.5 percent).

The benefit over an ETF is that an ETN eliminates the tracking error that occurs when an ETF attempts to replicate the identical movement of an index on a daily basis. The administrator of the ETF does its best to track the underlying index, but there are inevitably tracking errors, because the stock holdings that make up the ETF will never be the exact percentage as the index. The major risk of an ETN is that it is an unsecured debt instrument of the issuer, very similar to a bond. If the issuer of the ETN happens to file for bankruptcy, there is a chance the ETN will lose a large portion of its value because an investor is not only buying into the underlying index, but also the creditworthiness of the issuing firm. Most would think that Barclays, a company that has been around for centuries, will never default. But we all understand that cannot be guaranteed during this economic recession—nobody is 100 percent safe.

Why ETFs?

When an investor asks me why he should invest in ETFs instead of mutual funds or individual stocks, I make sure he has some time for me to list all of the reasons. The following are the major factors that have driven me to become enamored with ETFs and the possibilities of using them to make money for clients. The benefits of using ETFs include, but are not limited to, instant diversification, tax efficiency, intraday prices, low expense ratios, low fees, passive investment style, transparency, the ability to use leverage and sell short, and convenience.

Instant Diversification

The purchase of a single ETF gives investors exposure to a basket of stocks, greatly lowering the risk of buying an individual stock. An investor could purchase shares of ExxonMobil (NYSE: XOM) or, for the same price, buy the Energy SPDR ETF (NYSE: XLE) and gain exposure to Exxon as well as 39 other energy stocks. The purchase of the ETF lowers the company-specific risk of owning a single stock and at the same time allows investors exposure to the energy investment theme.

Diversification can be created for an entire portfolio as well. The purchase of 5 to 10 broad-based index ETFs could give an investor exposure to literally thousands of stocks in every sector around the world. The expansion of international and alternative investment ETFs has opened the doors to portfolio diversification with an ETF-only portfolio.

Tax Efficiency

Because of low turnover (buying and selling of stocks within the ETF), most ETFs do not have large capital gains that are paid out to investors at the end of the year, known as phantom income. Mutual funds, on the other hand, are synonymous with paying out year-end capital gains even if a mutual fund was down on the year. This creates a tax burden for the holder of the mutual fund during a year in which the investment has created an unrealized loss.

Many investors were shocked in 2008 to receive large capital gains payouts on their losing mutual funds. The reason this occurred is that the mutual fund industry continues to struggle and the redemption from investors soared in 2008. To generate cash for the redemptions, the mutual funds are forced to sell positions, some with large gains, and therefore, the gains must be passed along to the investors in accordance with U.S. tax regulations. An example is the Dodge and Cox International Stock Fund (DODFX), which lost 47 percent of its value in 2008 and paid out $2.52 per share ($1.52 in capital gains and $1.00 in ordinary income) on December 22, 2008. The payout was significant, considering that the mutual fund had a NAV of $21 (about a 12 percent payout) the investor is responsible to pay taxes on when the fund lost nearly half of its value.

There were a number of ETFs that had similar years to the Dodge and Cox fund, losing nearly 50 percent, but as far as tax efficiency, the majority did not pay any capital gains to investors.[2] An example is the iShares MSCI EAFE Index ETF (NYSE: EFA), a very similar investment, which also paid no capital gains for the calendar year 2008. ETFs are able to eliminate capital gains by using in-kind redemptions when they decide to sell a position within the allocation. This type of transaction helps to reset the cost basis higher by delving out the tax lots with the lowest cost basis.

Intraday Pricing

The biggest change from 2007 to 2008 was the increase in volatility of all markets from stocks to commodities. A triple-digit move on the Dow was at one time considered to be a volatile day, but even with the Dow cut in half, it is no longer eye-popping and has become the norm. The increase in volatility requires both traders and investors the ability to buy and sell during normal market hours. The problem with mutual funds is that that is not possible. Because mutual funds price only once per day, an investor can sell only at the end of day at the closing price, which is referred to as the net asset value (NAV). The benefit of ETFs is that they trade in the same manner as a stock on a major exchange. There is always a bid and ask price for investors to buy and sell throughout the market session.

Assume an investor comes home from work and realizes the government made an announcement that will affect the stock market the following day and wants to sell when the opening bell rings. If the investor owns an ETF, she can either sell at the opening bell or possibly in extended hours trading. The same investor will not be able to sell any mutual fund investments until the following day and will get the closing NAV of the fund. So, if the market opens down 1 percent and closes the day lower by 5 percent, the inability to sell intraday cost the investors 4 percent in one day.

Low Expense Ratios

The average annual expense ratio of an ETF is lower than that of similar mutual funds. For example, the Vanguard Emerging Markets ETF (NYSE:VWO) has an annual expense ratio of 0.3 percent. The category average for an emerging market's mutual fund is 1.83 percent. Giving up 150 basis points each year will take a large toll on annualized returns. In 2008, VWO was down 54 percent, right in line with the category average for the emerging market mutual funds, and therefore, the 150 basis points will result in a larger loss for the average emerging market's mutual fund.

The reasoning behind the larger annual expense ratios of mutual funds is that they are active versus passive and must pay their managers who attempt to beat the benchmark. More on passive versus active is just ahead.

Low Fees

The cost of buying and selling an ETF is the same as it would be for an individual stock. Most online brokerage firms charge about $10 both ways, resulting in $20 for the entire trade. On a $10,000 investment the total in trading commissions is 0.2 percent. A very small price to pay, considering a number of mutual funds not only charges a commission to buy and sell, but also loads.

I did not want to pick on one family of mutual funds in particular, but had to give you a real-life example. The American family of mutual funds are known for the ridiculous front-end loads they charge on their A-class shares of funds. The Growth Fund of America Class A (AGTHX) charges a 5.75 percent front-end sales charge along with its 0.65 percent gross annual expense ratio.[3] On a $100,000 investment, $5,750 is taken off the top for the fee, so the starting investment is now $94,250. In other words, your investment has fallen 5.75 percent before it even began. To get back to breakeven, the mutual fund must gain 6.1 percent.

So why would anyone in his right frame of mind pay a front-end or back-end sales load? Lack of education, ignorance, or maybe a very unethical salesperson. Regardless of why you may have purchased a load mutual fund in the past—*never* do it again. AGHTX has lagged the S&P 500 by 0.5 percent annually over the last three years. So again, why pay the upfront sales load—not only has the investor who purchased three years ago lagged the S&P 500, but the mutual fund is well below the market average because of its lower starting point. The introduction of no-load mutual funds, and now ETFs, could lead to the death of the load mutual funds—I hope!

Passive Investment Vehicles

Until 2008, all ETFs were passive investment vehicles that track a set index, and the composition of the ETF altered only a few times a year. Most mutual funds are actively managed, and the fund managers are therefore buying and selling on a daily basis in an attempt to beat the fund's benchmark. If the odds were with the actively managed mutual funds to beat the benchmark, it would be great. However, the truth is that approximately 80 percent of all actively managed mutual fund managers are unable to meet the performance of their benchmark.

In 2008, the introduction of actively managed ETFs was greeted with little fanfare and they have yet to take off like many thought they would. I personally have always been in favor of keeping the active management on the mutual fund side and let the ETFs concentrate on passive, index tracking. Most indexes that ETFs track are rebalanced either biannually or quarterly, and the turnover consequently remains low. By taking a passive approach, an investor knows what index she is tracking instead of betting on a mutual manager or team of managers behind closed doors. This takes us to my next benefit of ETFs: transparency.

Transparency

Because of the passive investment approach of ETFs, the holdings on any given day can be viewed by potential investors. Simply go to the ETF company web site and look at the holdings of the ETF that is being considered and you will know exactly what stocks you are gaining exposure to before buying. The same cannot be said for mutual funds because the holdings are updated only monthly and is a snapshot only at the close of that particular day. *Window dressing* is an investment term that refers to mutual fund managers who buy the best-performing stocks of the month on the last day of the month. When potential buyers look at the top holdings of a mutual fund they will see the best performers as top holdings and may be swayed toward buying the mutual fund. At the same time, the mutual funds will sell the losers so they do not have the worst performers in their list of top holdings at month-end.

Another way to view the transparency of mutual funds is by comparing it to an investment adviser. When I sit down with a new client, they find out about my investment style and realize that I will be managing his portfolio on a daily basis and he has access the buys and sells that occur. When you invest in a mutual fund, your hard-earned money is being trusted to a manager you never met and who could leave the fund at any time or pass off the investment decisions to a team of inexperienced traders. I understand the lure of mutual funds, but with the growth of ETFs, I no longer see a need for any mutual funds.

Leverage and Short Selling

Similar to stocks, most ETFs can be bought on margin, allowing investors to leverage their cash in a position. The majority of ETFs can also be shorted if an investor believes the ETF is due to fall and wants to profit on its demise. But when the subject becomes leverage and short selling, the introduction and continued parabolic growth of leveraged and short ETFs is the real story. The ProShares family of ETFs introduced their leveraged long and short ETFs that provide traders with more trading vehicles and investors with more ammunition to blow themselves up.

A leveraged ETF provides investors with instant margin. For example, the ProShares Ultra S&P 500 (NYSE: SSO) provides investors with two-to-one exposure to the daily movements of the S&P 500. If the S&P 500 were to gain 2 percent on the day, SSO will gain 4 percent, and vice versa. As great as this may sound to investors, it can be very dangerous, and if not used in the correct manner, can destroy a portfolio. An investor who bought SSO at $60 on September 19, 2008 after a two-day rally that some thought was the bottom, would have lost over 50 percent in less than one month. The average investor needs to be very careful when delving into the world of leveraged ETFs.

Short ETFs come in different sizes. There are short ETFs that track the exact opposite of the underlying index, such as the ProShares Short S&P 500 ETF (NYSE: SH). The ETF offers a one-to-one inverse relationship to the S&P 500. If the index is up 2 percent on the day, SH will be down 2 percent, and vice versa. The short ETFs also come with leverage and can be very dangerous if you decide to buy in a bull market. There is more on leveraged ETFs later in the chapter.

Convenience

All of the benefits of ETFs mentioned earlier can lend themselves to the convenience of the investment vehicle. Being able to buy and sell throughout the day makes it convenient to investors. Instant diversification, along with transparency, add to the convenience; you can throw in time savings, too. The tax efficiency can also be considered convenient to investors who do not want to worry about phantom income. Overall, the products are made for your convenience.

Exposure to Alternative and Niche Sectors

The growth of the number of ETFs has led to the introduction of new products that track very concentrated indexes. Everything from an ETF that invests only in Malaysia to an ETF focused on water-related stocks, the world of ETFs has most bases covered. The niche ETFs, as I like to call them, are one of the biggest benefits for me and my clients. The ability to buy in to a narrow portion of the market without taking the risk of an individual stock has changed the investment landscape for my business and for many other investors and advisers.

The water ETF is a great example, because as you know from Chapter 4, I strongly believe in the water industry as an investment choice. But within the water industry, I would like to gain exposure to the utilities, infrastructure, and landowners. To achieve this in the past, I would be required to buy at least three individual stocks. Now, there is a water ETF that encompasses all three areas with a basket of stocks that also lowers my investment risk.

Building an ETF Hedge Fund

The ability to invest in a hedge fund is reserved for high net worth investors who have the right connections to the best fund managers in the world. I will assume the average investor is not in the process of shopping around for hedge funds and I will therefore help you build your own hedge fund using just ETFs. There are many types of hedge funds that range from long and short funds to strategies that take advantage of statistical arbitrages. The ETF hedge fund I propose in this book is based on exposure to sectors and asset classes I believe will out-perform in the coming years.

The goal is to build an asset allocation using only ETFs that will allow the portfolio to beat the market with what will be less risk because of the conversification of the ETFs. By using only ETFs, the fees will remain low and there will be no need for a high-priced fund manager. You will also have control over your portfolio and will know on a daily basis how your personal ETF hedge fund is performing.

Domestic Equities

Investing in the United States is imperative because regardless of what the news media may portray, we are still the world's leader, for now. More innovation and production will come from the United States in the decades ahead and the hedge fund must have exposure to the country. I have chosen a large-cap growth ETF for two reasons. First, the large-cap asset class has lagged the smaller stocks for years and I believe the tides are about to turn in favor of the big guys. The second reason is because during a bull market you want to be invested in growth stocks that carry a high valuation that is reflected in a soaring stock price. Value investing could be profitable in the early stages of a bull market, but over time, the growth stocks will win.

iShares Morningstar Large Growth Index ETF

The iShares Morningstar Large Growth Index ETF (NYSE: JKE) is composed of 83 of the largest and best-known companies in the United States. The top holdings include Microsoft (NASDAQ: MSFT), Coca-Cola (NYSE: KO), Cisco Systems (NASDAQ: CSCO), and Apple, Inc. (NASDAQ: AAPL). Health care is the most heavily weighted sector (22 percent), followed by computer hardware (16 percent), and computer software (13 percent). The heavy exposure to tech-nology is not a surprise, considering they are considered growth plays within the large-cap arena. With a low expense ratio of 0.25 percent, the cost remains low to add JKE to the hedge fund.[4] All information regarding the ETF was taken from the iShares web site.

Figure 12.1   iShares Morningstar Large Growth Index ETF Has Begun
to Outperform the S&P 500 in 2009
SOURCE: TeleChart2007® or StockFinder® chart, courtesy of Worden Brothers, Inc.

On the chart, JKE has moved almost in lockstep with the S&P
500 and will not deviate too much from the large-cap U.S. index.
The ETF lagged the S&P 500, in 2008, falling 42 percent versus
a drop of 38 percent in the index (see Figure 12.1). Through the
first five months of 2009, JKE was up 13 percent, easily outpacing
the gain of 2 percent for the S&P 500. Going forward, I expect the
ETF to continue its outperformance, as growth stocks outperform
value stocks.

International Equities

The benefits of investing in the emerging and frontier markets was
highlighted in Chapter 10. One country in particular that I believe
has the ability to outperform both the United States and its peers
over the next decade is China. As early as the first two months of
2009, the Chinese stocks have begun to show a unique relative
strength. The Shanghai Composite Index gained 14 percent through
the first two months of 2009 versus a 19 percent loss for the S&P
500. Granted, the Shanghai Index was down 65 percent in 2008, but
the valuation has become reasonable and investors around the world
are recognizing the opportunities in China. For a more detailed look
into China, please refer to Chapter 13.

iShares FTSE/Xinhua China 25 Index ETF

Investors have a number of choices when it comes to investing in Asia and, specifically, China. I have decided to recommend the iShares FTSE/Xinhua China 25 Index ETF (NYSE: FXI). FXI is an ETF I have ownership in for clients of Penn Financial Group, and I compare it to owning the Dow Jones Industrial Average in the United States. The ETF as advertised is made up of 25 Chinese ETFs that are traded on the Hong Kong exchange—considered H Shares. Nearly half of the allocation is invested in Chinese financials, which have dealt with difficulties similar to those in the United States, but on a much different scale. The country continues to grow its GDP at a modest pace, and the banks are benefiting from continued borrowing to support the growth. The top five holdings include three stocks that are traded on the NYSE: China Mobil (NYSE: CHL), China Life Insurance Company (NYSE: LFC), and CNOOC (NYSE: CEO). All three suffered major losses from the high in 2007 to the low of 2008 and the ETF followed their lead. Even though the three stocks and the ETF is well off the 2008 low, it is not too late to use pullbacks to gain exposure to the long-term potential of China. The likelihood of FXI falling back below $30 is not good, so look for an entry in the low to mid-$30s (see Figure 12.2). The China investment play is not over and the hedge fund needs its exposure through a concentrated, yet diverse ETF. FXI is a great example of conversification.

Figure 12.2   iShares FTSE/Xinhua China 25 Index ETF Buying Opportunity of Lifetime Is Gone, but in the $30s Is Attractive
Source: TeleChart2007® or StockFinder® chart, courtesy of Worden Brothers, Inc.

Vanguard Emerging Markets ETF

Even though China is the favorite emerging market country for invest-ing, the hedge fund needs to gain exposure to other countries in the asset class. The cheapest and most efficient way to accomplish this is through the Vanguard Emerging Markets ETF (NYSE: VWO). The ETF is extremely diverse, with over 700 stocks from over 20 emerg-ing market countries. Brazil makes up the largest portion of the ETF with 15 percent, followed by Korea at 14 percent, and China at 11 per-cent. Along with the emerging markets, the ETF also has exposure to frontier markets like Egypt. With a minimal expense ratio of 0.25 per-cent, the ETF is the best low-cost ETF to gain exposure to the broad emerging markets arena.

Technically, the ETF formed a textbook double-bottom pattern in November 2008 and March 2009, offering a bullish buy signal. If you were too late for the buying opportunity when it was in the low $20s, do not fret; buying under $30 is still an acceptable investment (see Figure 12.3).

Commodities

When investing in commodities, an investor must make the distinc-tion between investing in the actual commodity futures contract or

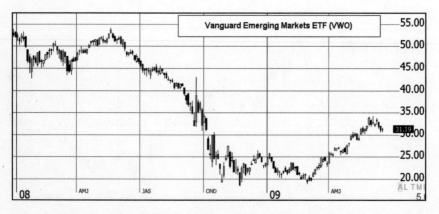

Figure 12.3   Vanguard Emerging Markets ETF Remains Attractive below $30
SOURCE: TeleChart2007® or StockFinder® chart, courtesy of Worden Brothers, Inc.

a company that is involved in producing the commodity. For example, an investor could buy a gold futures contract or a gold mining company.

PowerShares DB Commodity Index Tracking ETF

In the hedge fund, I would like to diversify into the futures markets through an ETF—the PowerShares DB Commodity Index Tracking ETF (NYSE: DBC). The ETF provides exposure to six commodities in the metals, agriculture, and energy sectors. The following is a list of the six commodities and their base weighting, according to the PowerShares web site.

Commodity	Base Weighting
Light Crude	35%
Heating Oil	20%
Aluminum	12.5%
Corn	11.25%
Wheat	11.25%
Gold	10.5%

The ETF offers diversity across three distinct areas within the world of commodities, even though it is heavily weighted toward the energy commodities. With the price oil well off the highs and the next bull market around the corner, it creates an opportunity for oil to rise back to the triple-digit level; the exposure through DBC will allow the hedge fund to profit from such a move. The 22.5 percent exposure to the agriculture commodities is another reason I chose DBC—this is another area that has been hit hard during the recession, but with a growing global middle class and inclement weather around the world, prices are expected to rebound sharply. In the end, DBC is an ETF that offers conversification to investors who want exposure to the commodity futures asset class.[5]

DBC has not rallied from the lows with the same magnitude as its peers, but the basing formation that includes new multimonth highs is a bullish signal (see Figure 12.4). Buying DBC in the low $20s is a long-term investment that I believe will pay huge profits during the Next Great Bull Market.

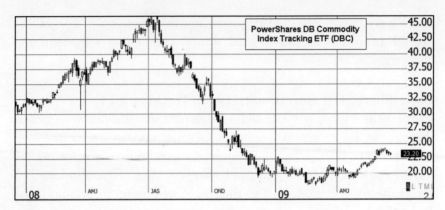

Figure 12.4   PowerShares DB Commodity Index Tracking ETF Has Been
Lagging the Market, but Is Ripe for a Purchase
SOURCE: TeleChart2007® or StockFinder® chart, courtesy of Worden Brothers, Inc.

PowerShares DB Precious Metals ETF

The one area within the commodities sector that is lacking in DBC is
the precious metals. Gold makes up a mere 10 percent, and silver has
no representation. Exposure to gold or silver is imperative for the hedge
fund because they can benefit from three of my major investment
themes: higher inflation, a falling U.S. dollar, safe investment. Instead of
simply buying the SPDR Gold ETF (NYSE: GLD), the PowerShares DB
Precious Metals ETF (NYSE: DBP) gives the hedge fund some wanted
exposure to silver futures. Even though gold accounts for 80 percent
of the ETF, the 20 percent exposure to silver increases diversification
within the precious metals—again back to our conversification investment strategy. For more on gold and commodities, refer to Chapter 7.[6]

The volatility in the price of gold and silver has increased in 2008,
and the spikes and sell-offs are more common for the metals. This can
be frustrating for the long-term investor, but what it does is create
opportunities to buy on pullbacks for new investors. Figure 12.5 shows
the two rallies to new highs in 2009 for DBP, and both were followed
by pullbacks. Do not chase the rallies; wait for weakness to enter DBP.

Currencies

The U.S. Dollar Index was in a downtrend for six years before ending its
bear market in 2008. After a year of rallying, I believe the longer-term

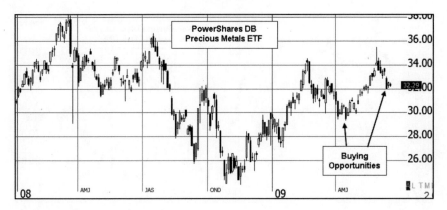

Figure 12.5   PowerShares DB Precious Metals ETF Is Pulling Back from
a 2009 High
SOURCE: TeleChart2007® or StockFinder® chart, courtesy of Worden Brothers, Inc.

trend of moving lower will continue for the index. As of June 2009, the
index was once again on the verge of breaking down to a new yearly low.

PowerShares DB U.S. Dollar Bearish ETF

The most direct investment to benefit from the fall in the U.S. dollar is
the PowerShares DB U.S. Dollar Bearish ETF (NYSE: UDN). The ETF
will give investors inverse exposure to the index that tracks the performance of the greenback versus the euro (57 percent), the Japanese yen (14
percent), the British pound (12 percent), the Canadian dollar (9 percent),
the Swedish krona (4 percent), and the Swiss franc (4 percent).

The biggest factor in the rally of the index has been the fall of the
euro from $1.60 to $1.25 against the U.S. dollar. The euro could continue to struggle for the same reason as the U.S. dollar, but at the end of
the day I believe the U.S. government will drive down the greenback
regardless of what the official policy is. The ability to buy into UDN in
the low-to-mid $20s is a privilege for investors who have a year or two
of patience to let the ETF move (see Figure 12.6). That being said, it
may take off quickly, and a profit should be booked.

Select Sectors

So far, most of the ETFs in the hedge fund have covered large asset
classes that encompass several sectors. There should also be a focus on

Figure 12.6   PowerShares DB U.S. Dollar Bearish ETF
Source: TeleChart2007® or StockFinder® chart, courtesy of Worden Brothers, Inc.

select sector ETFs that will give the hedge fund exposure to a more concentrated investment. Examples are ETFs that focus on nuclear energy, consumer staples, software, and many others. This is an area of the hedge fund that will change frequently, depending on which sector is offering attractive valuations at the time. A sector ETF that has several factors in its favor is MOO, and it is discussed in more detail next.

Market Vectors Agribusiness ETF

The most difficult ETF to choose was in the select sectors portion of the hedge fund. After narrowing the list down to approximately 10 very different ETFs, the Market Vectors Agribusiness ETF (NYSE: MOO) was the winner. MOO was the final choice because of its ability to move with the bull market and at the same time create diversity by investing in commodity-related stocks. As the bull market pushes stocks higher, the agribusiness companies in the ETF should benefit from increased demand for their products and higher commodity prices on the basis of global supply and demand.

MOO is made up of 41 agricultural stocks, and charges an expense ratio of 0.65 percent. Please refer to Chapter 7 for more details on MOO. Figure 12.7 shows the chart for MOO and its rally off the late 2008 lows. The combination of a weakening U.S. dollar, fears of inflation, and a turnaround in global demand for agriculture has led to its strong start in 2009.

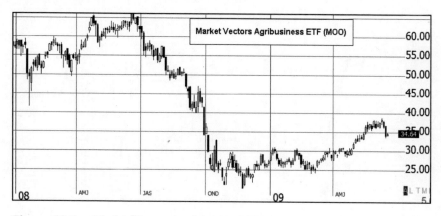

Figure 12.7   Market Vectors Agribusiness ETF
SOURCE: TeleChart2007® or StockFinder® chart, courtesy of Worden Brothers, Inc.

Fixed Income

Bubbles bursting have become a regular occurrence in the investing world, beginning with stocks and moving on to commodities in the last two years. I believe the latest bubble to burst was that of the U.S. government bonds. When the interest rate on a 10-year U.S. Treasury Note fell to 2.03 percent in December 2008 from 4.32 percent six months earlier, it was time for the bubble for Treasuries to burst. The yield and the price of a bond have an inverse relationship; therefore, at the same time yields were hitting multidecade lows, the bonds themselves were hitting new highs. The days of a 2 percent yield on the 10-year Treasury are over.

ProShares UltraShort 20+ Year Treasury ETF

The 30-year long Treasuries followed the 10-year to new multidecade lows on yields in December 2008 (see Figure 12.8). At the same time, the newly introduced ProShares UltraShort 20-Plus Year Treasury ETF (NYSE: TBT) was hitting a fresh low. TBT began trading in May 2008 when the 30-year Treasury was yielding 4.6 percent; in December, the yield fell to a low of 2.5 percent. The ETF bottomed out at $35 per share and has since established the December low as a bottom. The yields have continued to rise in 2009, and the price of the bonds are falling steadily. This has resulted in TBT hitting a multimonth high in

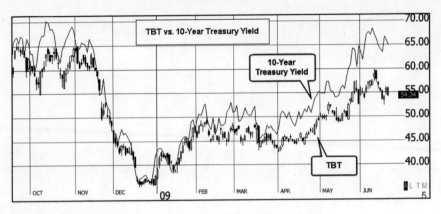

Figure 12.8   ProShares UltraShort 20+ Year Treasury ETF
SOURCE: TeleChart2007® or StockFinder® chart, courtesy of Worden Brothers, Inc.

June 2009. Use the volatility in TBT as a buying opportunity if you are considering buying the leveraged ETF.

TBT will give the hedge fund exposure to the continued bursting of the Treasury bubble that I believe will last for a few more years. TBT is an aggressive play because it is leveraged two-to-one to the inverse action of the long-term Treasury bonds. As the price of bonds fall, and yields rise—so does TBT. The reason TBT is in the hedge fund is because as Obama prints money 25 hours a day, the government will have to pay for the cash infusion. How do they pay? By selling bonds to foreigners, especially China. This sounds like a plan, but to entice China and other foreign countries to continue sending money to the United States, the interest rates must increase on the government bonds. As the rates increase, the prices of bonds fall and TBT rises.

SPDR Lehman High Yield Bond ETF

The SPDR Lehman High Yield Bond ETF (NYSE: JNK) invests 100 percent of its assets in below-investment-grade corporate bonds, also referred to as junk bonds. I realize it may sound odd to buy an investment that is known as junk on Wall Street; but someone's junk could be another person's treasure. This is the view I am taking on the junk bonds heading into the next few years because I believe there is a treasure waiting to be found in the sector.

Because of my belief that the Next Great Bull Market is now upon us and that 2009 and 2010 offer investment opportunities of a lifetime, junk bonds fall into the opportunity category. The junk bond market took a major hit throughout 2008 as several big name companies disappeared and left stock and bondholders out of the money. The fear of more companies with junk status filing for bankruptcy on the horizon sent junk bonds to levels not seen in years and yields skyrocketed. I cannot blame the fear that was instilled into investors of junk bonds, but the likelihood of even a large number of companies in junk status going bankrupt is very small.

However, when there is opportunity, it is created by irrational thinking, the type that has sent junk bond yields up to double digits and the actual bonds trading at 60 to 70 cents on the dollar. Buying into junk bonds at current levels allows investors to lock in very high yields and also the opportunity for capital appreciation of the underlying bond. Another reason I want to position the hedge fund in junk bonds is because my thinking is that when big money comes back into the market, it will be into corporate bonds first and then common stock. If you can buy the bond of a corporation at a 30 percent discount, bring in a double-digit annual yield, and have less risk than the common stock—why would you not buy the bond?

There are a number of ways to play the junk bond market through ETFs, and my favorite is JNK. The ETF is composed of more than 100 corporate bonds, all in junk status with a yield of 14.3 percent. After careful consideration of the top holdings in JNK, I thought it was a prudent choice to buy for my portfolio management clients in early 2009 as a play on the recovering equity market. The chart in Figure 12.9 shows the beginning of the bull market in junk bonds off the March 2009 low. A 35 percent rally in only three months has JNK at a fresh eight-month high in June 2009.

PowerShares Emerging Markets Sovereign Debt ETF

The decline in the U.S. dollar began in early 2002 and continued all the way through 2008. The drop of more than 40 percent in the value of the U.S. Dollar Index was both a blessing in disguise and a hindrance for companies based in the United States. The large multinationals that generate a sizable portion of their sales overseas benefited from

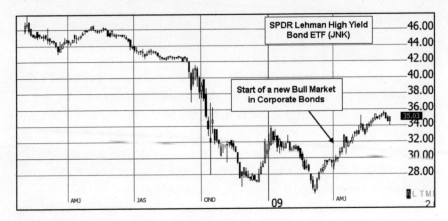

Figure 12.9   SPDR Lehman High Yield Bond ETF
SOURCE: TeleChart2007® or StockFinder® chart, courtesy of Worden Brothers, Inc.

the weak U.S. dollar as sales increased. Also benefiting were investors in foreign debt, because they could benefit from the currency conversion back into U.S. dollars. The income generated from the bonds in foreign income could be converted back into a greater number of U.S. dollars as the value of the foreign currency increased.

My thought process is that the U.S. dollar will once again resume the downtrend it began in 2002, due, once again, to the printing press in Washington. The value of the greenback will fall as foreign currencies, specifically the non-euro, emerging market currencies. To take advantage of this investment theme, the hedge fund will invest in the PowerShares Emerging Markets Sovereign Debt ETF (NYSE: PCY).

PCY invests in debt issued by emerging market countries and has exposure to approximately 22 different countries. Within the top 10 holdings, there is not one country that is represented more than once, highlighting the diversity with the allocation. The largest holding is a 7.1 percent bond issued by the Republic of Chile, and number two is a Republic of South Africa bond with an interest rate of 5.9 percent. The ETF pays an annual dividend yield of 6.3 percent and has been a fairly stable performer, with the exception of a major drop in October 2008. The ETF has since worked its way back from the drop and has worked its way back into a narrow trading range (see Figure 12.10). When pulling in a sizable dividend, a sideways movement during a

Figure 12.10 PowerShares Emerging Markets Sovereign Debt ETF
SOURCE: TeleChart2007® or StockFinder® chart, courtesy of Worden Brothers, Inc.

rough market is acceptable. I expect both capital appreciation and a sizable dividend once the bull market takes off.[7]

Now that you have a solid starting point to building your very own ETF hedge fund, the next chapter provides more details on how to profit in the bull market. Chapter 13 focuses on the opportunities in the stock market that have arisen after President Obama was elected into office. Also in the chapter is a discussion of the booming middle class around the world and specific investments that will profit from the demographic shift.

Chapter 13

More Themes
to Consider:
Investing and the
Obama Administration

A s the new U.S. president in the White House, Barack Obama
will be out to implement both his social and economic agen-
das. There is no doubt in my mind that President Obama has
his mind set on an agenda that will greatly alter the economy and present
investment opportunities as well as pitfalls investors must avoid.

One area that could be affected dramatically is health care, which
is a major focus in the first year of the new administration. There will
be winners and losers that come out of the new health care bill that
will eventually make its way to Obama's desk. As the discussions about
a new approach to health care heat up, the related stocks have been

stuck in neutral. When there is major uncertainty surrounding a sector, it will have difficulty attracting buyers, and sellers typically sit on their hands. Until a resolution is reached, the health care sector will struggle to break out and join the rally of the overall market.

A number of the investment ideas throughout the book are related to the new Obama administration and the direction the United States is going. That being said, I will not put all of my eggs into one basket because Obama's reign at the top will likely only last four years and another shift may occur in 2012. That is why the other investment ideas I discuss are based on underlying fundamentals and long-term themes.

Investment themes discussed in this chapter are based on trends that have occurred in the early stages of the Obama administration and I believe will continue for the remainder of the four-year term. They include the printing of more money by the U.S. Government Printing Office, higher interest rates, a weak U.S. dollar, the numerous bailouts of major corporations, and the redistribution of wealth. The chapter also touches on demographic shifts outside the United States and related individual stock opportunities.

In Figure 13.1, the stock market reaction to the Obama administration is highlighted. After a very rough start, the S&P 500 was able to make a comeback from its March 2009 low. Through the first four months, the index was up 6.5 percent, which is not bad, considering

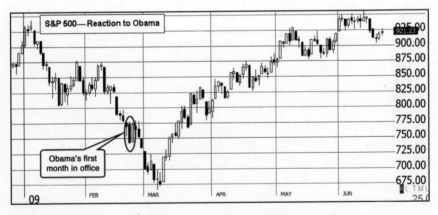

Figure 13.1   The Market's Reaction to a New President
SOURCE: TeleChart2007® or StockFinder® chart, courtesy of Worden Brothers, Inc.

the performance in 2008 before Obama took office. In reality, four months is too short a time to judge the administration's effect on the stock market.

The D.C. Printing Press

If you listen quietly at night, you can hear the sounds of an old-fashioned printing press coming from President Obama's room in the White House. There is only one way to pay for all the bailouts, tax cuts, and programs on the new president's agenda—print more money. When a nation floods its economy with large amounts of currency, the end result 99 percent of the time will be inflation. As you already know from Chapter 9, inflation is a major concern of mine and is inevitable as long as the American government continues to throw money at its problems.

The end result along with inflation will be a lower U.S. dollar and higher interest rates, both of which are discussed in this chapter. I do not rehash the inflation argument and the specific investment opportunities associated with rising prices. That being said, please realize how adamant I am about inflation and the need to position your portfolio accordingly. I have been allocating clients' portfolios at Penn Financial Group throughout 2009 to prepare for the coming rise in inflation, and I suggest you do the same.

Higher Interest Rates

The yield on the 10-year Treasury note fell to 2.04 percent in December 2008, the lowest in decades. This was caused by an overwhelming amount of money going into bonds as a safe play amidst the nasty stock market sell-off. The demand for bonds increased, resulting in the price of bonds to move higher. Because bond prices and bond yields have an inverse relationship, it caused the yields to fall as the bond prices increased.

As the stock market began to consolidate after the November 2008 low, the yields started to inch higher, little by little. The stock sell-off in March sent yields lower again on the 10-year, but only down to 2.46 percent. After a quick pullback in yield in March, bond prices

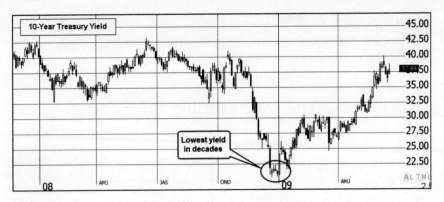

Figure 13.2 10-Year Bond Yield Drop and Rally Back
SOURCE: TeleChart2007® or StockFinder® chart, courtesy of Worden Brothers, Inc.

began to fall and the yields moved higher in a straight line. The increase in the yield can be attributed to investors moving out of bonds as the stock market improved and rallied 40 percent off the March low. In Figure 13.2, the chart of the 10-year yield shows the dramatic drop-off in December before rebounding in early 2009. If the yield breaks through the psychological level of 4.0 percent, it could send bonds lower and the yield much higher.

There is another underlying factor, however, that may be the true reason behind the rise in yields. As the United States continues to spend like a drunken sailor it can pay for the costs by printing more dollars and by issuing new debt, mainly to foreign countries. China is currently one of the biggest buyers of U.S. debt and has been starting to jawbone about a weak U.S. dollar. The government will have to increase the yields it offers on its bonds for it to continue enticing the Chinese and other foreign countries to buy U.S. debt. At the end of the game, it is simple economics. If the demand for the bonds decreases, the U.S. government will increase the yield to attract more debt buyers.

Investors who want to profit from rising bond yields should not lock in a large amount of their portfolio into fixed income, because prices will fall as more attractive yields arise. To directly make money from falling bond prices and rising yields, there is the ProShares UltraShort 20-Plus Year Treasury ETF (NYSE: TBT). The ETF offers a return that is twice the inverse to the long Treasury bond prices as tracked by the Barclays Capital 20-Plus Year U.S. Treasury Index.

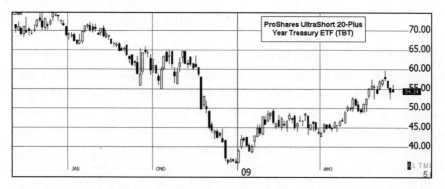

Figure 13.3   ProShares UltraShort 20+ Year Treasury ETF
Source: TeleChart2007® or StockFinder® chart, courtesy of Worden Brothers, Inc.

Figure 13.3 is a chart of the ETF and is a display to the volatility leveraged ETFs offer. The line on the chart is the yield on the 10-year, and the inverse correlation is evident. I do not typically advocate leveraged ETFs as long-term plays, but TBT may fall in to that category as a long-term trade, but not as an investment. Investors who continue to believe in buy-and-ignore, this ETF is not for them; it will benefit active investors willing to buy and sell every few weeks or months.

The Weak U.S. Dollar

The mantra during the Bush administration was always, "Strong Dollar, Strong Dollar." Well, actions speak louder than words because the U.S. Dollar Index fell for seven straight years, beginning in 2001. The greenback rallied just after the Obama administration took office, but has since backed off. The index hit a fresh six-month low for a short period in early June and I believe it is only a matter of time before the downtrend in the U.S. dollar continues.

A weak U.S. dollar can be beneficial to a number of sectors that have already been mentioned throughout the book as investment ideas. The most well-known of the anti-dollar investment strategies is investing in commodities, which was discussed in Chapter 7. Other sectors that benefit from a weak U.S. dollar include U.S.-based multinationals, foreign-based companies, foreign currencies, and foreign bonds.

U.S.-Based Multinationals

A trend in large-cap stocks based in the United States involves expanding overseas at some point, because that is where the growth opportunities are found. As mentioned in Chapter 3, companies such as McDonald's Corporation (NYSE: MCD) realized this years ago and now find themselves in a situation in which more than half of their revenue is generated from outside the United States. The Illinois-based fast food restaurant is known from China to Latin America and nearly everywhere in between. In Figure 13.4, the chart of McDonald's displays choppy action, but considering what was going on around it, the action is very impressive.

Not only has the stock been a leader during the recession, it is also a candidate to benefit from a weak U.S. dollar. When McDonald's reports quarterly earnings, it has to include the currency conversion from sales in local currency around the world back to U.S. dollars. When the foreign currencies are stronger, it allows for a more favorable conversion ratio into U.S. dollars and helps the bottom line for the company. During the fourth quarter of 2008, the bottom line for McDonald's was slightly impaired because of a rise in the U.S. dollar. If the U.S. dollar revisits the downtrend and tests the lows, it will be a boost to all multinationals' bottom line, and the sector is therefore a hedge against a weak U.S. dollar.

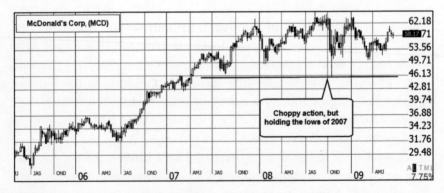

Figure 13.4 McDonald's Corp Bouncing around after a Multiyear Uptrend Was Halted by the Recession
SOURCE: TeleChart2007® or StockFinder® chart, courtesy of Worden Brothers, Inc.

Profiting from Bailout Money with Financial Stocks

The United States has always been a nation that gives second chances, but this has recently gotten out of hand; from the financial institution bailouts to the bailout of AIG to the bailout of the auto industry. Nearly every sector has had its hands out to Washington. I cannot blame them because as long as the government is drunk on spending, why not take the money? It has been made clear by both the Bush and now the Obama administrations that there are certain companies that are too big to fail. The one sector that has received the largest portion of bailout money has been the financial stocks and that is where I turn for an investment opportunity based on the theory of bailout nation.

Two financial companies that did take money from the Troubled Asset Relief Program (TARP), but were not in danger of going the way of Bear Stearns or Lehman Brothers are Goldman Sachs (NYSE: GS) and Morgan Stanley (NYSE: MS). Both companies are leaders in their sector and had the diversity to make it through the recession and will ultimately be two of the small group of players that will flourish when the Next Great Bull Market begins. If I was forced to choose just one of the companies for my portfolio, the choice would be Goldman Sachs.

Goldman Sachs is best known for its trading desk, which houses some of the best traders in the world. In both up and down markets, these traders have the ability to make the company very profitable, and once the sector gets back to using riskier leverage, it will benefit Goldman more than any other company. Goldman is now a bank holding company after a conversion in late 2008 that allowed the company to receive government bailout money. Along with the banking division, which offers mortgage originations and loans, the company is also a market maker, asset manager, investment banker, and much more. Figure 13.5 shows the rebound in the stock from the November 2008 low, and at the same time the amount of ground it needs to make up to get back to its 2007 high. There is definitely more upside left for the leader in the industry.

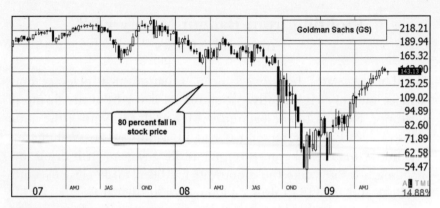

Figure 13.5   Goldman Sachs Bouncing Off the Multiyear Lows and Poised to Begin New Long-Term Bull Run
SOURCE: TeleChart2007® or StockFinder® chart, courtesy of Worden Brothers, Inc.

The Redistribution of Wealth

As it becomes more apparent that the current Obama administration is either willing to accept a move toward socialism or it is their ultimate goal, investors must realize the ramifications it will have on the demographics in the United States. The redistribution of wealth will be initiated by higher taxes on the wealthy, who are already paying the majority of the taxes in the United States. This could have a negative effect on the upper echelon of taxpayers that will ultimately trickle down to the middle and lower classes.

The wealthy who will see their taxes raised are not only big spenders in the U.S. economy, but many also own small companies that employ the middle- and lower-income classes. If the goal is to redistribute wealth from the wealthy, it will overwhelmingly fail as the small businesses lay off employees who, for the most part, are in the two lower-income groups, and the unemployment rate will increase as a result. Would a middle class family choose to have two working parents or one in the unemployment line for an extra few hundred dollars in tax savings?

Growth of Global Middle Class

As the Obama administration attempts to save the middle class in the United States, the middle class is flourishing around the world in emerging markets such as China and India. The World Bank estimates the global middle class will likely grow from 430 million in 2000 to 1.15 billion in 2030. Even more amazing is that in 2000 the developing nations were home to 56 percent of the global middle class, but by 2030 the developing nations will account for 93 percent. These figures back up my argument that the real middle class growth is in nations such as China and India. The World Bank goes on to say that China and India will account for two-thirds of the expansion.

The McKinsey Global Institute projects China's middle class will increase from 43 percent of the population in 2008 to 76 percent in 2025. India's middle class will explode from 50 million in 2008 to 583 million in the next two decades. The expansion within India will create the world's fifth-largest consumer nation, up from number 12 today. I can continue to throw out mind-bending statistics in regard to middle-class growth in the developing nations. The bottom line is that more people with disposable money will result in greater demand for necessities such as food as well as discretionary products and services.

The Fight for Food

As the population grows and, more importantly, joins the middle class, there will be more mouths to feed and fewer people living in poverty. This will result in a higher demand for food around the world, and if the supply does not meet the demand, there could be serious ramifications. There will also be an increased demand for better and more nutritious food. As I mentioned in Chapter 4, water could be a commodity that eventually will be a reason for war between countries. Food is not far behind and has already been linked to fighting among civilizations. There are some agricultural companies that are ahead of the game in preparing to feed future generations, and they offer interesting opportunities for the forward-thinking investor.

Monsanto Company

Monsanto (NYSE: MON) is an agricultural chemical company that strives to help farmers produce more while conserving more. The goal of the company through a variety of products is to help farmers increase their yield without making a negative impact on the environment. Some of the company's leading brands include Roundup herbicide, which has been used by farmers for decades to eliminate weeds, and Seminis,

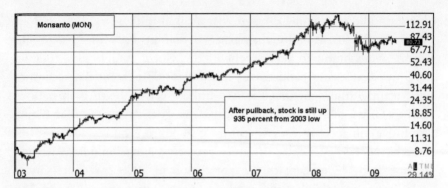

Figure 13.6   Monsanto Stock Takes a Break from the Long-term Uptrend
SOURCE: TeleChart2007® or StockFinder® chart, courtesy of Worden Brothers, Inc.

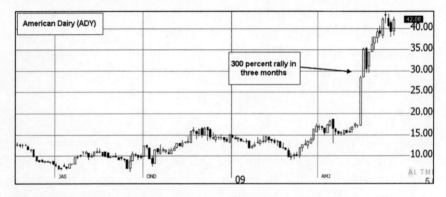

Figure 13.7   Parabolic Move in American Dairy
SOURCE: TeleChart2007® or StockFinder® chart, courtesy of Worden Brothers, Inc.

which is the world's largest developer, grower, and marketer of vegetables and fruit seeds. The long-term chart of Monsanto in Figure 13.6 displays the uptrend the stock has been in for years and also the short-term pot-hole it hit during the recession. I expect the uptrend to continue and bought shares of the stock for clients in early June 2009.

American Dairy, Inc.

Another agricultural company to observe is American Dairy, Inc. American Dairy (NYSE: ADY) is a Chinese company that specializes in producing and distributing milk powder, soybean products, rice, walnuts, and infant formula milk in the country. The stock has been one of the best perform-ers in the market in 2009, rising from a low of $9 in March 2009 to a high above $40 just three months later, as you can see in Figure 13.7. The move in the stock was fueled by the company's earnings report that was released on May 14, 2009. Sales for the first quarter increased by 191 percent to $113.8 million and net income surged 282 percent to $27.8 million from $7.3 million one year earlier. The promise going forward will be based on sales of the infant formula sector in which American Dairy is a premium player. The CEO of the company projects the Chinese market for infant formula to grow from about $5.5 billion to $12.0 billion in the next five years. If this is the case, expect American Dairy to capture a large portion of the growth and to continue with an increasing stock price.

Increasing Disposable Income

As the middle class grows around the world, the amount of disposable income will increase for the lower middle and middle class populations. This demographic and economic shift will result in purchases of goods and services that were not available to them in the past. The most apparent changes will occur in developing nations such as China and India, where in the past all resources were poured into food and survival. The emergence of the middle class will have a population with newfound money searching for fun and exciting ways to spend its extra income.

Within China, one of the areas that is abuzz among teens and young adults is computer gaming. There are three stocks that trade in the United States that are major players in the gaming industry in China, and all three have experienced superior growth and big runs in their stock price in the face of a global recession. According to Pearl Research, the China online game market brought in $2.8 billion in 2008, a 63 percent increase from 2007. The research company showed that 65 percent of online users in China played online games and 70 percent of the 298 million Internet users in China are under the age of 30; these are both impressive numbers for the sector. Spending money on gaming may not be the first choice for fun by U.S. residents, but the Chinese love their gaming and with millions already playing and wanting to join the craze, the three companies discussed next could continue to flourish.

Shanda Interactive Entertainment LTD

Shanda (NASDAQ: SNDA) is a leader in China in the interactive entertainment media sector, offering multiplayer online role-playing games, casual online games, and online board games. The two big games are

"The Legend of Mir II" and "The World of Legend," which generate about 75 percent of the revenue. Players of the games pay a subscription fee to play the games online.

During the first three quarters of 2009, the company reported revenue that rose 42 percent to 1.1 billion yuan ($160 million). Net income increased by 25 percent to 361 million yuan. This is amazing growth during one of the toughest quarters for earnings in decades. The most recent estimates have Shanda earning $3.32 per share in 2009; based on a share price of $54, it puts the P/E ratio in the midteens. This valuation is extremely attractive for a company with such high growth potential.

NetEase.com

NetEase.com (NASDAQ: NTES) also offers multiplayer online role-playing games similar to Shanda. The big difference is that NetEase is a more diversified company that also offers a web portal with an online community and e-commerce services. The company also sells advertising on its web site. This diversity takes the reliance off the gaming sector and lowers the potential risk to investors.

According to the company's quarterly earnings report that was released on May 20, 2009, NetEase earned 47 cents during the first quarter, up from 30 cents a year earlier, but lower than the 65 cents in the fourth quarter of 2008. Revenues rose by 20 percent to $114.4 million, but advertising revenue fell to $6 million from $11.3 million one year earlier. The gaming revenue made up for the fall in ad revenue by increasing 30 percent to $106 million from $81.4 million in 2008. The most recent quarter is a situation in which the diversity in advertising actually hurt the company as gaming continued to grow.

The big news with NetEase has been the contract it signed in April with Blizzard Entertainment, a unit of Activision Blizzard (NASDAQ: ATVI), to distribute in China the widely popular online game, "World of Warcraft." There were no monetary details of the exact licensing fee at the time this chapter was written, but some analysts have predicted it could generate revenue of up to $300 million per year for the company. In the three months following the deal the stock price of NetEase rose by over 30 percent.

Changyou.Com LTD

Changyou.com (NASDAQ: CYOU) had an IPO in early 2009 and began trading on the NASDAQ in April 2009. The company was formed when Chinese media company Sohu.com (NASDAQ: SOHU) spun off its gaming unit. The majority of the revenue for Changyou comes from its most popular game, "Tian Long Ba Bu," which has nearly two million users, according to Hoovers. The company was a division of Sohu.com when it began its operations in 2003 and became a stand-alone unit in 2007 before the IPO in 2009.

The company boasts year-over-year revenue of 187 percent between 2007 and 2008; a number that is tough to argue with. The quarterly report released by the company in April 2009 for the first quarter of 2009 showed total revenue at $61.6 million, up 50 percent from last year. The GAAP net income hit a record during the quarter of $33.5 million, an increase of 120 percent year over year. The numbers go along with the rise in the stock price from the time it began trading. A move from the high teens in early April to the mid-$40s in June is more than impressive. The stock will show heavy volatility and is only considered a buy on pullbacks for aggressive investors. The chart of Changyou in Figure 13.8 gives an indication of the volatility

Figure 13.8 Changyou.com LTD: A Winner from Day One
SOURCE: TeleChart2007® or StockFinder® chart, courtesy of Worden Brothers, Inc.

and interest it has attracted from investors from the day it began trading. Patience is a virtue when looking for an entry point on a stock such as Changyou.

Time to Execute

Now that your head is filled with a plethora of investment ideas that range from water companies to Chinese gaming stocks, it is time to put the new information into action. Execution is integral to make money in the coming decade when the Next Great Bull Market comes upon us. Patience and planning are two key skills successful investors need, and they are discussed in detail in Chapter 14.

Chapter 14

Having a Plan

How do you know when you've really made it? I always thought it would be an invite from Hugh Hefner to the Playboy Mansion, but the more I think about it, it might be when you invent a new word. Well, I have yet to achieve either, so I guess I better keep writing and hope that both will come to fruition at some point in my life. I explain the two traditional investment strategies of concentration and diversification in this chapter and why using a mixture of the two just might be the best approach to investing. The word I use for this approach is *conversification*, which I first introduced to you in Chapter 11.

You'll learn the different types of sell orders as well as three sell strategies for knowing when it's time to sell. Lastly, it's important to remember that a time will come when you must cut your losses. I close the chapter with a section on buying, using a specific example from Chapter 5.

The Concentration Approach

The problem with taking a concentration-only approach to investing is that the investor is putting all the eggs in one basket. If that basket happens to fall, all the eggs break and a large loss could be incurred. On the other hand, if the bet is right and the correct sector is chosen, the portfolio will greatly outperform the market. Looking back on 2008 is a good way to get my point across about the potential windfall and pitfalls of concentration.

Assume you felt the financial sector had come down enough from the 2007 highs and that after losing one-third of its value, January 2008 was an opportunity to buy into the sector. If you wanted to invest in the entire sector with an ETF one choice would be the SPDRs Select Sector Financial ETF (NYSE: XLF). The ETF fell to $25 in mid-January 2008 from a high of $38 in 2007. By November 2008, the ETF was in the single digits and down more than 60 percent. Imagine if you decided to pick an individual stock such as Citigroup (NYSE: C) because you felt at $25 it was a bargain you could not pass up and the financial crisis would not last much longer. Buying Citi at that time would have resulted in a loss of nearly 90 percent.

Now let's play the other side of the trade and assume you felt the market was in for a rough 2008 and you decided to buy into bond ETFs as a hedge. The iShares Barclays 20-Plus Year Treasury Bond ETF (NYSE: TLT) tracks the price of long-term U.S. Treasuries and pays a solid dividend of approximately 4.7 percent. If you decided to purchase TLT instead of XLF in January 2008, the 60 percent loss could have been replaced by a 20-plus percent gain by the end of that year.

Buying TLT in January 2008 seems like a logical purchase when looking back from 2009; hindsight is always 20/20, though, especially in the stock market. Holders of TLT from 2003 through 2007 experienced little to no gain as the S&P 500 doubled. So, even though you would not have suffered big losses by making the wrong choice with TLT in 2003, the opportunity cost of doubling your portfolio in the market is significant.

While concentration can provide an investor with excitement and something to talk about at a cocktail party, the average investor will struggle to pick the right investment at the right time. Unless you are a seasoned investor or have a large appetite for risk, concentration is not the most prudent strategy for the average individual investor.

And Then There's Diversification

Diversification on the other hand is the exact opposite of concentration. According to dictionary.com, the word *diversify* means "to distribute (investments) among different companies or securities in order to limit losses in the event of a fall in a particular market or industry." The first half of the definition is true; the second half is up for debate. Assume your portfolio was diversified in 2008 through investments in 10 different ETFs that covered the major sectors as well as international exposure. Do you think your portfolio would have been able to "limit losses" as the definition suggests?

The Select Sectors SPDRs offer nine ETFs that invest in a broad range of sectors and give an investor exposure to more than 650 stocks. (See Table 14.1.) The final ETF in the diversified portfolio is the iShares MSCI EAFE Index ETF (NYSE: EFA), which gives investors exposure to Europe, Asia, and Australia. Assume the portfolio was equally weighted among the 10 ETFs. To most investors' surprise, the return

Table 14.1 2008 Returns of the Diversified Portfolio

ETF	2008 Return
XLK, XLB	−42%
XLI	−40%
XLU	−31%
XLP	−17%
XLV	−25%
XLE	−40%
XLF	−57%
XLY	−34%
EFA	−36%

for 2008 would have been a negative 36.7 percent. Considering the S&P 500 lost 38.5 percent, I do not consider an outperformance of less than 2 percent to be limiting the losses.

Even though the diversified portfolio had exposure to nearly every niche sector within the market, being overly diversified sent the return of the portfolio back to the mean. That is the major problem with diversification—most investors overdiversify, assuming the risk will be lower and returns will not suffer; this is a misunderstanding. There are endless studies going back to Burton Makiel's *Random Walk Down Wall Street* that discuss how many stocks are needed to diversify a portfolio. The consensus is that approximately 15 stocks will remove a large portion of individual stock risk. Any stocks above and beyond the 15 will not significantly lower risk, and they are therefore not needed to further diversify a portfolio. Keep in mind that owning 10 different ETFs gives investors exposure to hundreds of stocks, creating instant overdiversification. If you own a handful of mutual funds, you are in a similar position and it is time you change your strategy immediately.

A myth about diversification that many investors fall victim to is that if you buy at least 15 stocks, your portfolio is suddenly diversified. Even though the numbers do prove this, there are stipulations behind what type of stocks are bought. If your portfolio was composed of only mega-cap stocks or only energy-related stocks, where is the diversification? To be truly diversified with 15 stocks, the portfolio must be carefully constructed to give a proper representation of the overall market.

Reintroducing Conversification

A word that I have been using to describe one of my investment strategies is conversification. As I defined it in Chapter 11, conversification is the perfect mixture of concentration and diversification. What I mean by that is to concentrate on the sectors of the market that are outperforming, and at the same time diversify across the same sectors. In theory, conversification will produce results that are much greater than that of a portfolio that is diversified and offer less risk than a portfolio that is concentrated. By taking the best of what diversification and concentration have to offer, conversification presents the most attractive reward-to-risk scenario of the three investment strategies.

Knowing When to Sell

Whether you use a concentration-only approach, diversification, or a mixture of the two, determining when to buy a stock can be painstaking for most investors because it involves a number of factors. From the fundamentals to the charts to the state of the overall stock market, all are equally important and they do not always tell the same story. Equally important, if not more important, is knowing when to sell a stock, whether it be locking in a gain and attempting to sell near a high or a forced sale of a position because it continues to fall and it is time to cut the cord and take a loss.

The next section helps you determine when to buy and when to sell the exciting new stocks and ETFs you were introduced to in the first 13 chapters of this book. Unfortunately, it is not as easy as buying and walking away; as an interested investor, you need some time and knowledge of when to buy and, more importantly, when to sell.

Until an investor can come to grips with the concept of taking losses and moving on from a failed investment, it is impossible for that investor to find success over the long term. I can use baseball as an analogy. Some of the best hitters in the Baseball Hall of Fame finished their careers with batting averages around .300. The most successful hitters were able to realize failure was a part of the game considering they were able to get a hit only 3 out of every 10 at bats. If you are a swing trader or a day trader, you can also be very successful at batting .300 with the right plan. The key is to incur small losses and book big wins, which goes back to knowing when to sell both winners and losers.

Before listing specific buy signals, investors need to realize that the way the human brain is wired makes selling more difficult than buying. As hard as it is to sell a losing position, exiting a winner is just as difficult. When a stock is rising, you feel good about the stock and no one wants to sell when the feeling is good and optimism is percolating—but that is typically the time to sell. Even if your original target is reached on a stock, it is natural to not sell and look for a bigger profit. Psychologists refer to this behavior as greed, and they are somewhat correct. Along with greed is the thought process of why end something when the going is good; let's try to ride this stock as high as it will take us. The one problem with the ride-the-train strategy is that eventually the train will stop and begin to head back to its origination point.

To combat the possibility of giving back the profit, there are three different strategies investors can implement. They involve slightly more complex sell orders, and more work from the investor. These strategies will allow you to maximize the profit as best as you can and help eliminate the emotion involved in the selling process. Quickly, before jumping into the specific sell strategies, I need to offer a brief explanation of the types of sell orders available to investors.

Types of Sell Orders

Knowing your options is an important first step. The six types of sell orders available to investors are market order, limit order, stop order, stop limit order, trailing stop order (percentage) and trailing stop order (dollar amount).

- *Market Order:* An order that will sell the stock at the prevailing bid price. The order is typically filled within seconds during normal trading hours. The risk is that the stock moves from the time you originally place the order; this is more relevant for illiquid stocks.
- *Limit Order:* An order that will only fill if the limit price is reached. The sell limit price will be placed above the current price. For example, if ABC is currently trading at $40 per share, a limit order for $41 could be entered. If ABC trades up to $41, the stock will be sold. ABC will never be sold for less than $41 per share.
- *Stop Order:* An order that is placed below the current market price of a stock to protect against downside risk. If ABC stock is trading at $40 per share, a stop order could be placed at $39. If ABC falls below $39, the stop order will be triggered and the stock will be sold at the market price. The risk is that the stock falls rapidly through the $39 stop price and when the market order is triggered, the stock could be sold at a much lower price than $39.

- *Stop Limit Order:* An order that is similar to the stop order except along with the stop price ($39), there must also be a limit price entered. Instead of turning into a market order after the stop is triggered at $39, a limit order will be initiated. Going along with the same example, the stop is at $39 and the limit is at $38.50. This is telling the broker to trigger a limit order of $38.50 if the $39 price is broken. In essence, what this is doing is protecting against a rapid fall in the stock or overnight risk. An example of overnight risk is ABC closing at $40 and reporting earnings after the market is closed that were much worse than expected. The stock will open lower the next day at $35 per share because of the news. With a normal stop order at $39, the order will be triggered on the open because the stock is below $39 and a market order will be placed—selling the stock near $35. If the stop limit order was placed instead, the stop will be triggered because the stock is below $39. The stock will not be sold, however, because the stock is trading below the limit price of $38.50. At the time, there is no indication as to which order will result in the better outcome; only time will tell. The bottom line is that the stop order sold the stock and the stop limit order did not sell the stock because it is below the $38.50 limit price.
- *Trailing Stop Order (Percentage):* An order that will allow a stock the ability to continue moving higher, but with downside protection. Assume ABC is at $40 and you believe there is a possibility it could go to $50, but do not want to give up the gain already achieved. The investor could place a trailing stop order based on a percentage basis. A trailing stop order of 5 percent tells the broker to place a stop order 5 percent below the current price, resulting in a stop order at $38 (5 percent below the current price of $40). Because the order is a trailing stop, it will move with the price of the stock. Assume ABC moves to $45 in the next week. The trailing stop order will move with the price of the stock and is now at $42.75 (5 percent below the current price of $45). The level of the trailing stop will be raised when the price of the stock increases and will be determined by the high water mark of the stock after the order is placed. The stock may continue to $50, but after hitting $45, the stock pulled back below $42.75 and the stop order was triggered.

- *Trailing Stop Order (Dollar Amount):* An order that is nearly the same as the trailing stop order (percentage), expect the trailing figure is based on a dollar amount. Instead of placing the trailing stop order 5 percent below the current price, an investor has the choice of placing it $2 below the current price.

Sell Strategies for Winning Positions

The three strategies for winning positions are to sell when the original target is reached, use trailing stop-loss sell orders, and sell half and let the other half run. These strategies, discussed in detail next, involve complex sell orders and require careful work by the investor, but will go far to help protect profits.

Sell When the Original Target Is Reached

An easy way to assure emotions are eliminated and the profit is banked is to sell when the original target price is reached. This sounds simple because it is. Investing does not have to be complicated, and the best investors are often those who keep it simple and limit the emotional decisions. I am sure you have heard of the acronym KISS—Keep It Simple, Stupid. Following the funny, yet helpful acronym will help you become a more successful investor. Selling when the target is reached will also allow the investor to move on to the next potential winner.

Use Trailing Stop-Loss Sell Orders

The exact opposite of selling the entire position is holding onto the stock. That being said, there is a strategy behind not selling when the target is reached. Assume the target is reached and the action of the stock is bullish along with the recent news out of the company. It is reasonable to believe there are a few more points on the upside, so why not let the stock continue moving higher and bank a larger profit in the future. The one problem with that thinking is based on the accuracy of bullish prediction. If the stock fails to move higher, the investor needs to be prepared to sell before losing the entire gain on the stock. A simple way to ensure this is to place a trailing stop-loss sell order that will be triggered if the stock falls a predetermined amount from the current price.

Sell Half Now and Let the Other Half Run

Because it is difficult for an investor to make a yes-or-no decision, this third strategy involves a compromise. Sell half the position when the target is reached, satisfying the logical thinking side of your brain. By keeping the other half of the position, this allows the investor to remain in the stock in the event the rally continues; this satisfies the greed part of the brain. It is important to implement a stop-loss strategy for the remaining half's position.

Cutting Your Losses

Even though the previous section made it out to be a difficult situation when a position is profitable, the real problem occurs when a stock goes against you and a loss has to be incurred. When selling a losing stock position, there is a feeling of giving up and admitting the investment decision was a failure. And because no one likes to admit to failure, hitting the sell button knowing a loss will be incurred is one of the most difficult, if not the most difficult, decisions in investing.

One of the most important lessons I learned in my early years of investing is that it is okay to take a loss. Along the same lines, I also realized that even if every buy indicator is in my favor, there will be situations in which the investment does not work out and a loss must be taken. Investing is a game of percentages and, unfortunately, no strategy is correct 100 percent of the time. I suggest you learn from both your winning and losing investments, but do not dwell on the past because it will affect future investment decisions.

An adage used on Wall Street more often these days is, "Take small losses and big gains." This is much easier said than done, especially considering the market action over the last few years. I do agree with the adage and try to live by it as closely as I can for my own portfolio as well as for clients of the Penn Financial Group. I believe there is a fiduciary obligation to not let any one position affect the portfolio too much on the downside.

To appropriately implement a strategy that involves taking small losses, the key is to have parameters in place to signal when it is time to sell. Before entering a new investment, the investor must determine the entry price before placing the order. I also suggest a price be determined that will be the stop level that, if breached, will signal it is time to take a small loss and move on to the next possible winner. Not to harp on this, but I strongly suggest you determine the stop price before buying, because once the stock goes against you and begins to move lower it becomes nearly impossible to make a decision without emotional factors.

Sell Signals

There is no right or wrong answer when asked how you determine when to sell a position. As long as you have a plan to alert you when it is time to sell, you are aware of the need that selling must occur. The following is a list of sell signals that can be used to determine if it is time to sell a position.

The original reason has changed. If a stock was purchased because you felt its new product would be a game changer in the industry and you were wrong, it is time to sell. Any time the original reason for purchasing is no longer valid, it is time to sell the stock, whether it is a winner or loser.

Technical analysis. There are traders who make a living purely from using the charts to determine when to buy and sell. I am a big believer in technical analysis and include it in every buy and sell decision I make. Without getting overly complicated, there are two simple chart sell signals for investors. The first involves the current trend of the stock: If the uptrend (a line connecting a series of higher lows) is broken, a sell signal is initiated. The second involves moving averages: If a stock trades below the 50-day and 200-day moving averages, the stock should be sold.

The company cuts its dividend payout. During the recession, it was not uncommon to have a handful of stocks cutting their dividends each day as they attempted to horde cash. Once the economy and market get back to normal, the payment of dividends will once again become important, and most companies should be able to increase the payout. If the company you own stock in cuts a dividend, it typically suggests there is a cash flow issue and selling the stock should be considered.

Valuation. The most common way to determine valuation is by using the price-to-earnings ratio (P/E ratio). Even though this is industry procedure, selling a stock based only on a P/E ratio is crazy. A company that is growing should not be compared with a company that is mature and no longer in the growth stage. An example is Microsoft (NASDAQ: MSFT) and Google (NASDAQ: GOOG). Microsoft has a P/E ratio of 12 and Google is trading with a P/E ratio of 31. Both companies are two of the largest in the technology industry and should be compared with each other and therefore Google should be sold because of its lofty valuation—Wrong! Growth rate must also be taken into consideration and the P/E ratio should be divided by its growth rate to generate the PEG ratio. The PEG ratio on Microsoft is 1.21 and Google is 1.1, suggesting that Google is undervalued in comparison with Microsoft. When selling on the basis of valuation, I suggest the PEG ratio to be your basis and it should only be compared with companies that are regarded as being in the same business space.

Relative weakness. If a sector is booming and the majority of the stocks are moving higher, but your stock is lagging, it is displaying relative weakness and should be sold. An example occurred throughout 2007 and into early 2008 when the teen retail sector was booming because the consumer was still spending. During 2007, there were three stocks in particular that I followed and two of the three were performing well as the third struggled to make headway. The two companies moving higher and hitting highs on a regular basis were Aeropostale (NYSE: ARO) and The Buckle (NYSE: BKE); Abercrombie & Fitch (NYSE: ANF) throughout 2007 and early 2008 failed to break out to new highs. In early 2008, Abercrombie & Fitch began a sell-off that took the stock from a high of nearly $90 in 2007 to a low of $13 in 2008. The other two stocks also took big hits during the recession in late 2008, but they both moved either above or within a few dollars of their prerecession highs in 2009. Abercrombie & Fitch, on the other hand, remained 60 percent off its prerecession highs in mid-2009. If the investor was aware that Abercrombie & Fitch was showing relative weakness in 2007 and 2008, it would have resulted in an early and appropriate exit.

Target is reached. When a new investment is bought, there is only one thing an investor asks for—send the stock to the target price. What is amusing and interesting is that when the target is reached, the last thing the investor wants to do is sell. Even though the target was determined on the basis of charts and fundamentals, it is not easy to be happy with selling a stock knowing it could continue higher after it is sold. Unfortunately, investors too often do not sell at the target price and, in the end, sell their position at a lower price.

Stop loss order is triggered. If you place a stop order for a position, whether it results in a winning or losing investment, please abide by it. The stop loss was placed when you were emotionally stable regarding the position and should not be changed when the stock begins to fall. The goal of the stop order is to minimize any further loss in the position and, as an investor, you should step back and let nature take its course.

Portfolio rebalance. This is a good problem to have. When an individual investment dramatically increases in price, it will grow to become a larger portion of the overall portfolio and eventually to a level that is not consistent with the asset allocation. An example would be if you bought $10,000 of a stock in a $100,000 portfolio and it doubled in the next year while the other positions in your portfolio remained unchanged. The stock would have increased from 10 percent of the portfolio allocation to 18 percent, resulting in too much concentration in one position, so all or half of the stock should be sold.

Overall market is weak. This sell signal is a major component of the top-down approach that I implement in my investment strategy. When the overall market is in a bearish situation, the probability of an individual stock moving higher is low. It is therefore imperative that a few positions in the portfolio be sold to lower the exposure to the actions of the overall market. The most recent bear market is a great example of how even strong stocks fell, and it was due mainly to investors selling everything and anything.

Competition or product change. If you wake up one day and Microsoft announces a product that will rival the iPod for supremacy at half the price, it may be time to consider selling shares of Apple (NASDAQ:

AAPL). The same could be said if one day Apple announced that any-one using the iPhone will lose all of their hair because of radiation from the phone, the product has changed, and the stock must be sold. Both of the examples are extreme, but they get my point across.

On the cover of a magazine. When you finally make the cover of *Rolling Stone*, it means you've made it as a rock band. When a company is featured on the cover of *Business Week*, it often marks the end of the bull market for that stock. Once a company is featured on the cover of a prominent magazine, it suggests that everyone knows about the stock and the upside is now capped. Sell when you see your company on the cover.

Now that you understand how and when to sell a position, it is only right for me to share the insights into the buying process.

It's Time to Buy

The first step in the buying process is deciding on the stock you want to buy, which has already been done for you in the previous chapters. I realize prices of stocks change dramatically over time, and depending on when you are reading this book, the prices of the recommended investments may be much higher or lower.

To try to make the process easy to understand and real, I have decided to use an example of a stock discussed earlier that I did not own at the time this chapter was written. Chapter 5 concentrated on the infrastructure boom and stocks that will benefit from the worldwide spending spree of governments. AECOM Technology Corporation (NYSE: ACM) is a stock that I have been watching for months and after a nice rally through the first five months of 2009, it had risen to the top of the buy list. The only problem is that the stock had already risen from a low of $20 in March 2009 to a high of $32 in May 2009.

Because of the gain of more than 50 percent in two months, it is not prudent to chase the stock in the low $30s. This is where patience and knowledge of knowing when to buy is very integral to entering the stock at an acceptable price. Ideally, the goal is to enter the stock

Figure 14.1   Determining the Buy Point for AECOM
SOURCE: TeleChart2007® or StockFinder® chart, courtesy of Worden Brothers, Inc.

at the lowest possible price, but you know by now that buying at the lows and selling at the highs is merely a fantasy of unsuccessful investors. I would prefer you look for the sweet spot in the stock, which is a point at which the stock can be purchased at a reasonable price near an important support level.

Figure 14.1 shows the chart of AECOM during the first week of June 2009 as I prepared to place an order to buy the stock. The chart shows the stock has been in the $32 range in the past and it has pulled back each time over the subsequent weeks. So, with the stock in the $30s, it does not appear to be in its sweet spot, and so buying it immediately would not be a good idea. There appears to be support on the charts at the $28 mark and that is where I have determined the buy zone is located. Only time will tell if the stock pulls back to my entry point at $28 in the coming weeks.

If the stock does not pull back to $28 and continues its uptrend, there is a chance that AECOM will never be bought. With thousands of stocks available on the major exchanges, there is no reason to chase the price of a stock. There are a number of alternative investments in Chapter 5 for investors who may have missed out on AECOM.

A mistake that most investors make, myself included, is chasing the price of a stock because the feeling of missing out on buying cancels out all rational thinking. Patience is a virtue in the world of investing and thankfully, I have quite a bit of it; unfortunately for everyone around me outside of my office, my patience is nonexistent. So I can understand how investors do not want to practice patience when attempting to buy a stock. The argument I hear most often about buying goes like this: "Why not buy AECOM at $30 and be done with it? The stock will be $40 in the future, so why risk missing it for the $2 you are saving with a purchase price of $28?" The investor makes a valid point, but there are two variables in the argument. First, who is to say the stock will not pull back to $28 and second, there is no guarantee the stock goes to $40 and could have already hit a high and is on its way back down to $20. A purchase price at $28 versus $30 lowers the downside risk if the stock does not act in the manner predicted. In the end, it is all about reward to risk.

To take the reward to risk one step further, please refer back to Figure 14.1, the chart of AECOM. If the purchase price is $28, it allows for $6 to the upside before the stock runs into resistance at the all-time high of $34 set in June 2008. The intermediate-term support is between $25 and $27, making the risk $3, a two-to-one reward-to-risk setup. A purchase price of $30 is a reward of $4 and the risk is now $5 because support is at $25; the setup is not in favor of the investor at that point and that is why we will wait for the stock to pull back before buying. When determining if an entry price is attractive enough to purchase, I require the reward to risk to be a minimum of two-to-one, and typically look for a higher number.

Remember that knowing when to sell is the most important aspect of managing an investment, and choosing the correct entry point can also play a crucial role in determining a successful investment.

The next chapter lays out why it is important for investors to begin investing now for the Next Great Bull Market. If history is a barometer for what lies ahead, the Dow found its low in March 2009 and there is big money to be made in the decade ahead. Find out what the charts from the 1970s tell us about the next 20 years.

Chapter 15

It's Time to Buy;
History Says So

The stock market will move higher over time, but as you probably know by now, it does not go up in a straight line. There will be more bear markets in your lifetime and if the long-term pattern of the U.S. market holds true, we could be in the middle of a 16-year sideways pattern. With that being said, investors need to realize money can be made when the major market indexes rise or fall. In Figure 15.1, a long-term chart of the Dow highlights the pattern of bull markets followed by years of sideways movements. The time frame of the patterns are approximately 16 to 18 years in length and occur like clockwork.

The Dow is now in its tenth year of consolidation after peaking in 1999; since that time the index has moved sideways with furious moves to both the upside and downside. The action during the last 10 years is eerily similar to that of the late 1960s and early 1970s. After hitting a high in 1966, the Dow fell into a bear market and a few years later hit a new multiyear low, similar to the action from 1999 through 2002.

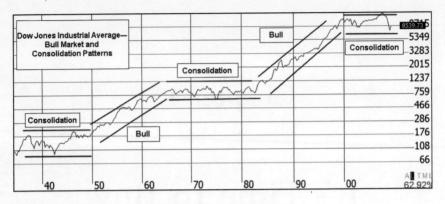

Figure 15.1 Dow Jones Industrial Average Patterns
SOURCE: TeleChart2007® or StockFinder® chart, courtesy of Worden Brothers, Inc.

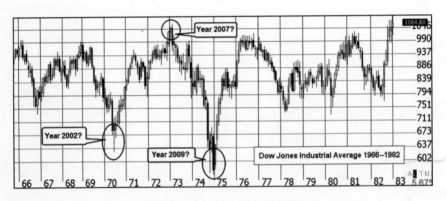

Figure 15.2 Dow Jones Industrial Average 1966–1982
SOURCE: TeleChart2007® or StockFinder® chart, courtesy of Worden Brothers, Inc.

A rally ensued off the lows of 1970 and the index briefly hit a new all-time high in 1973; the current situation is again very similar, with the rally from the 2002 low to the 2007 high. After hitting a high in January 1973, the Dow began a drastic sell-off that sent the index from a high of 1067 to a low of 570 in December 1974, a fall of 47 percent in just under two years. Amazingly, the Dow once again tracked the performance of the mid-1970s by falling from a high of 14,198 in October 2007 to a low of 6469 in March 2009, a drop of 54 percent (see Figures 15.2 and 15.3).

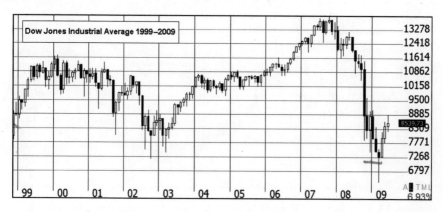

Figure 15.3 Dow Jones Industrial Average 1999–2009
Source: TeleChart2007® or StockFinder® chart, courtesy of Worden Brothers, Inc.

If the pattern continues to hold true, the Dow should have found its low for this decade and investors should be prepared to begin buying as the next great bull market is right around the corner. The rally that began in 1974 was from a level not seen in 10 years, just as the Dow hit a decade low in March 2009. If the Dow is on its way back to the old highs as the index did in the mid-1970s, there will be investment opportunities of a lifetime that cannot be passed up. The great bull market that ran through the 1980s and 1990s was a time when average investors became millionaires and millionaires became multimillionaire philanthropists.

The key then and now is knowing when and how to invest your money in the market. This book has laid out numerous investment ideas I believe will be the leaders of the Next Great Bull Market, and if the trend of the Dow continues, you better prepare for a large financial windfall in the years ahead.

Volatility Is Baaacckkk

It was not uncommon to have 200-point swings in the Dow Jones Industrial Average on a daily basis during the height of the financial crisis. After years of abnormally low volatility, the recession and collapse of several financial institutions brought back the volatility of the

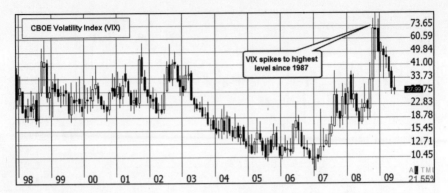

Figure 15.4   The VIX Shows Volatility at Highest Level in Over a Decade
SOURCE: TeleChart2007® or StockFinder® chart, courtesy of Worden Brothers, Inc.

early 2000s. Volatility as measured by the CBOE Volatility Index (VIX) spiked to the highest level since the 1987 stock market crash (see Figure 15.4). The higher the reading on the VIX, the more fear that is in the market, and from a contrarian point of view, this is bullish. This is where "when the VIX is high, it is time to buy" comes from.

Another angle to measure the amount of volatility in the market is to analyze the number of triple-digit closing changes in the Dow. For the entire year of 2007, the Dow either closed up or down by triple-digits a total of 78 times. In 2008, that number nearly doubled to 146. Through the first five months of 2009, the Dow has achieved the triple-digit close a total of 54 times and was on pace for 132 for the entire year. Through the first five months of 2007, the Dow hit the mark only 16 times versus 75 in 2008.

One argument is that the Dow was trading at a higher level and, therefore, triple-digit gains are not as meaningful. Wrong. The Dow traded higher in 2007 than it did in 2008 and the majority of the triple-digit moves in 2008 came with the Dow below 10,000, when in 2007, the index was above 13,000 for most of the year. That is why the VIX spiked to an all-time high amid the huge one-day gains in stocks and the fear that was running rampant on Wall Street. The bottom line is that volatility is back in the market and is here to stay for the foreseeable future.

Volatility Is Your Friend

The volatility during the heart of the bear market was enough to drive large hordes of investors out of stocks and into cash. The reason was that most of the volatility involved daily swings that resulted in the market closing lower at the end of the day. There came a point when the triple-digit swings were simply too much for average investors to stomach and they threw in the proverbial towel.

From the perspective of a long-term investor, the volatility can create a situation that is difficult to handle. This, in turn, leads to emotional decisions that over time may turn out to be poor. When the VIX spiked in November 2008 to close at the highest level in decades, it was coinciding with the market finding a short-term bottom. In the three weeks after the high on the VIX, the S&P 500 was higher by more than 20 percent. The index eventually gave back the gains and closed at a new low in March 2009, but many investors let the volatility make the decision to sell in November and remain on the sidelines (wishing they did not sell).

Short-term investors and traders have a love-hate relationship with volatility; some days, it could be their best friend, and on other days, it is the number one nemesis. It comes down to being on the right side of the trade when volatility is high. The result for traders is often large gains or large losses. During the bear market, the traders who were able to play the short side of the market enjoyed huge profits as the traders on the other side of the trade are probably no longer employed as traders.

Instead of fearing volatility, long-term investors must embrace it and use it to their advantage. I discussed in the previous chapter the art of knowing when to buy and setting target prices at which a stock should be purchased. When the market is displaying high volatility, there are individual stocks that could be experiencing even larger daily swings. When looking to enter a new position, it is imperative to show patience because when volatility is high, the odds of the stock falling to the entry price is high. The pullback to the entry price may occur for a few hours before it spikes higher once again. This is why investors need to be ready with a price they are comfortable buying a stock and use the volatility as a tool to enter the position.

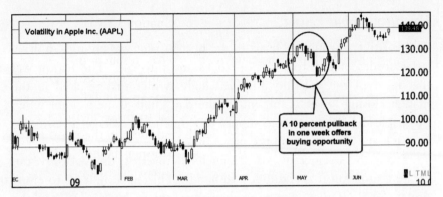

Figure 15.5   Volatility in Apple Stock Creates a Buying Opportunity
SOURCE: TeleChart2007® or StockFinder® chart, courtesy of Worden Brothers, Inc.

In Figure 15.5, Apple stock was on fire after hitting a low in March 2009 and it appeared the stock would never pull back for new investors to buy at a reasonable price. The stock hit a high above $130 in early May 2009 and the stock could not be purchased on the basis of the chart, so a pullback to the $120 support level became the designated point of entry. There was a burst of selling and one week later, the stock fell 10 percent to the $120 level and the stock could have been purchased. By early June, the stock was at $140 and the patient investor was sitting with a profit of $20 (18 percent) versus the impatient investor who bought at $132 and has a gain of only $8, or 6 percent.

The Reason for Volatility Today

So why has volatility come out of nowhere to ravage the steady and slow-moving U.S. stock market? I blame it on a number of factors, but the most prevalent is the abundant availability of information on the Internet. I agree that the Internet is probably the most amazing invention of our lifetime, but it has also opened a Pandora's box for the world of investing.

Information that was once available only to professionals who work on Wall Street is now readily available to anyone with an Internet connection. This is not necessarily a negative for investors and the stock market, but if the information is not used correctly, it could result in dire consequences. What I mean by that is that an uneducated, amateur investor now has the ability to garner information that could lead to poor investment decisions.

The introduction of investment blogs has resulted in not only potentially helpful information, but also blatantly false stories strewn throughout the World Wide Web. How can an individual investor determine what information has the potential to make them the next Warren Buffett and what information will land them in the poorhouse? Because some investors interpret the information as bullish and others as bearish, the amount of buying and selling has picked up, leading to more volatility.

The timing of the information on the web and from the television media has also added to the volatility. Economic releases, earnings, and any breaking news are streamed across every medium available, and the average investor at work now has the ability to trade on that information. This is a scary thought for me, considering it is difficult for professional traders to make money on short-term swings and now the Average Joe is entering the ring.

In the mid-2000s, my clients were focused on investing for the long term and finding quality stocks that would grow over time. In the last two years, the focus has done a 180-degree turnaround: My clients would now rather buy a stock and sell it in a few months after a gain has been generated. Their patience with the market and long-term investing has worn thin and the belief that holding for the long term is the best strategy has disappeared. Much of the blame can be put on the media for overexasperating the volatility and portraying the trading aspect of investing as the strategy for the future. I do not disagree that market timing is integral for a successful investor, but the average investor will be wrong when timing the market the majority of the time, thus resulting in more buying and selling, attempting to catch the ups and downs of the market. This creates even more volatility.

A fairly recent introduction into the world of investing has been leveraged exchange-traded funds (ETFs). Leveraged ETFs are covered in greater detail in Chapter 12 if you need a full explanation of how they work. Whether the leveraged ETF is up or down, trading more money in them results in more volatility in the market. The ProShares UltraShort Financials ETF (NYSE: SKF) is a great example of the volatility in the market.

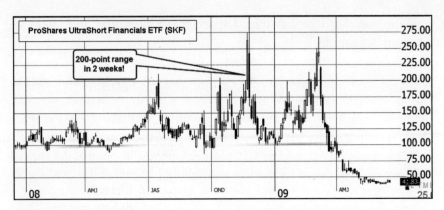

Figure 15.6   Volatility in ProShares UltraShort Financials ETF Is Not for the Weak-Stomached Investor
SOURCE: TeleChart2007® or StockFinder® chart, courtesy of Worden Brothers, Inc.

· In Figure 15.6, the ProShares UltraShort Financials ETF is a display of the volatility that swept the market in 2008 and into 2009. There were several instances in which the ETF doubled in value in a short period of time, only to give back all the gains just as quickly. From May 2008 through July 2008, the ETF doubled from $100 to $200 per share. A mere two months later, the ETF was back below $100 again. Two months after that, the ETF trading at $300 and an amazing three weeks later back down to $100.

The short-term swings are even more mind-blowing and detail the intraday volatility that has never been seen before in the markets. The ETF hit an intraday high of $303 on November 11, 2008, before closing at $244. The next day, the ETF closed at $173, an astonishing $130 points off the high of one day earlier. And yes, there were buyers at $303 thinking the ETF was going to go to $400 and they were wrong. Within a time of just over 24 hours, traders in the SKF could have been down more than 50 percent in their portfolio. Scary indeed.

As you read this chapter on volatility, I do not want to scare you away from the market. What I really want to get across is the understanding that it is now a part of the investment landscape and you need to know the realities of the effects it will have on your portfolio. It is okay to trade the leveraged ETFs as long as it fits into your risk profile and you are aware of the volatility associated with them. In the end, volatility can be our friend when it is understood and used in a diligent manner.

Covered Calls: A Strategy to Take Advantage of Volatility

Because of the rise in volatility, premiums on options have also spiked, making it more expensive for investors to buy calls and puts. At the same time, the sellers of the options are bringing in larger amounts of income with the higher implied volatility. To take advantage of the higher premiums in the call options in particular, I have begun to offer a new service to my clients—the PFG Covered Call Strategy.

The strategy may be new for some, but is something that I have been implementing for years on and off, when the environment calls for it. The goal of the strategy is to create monthly income as the cost basis for a long-term position is lowered. One of the factors that makes the strategy attractive is that investors who range from conservative to aggressive can participate. Because the option is covered by owning the underlying stock, the risk is very small and the truth of the matter is that it is less risky than simply owning an individual stock.

I realize that as soon as the topic of options is brought up, it alienates one half of investors who are risk averse and believe options are evil. The other half, who are considered risk junkies see their blood pressure rise in excitement. I will attempt to explain the strategy in extremely simple terms, or two steps, so even the novice can understand that all investors should be taking advantage of the volatility in options.

The first step of the PFG Covered Call Strategy is the purchase of a stock that is viewed as a long-term investment on the basis of both fundamental and technical analysis. The second step involves looking at the available front-month options available on the stock.

Step One: Purchasing a Stock

Once a call option is chosen, the appropriate amount of contracts is sold to match the number of shares of the stock. For example, if 500 shares of ABC are purchased, five contracts will be sold (one option contract is equal to 100 shares of the underlying stock). The covered call position is now established.

There are several possible outcomes when the call option expires on the third Friday of the next month. If the stock is trading above the strike price of the option, the stock will be sold at the strike price and a gain will be banked in a few weeks. This is a positive scenario because it guarantees a profit for the portfolio and frees up cash for the next investment.

The second scenario results when the stock is trading below the strike price of the call option. The call option will expire and the shares of the stock will remain in the portfolio with the new cost basis. This is positive, because if the stock were simply bought and a call option was not sold, the stock position would have a higher cost basis than it does after making money on the call option that expired.

If the stock fell dramatically, it could be below the new cost basis and an unrealized loss could be the result. The investor now has the option of selling the stock and taking a loss or selling another call option to lower the cost basis once again. About 9 times out of 10, a new call option is sold and the cost basis continues to be lowered because the stock was originally bought as a long-term investment and nothing has changed to force a sale of the stock. The following example highlights both scenarios and will give you a better understanding of the covered call strategy.

Step Two: Buying the Stock and Selling the First Covered Call

The only true way to give investors a feel for how the strategy works is to provide a real-life example from my account. On October 24, 2008, 500 shares of Foster Wheeler Ltd (NASDAQ: FWLT) were purchased at $22.50. As I mentioned earlier, one of the prerequisites for a stock to be a covered call candidate is that it must be viewed as a potential long-term investment suitable for the portfolio. FWLT met that requirement because it was a play on infrastructure and the valuation was deemed acceptable as a buy opportunity.

On the same day (October 24, 2008), five November $22.50 call options were sold for $3.10, thus lowering the cost basis for FWLT down to $19.40. On November 21, the day the option expired, the stock closed at $16.24 per share, well below the strike price of $22.50. Therefore, the call expired as worthless and the 500 shares remain in my account with an adjusted cost basis of $19.40.

There are two scenarios that could have taken place on the day the option expired. The first was the outcome that occurred; the stock was not sold and the option expires as worthless because the stock was trading below the strike price. The person who bought the call option from me had the option of buying FWLT at $22.50. Because the stock was trading below $22.50, the option buyer will not exercise the option and the end result is the premium paid by the buyer remains in my portfolio and lowers the cost basis of the FWLT position.

The second scenario involves FWLT closing above $22.50 when the option expired on the third Friday of November. The close above the strike price gives the buyer the right to purchase FWLT at $22.50 from me and could turn around and immediately sell it for the difference between the current price (above $22.50) and $22.50. More on the second option in step two.

Step Three: Selling Another Front-Month Call Option on the Stock

Front month refers to the next set of options to expire on the stock. For example, if a stock was purchased during the last week of May, the front month contract would be the June options. All equity options expire on the third Friday of the month. In our example, the third Friday in November has come and gone and FWLT remains in my portfolio. I am okay with the situation because FWLT was a stock that I felt was a solid long-term play, but obviously my timing of the purchase was not perfect. Thankfully, the call option was sold because it lowers the unrealized loss on the FWLT position. Step two is to sell another call option against the 500 shares of FWLT to once again lower the cost basis of the stock and generate income for the portfolio.

On November 25, five December $20 call options were sold against the 500 shares of FWLT at a price of $2.00. This transaction lowers the cost basis of FWLT down to $17.40, and if FWLT is above $20 on the third Friday of December, the stock will be sold at $20. On December 19, the third Friday of December, FWLT closed the week at $23.82 per share. Because the stock was trading above the strike price of $20, the 500 shares were called away (sold) at $20 the following Monday morning. Figure 15.7 shows a chart of FWLT with the timeline of when each trade took place for a more detailed look.

Figure 15.7   Foster Wheeler Covered Call Trades
SOURCE: TeleChart2007® or StockFinder® chart, courtesy of Worden Brothers, Inc.

The end result was a per-share gain of $2.60, or a profit of 15 percent, not including commissions. This may not sound like a large gain, but considering the entire trade was two months, the annualized return, not including compounding, is 90 percent. Another way to view FWLT is to analyze the position without selling the options against the position. Remember, the stock was bought at $22.50, so if the covered call strategy was not incorporated, the unrealized gain on the third Friday of December would have been $1.32 per share versus $2.60 with the PFG Covered Call Strategy.

Trading versus Investment Strategy
The example of Foster Wheeler was used because it is representative of the average covered call investment I have initiated over six months' time. Several have netted large gains as others resulted in small losses. Overall, the strategy has been very profitable and has even exceeded my projections. This is why I have been aggressive in attempting to explain the strategy to my clients so they can also profit from the volatility in the options market.

The question that arises is whether the PFG Covered Call Strategy is designed for traders or investors. What is great about the strategy is that it can be used by both types of investors in the same manner. The strategy was originally designed to generate income appreciation of approximately 10 percent a month and have the stock called away when it closed above the strike price. According to the Rule of 72, if the proceeds were rolled into a new covered call at the end of each month, it would take 7.2 covered calls to double the initial investment. Keep in mind that it never works out perfectly, and in the case of FWLT, it took two months to generate 15 percent. Assume a trader is able to achieve the 10 percent three times per year; it would result in a gain of 33 percent at the end of 12 months. Not a bad return at all, and over time would result in a large windfall.

In this market environment, I now use the PFG Covered Call Strategy as an income generator and a way to lower the cost basis on what could be long-term positions. The Foster Wheeler investment was an example of a stock that I was comfortable holding onto for the long term because of its exposure to infrastructure spending and, technically, it was forming a bottoming pattern. The downside risk is that the stock can be called away and the investor is giving up the potential for large gains. The cost basis is being lowered dramatically at the same time, lowering the downside risk. To step away from the investment world, what is really happening is that the investor is giving up large gains to immediately lower the loss potential.

This strategy may not be for everyone, and it certainly is not appropriate for every position in a portfolio. That being said, my success with the strategy in the current volatile environment is proof enough that it should be considered for a portion of a portfolio. What makes the strategy even more compelling is that it can be implemented in retirement accounts to mitigate tax implications. If the government allows covered calls in retirement accounts (where you are not even allowed to short stocks), it proves the risk level cannot be excessive.

The Magic of Compound Interest

Compound interest—two words that do not sound overly exciting, but once you realize what they can do, you will be as giddy as I am when I say them out loud, "Compound interest!"

A simple way to think about compound interest is by using the Rule of 72. This will help you determine how many periods it takes for an investment to double in value. For example, if an investment returns 8 percent annually, it will take nine years for the investment to double. The number 72 is divided by the annual percentage gain and the resulting number is the amount of periods, in this case years, to double in value. (See Figure 15.8.)

Assume you invest $100,000 into ABC stock and it returns 8 percent annually; after nine years, the stock will be worth $200,000 as long as no shares were sold along the way. If, on the other hand, you remove the 8 percent gain each year, the total profit would be only 72 percent. This is because the $8,000 removed at the end of each year will lower the initial investment the next year back to the original $100,000. The original investment after the second year in the first example would be $108,000 versus $100,000. In the end, after nine years, the effect of compound interest increased the profit by 28 percent, or 39 percent more than without compounding interest.

By simply reinvesting the principal plus the gains from an investment, it increases the amount of the new initial investment. And the larger the amount of the initial investment, the larger the gain will be compared to a smaller investment with the same percentage return. For example, a 10 percent return on a $10,000 investment is $1,000; a 10 percent gain

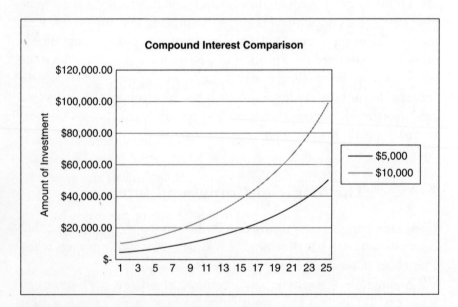

Figure 15.8   Effects of Compound Interest
SOURCE: Penn Financial Group LLC.

on a $15,000 investment is $1,500. The difference between the two starting investments was $5,000, but when it is time to reinvest the principal
and gains, the difference will be $5,500. This number is calculated by tak-
ing the difference between $16,500 and $11,000, the total after the gains
are added to the original investment.

Reasons to Believe in the Next Great Bull Market

This book is coming to a conclusion, and most readers are probably bullish on the market by now or at least on specific sectors. Before letting
you close the book, I want to recap the factors behind my bullish view
and why I believe we are on the verge of the Next Great Bull Market.

- Emerging markets are leading the rally off the lows. Money has
  found its way back into high-risk sectors that do well during bull
  markets.
- Economic numbers have stopped the deterioration and have either
  started to rebound or are moving sideways. Everything from consumer confidence to manufacturing numbers have improved from
  the lows of the first quarter of 2009 and the stabilization is the first
  signal of a bottom.
- Psychology among investors has improved dramatically now that most
  realize the United States is not going into the next great depression.
- Housing market bottom—The downward spiral in home prices
  has slowed and in certain regions of the country there has been a
  pickup in sales. By the end of 2009, I believe the housing market as
  measured nationally will have bottomed, leading to an increase in
  consumer confidence and slowing of foreclosures. If mortgage rates
  can remain near historic lows, it will be one of the major catalysts
  behind the housing bottom along with real estate vultures.
- The infrastructure bill, though far from perfect, will eventually lead to
  the unemployment rate bottoming in late 2009. Remember that the
  employment numbers are a lagging indicator, and by the time they
  begin to improve, the economy, and especially the stock market, will
  be well off the lows.

- Cash looking for somewhere to go. There is more than $3.5 trillion in money market accounts, according to the *Wall Street Journal* for the week of June 15, 2009. As the market begins to improve and interest rates on money markets remain low, the best investment opportunity will be stocks. Also, consider that most people are followers and believe in the herd mentality. As the market begins to move higher and more money moves into stocks, there will be a mad rush of cash into the market, resulting in an imbalance of buyers versus sellers and the end result will be higher stock prices.

- The financial crisis is in the late stages. The height of the financial crisis was between late 2008 and March 2009. Since that time, the major financial firms have done much to clean up their books and most are on the path to right themselves from the crisis. With the worst behind us and the future looking much better, the related stocks in the sector should be one of the leaders of the next bull market, and at the very least, not weigh on stocks and hold back the rally. Within the financial crisis was a credit crunch that saw banks halt lending and sit on the cash. That situation has also improved greatly, as the LIBOR overnight lending rate has returned close to normal levels from historically high levels in late 2008.

- Corporations have been able to raise capital in the private sector and investors are willing to buy their debt once again. Now that the irrational fears of a wave of bankruptcies of major firms has passed, companies are able to issue debt with reasonable rates. The improvement in the corporate debt market is an investment theme I touched on in the book and a signal the Next Great Bull Market is around the corner.

- The hedge fund industry has been altered dramatically and several of the largest funds have shut their doors. The hedge funds that remain are in a situation in which sitting on cash (and they have a lot of it) is no longer an option and they are looking to invest in the market and make money once again. If I am correct, this will create an influx of cash into stocks and commodities and be some of the fuel for the sustainable long-term bull market.

- From a technical and historical perspective, the stock market has generated several long-term buy signals, and investors who have the patience to ride the ups and downs for a few years will be rewarded greatly.

I hope all of you enjoyed this book as much as I enjoyed writing it. I truly wish you much success in your investment endeavors in the Next Great Bull Market.

Notes

Chapter 3: Globalization of the Stock Market

1. "Brazil Forecast, Outlook for 2009–2010," *Economist*, August 7, 2009. www. economist.com/countries/Brazil/profile.cfm?folder=Profile-Forecast.

2. "Brazilian GDP Grows 5.1% in 2008," Agence France-Presse, March 11, 2009. www.industryweek.com/articles/brazilian_gdp_grows_5-1_in_2008_18652.aspx.

3. "Russia Forecast, Outlook for 2009–2010," *Economist*, August 7, 2009. www. economist.com/countries/Russia/profile.cfm?folder=Profile%2DEconomic% 20Data.

4. "India Economic Data," *Economist*, August 7, 2009. www.economist.com/ countries/India/profile.cfm?folder=Profile%2DEconomic%20Data.

5. "China's GDP Up 6.1% in Q1 2009," *China Daily*, April 16, 2009. www.chinadaily .com.cn/china/2009-04/16/content_7683625.htm.

6. "China Cheers, but Not Too Loudly, after Bubbly Q2 GDP," Reuters, July 16, 2009. www.reuters.com/article/ousiv/idUSTRE56F0CR20090716.

Chapter 4: Water: The Next Great Commodity Rally

1. "State of the World 2005: Redefining Global Security," Worldwatch Institute, January 2, 2005.

2. "Drinking Water Infrastructure Key Points," Aqua America web site. www .aquaamerica.com/Pages/InfrastructureFacts.aspx.

3. "Australia in the Grip of Worst Drought in 100 Years, Prime Minister Says," Associated Press, October 13, 2006. www.climateark.org/shared/reader/welcome.aspx?linkid=61942.

4. "Water Crisis," World Water Council web site. www.worldwatercouncil.org/index.php?id=25.

5. "Water Scarcity and Its Effects," The Water Project web site. www.thewaterproject.org/water_stats.asp.

6. "Drinking Water Infrastructure," Aqua America web site. www.aquaamerica.com/Pages/Infrastructure.aspx.

7. "Northwest Pipe Reports First Quarter 2009 Results," press release from Northwest Pipe Company, April 28, 2009. http://finance.yahoo.com/news/Northwest-Pipe-Reports-First-iw-15051875.html.

8. "Northwest Pipe Company Announces First Quarter 2009 Earnings Release Conference Call," press release from Northwest Pipe Company, April 21, 2009. www.nwpipe.com/News__Events/.

9. "Ameron Reports Stronger-Than-Expected Fourth Quarter and Solid 2008 Results," Reuters, January 29, 2009. www.reuters.com/article/pressRelease/idUS97374+29-Jan-2009+BW20090129.

10. Jonathan Heller, "Dipping a Toe into Aqua America," TheStreet.com, November 13, 2008. http://finance.yahoo.com/news/Dipping-a-Toe-Into-Aqua-tsmp-13556362.html.

11. "Aqua America Upgraded to 'Buy' on Strong 1Q Profit," Associated Press, May 19, 2009. http://finance.yahoo.com/news/Aqua-America-upgraded-to-Buy-apf-15290757.html?.v=1.

12. "American Water Works Company, Inc. (AWK)," Yahoo! Finance company profile. http://finance.yahoo.com/q/co?s=AWK.

13. "About Cal Water," California Water Service Company web site. www.calwater.com/about/index.php.

14. California Water Service Company description, Hoovers web site. www.hoovers.com/california-water-service/--ID__12878--/free-co-factsheet.xhtml.

15. "Water Industry Stays Afloat in Economic Downturn," The Wall Street Transcript Online, June 2, 2009. http://finance.yahoo.com/news/WATER-INDUSTRY-STAYS-AFLOAT-twst-15413892.html?.v=4.

16. "Core Businesses," Pico Holdings web site. www.picoholdings.com/core-businesses.html.

Chapter 5: Global Infrastructure Build-Out

1. Steve Gelsi, "Power Firms Grasp New Tech for Aging Grid," MarketWatch, July 11, 2008. www.marketwatch.com/news/story/power-firms-grasp-new-tech

nology/story.aspx?guid=%7B3BB486EE-6B51-4B5D-9E91-0099ED4ED29
   1%7D&dist=TNMostRead.

2. "Obama Pledges to Flood Economy with Stimulus Money," Fox News, June 8,
   2009. www.foxnews.com/politics/2009/06/08/obama-promises-stimulus-jobs/.

3. Tom Coburn, "100 Stimulus Projects: A Second Opinion Senator," June
   2009. http://coburn.senate.gov/public/index.cfm?FuseAction=Files.View&
   FileStore_id=59af3ebd-7bf9-4933-8279-8091b533464f.

4. David Barboza, "China Unveils Sweeping Plan for Economy," *New York Times*,
   November 9, 2008. www.nytimes.com/2008/11/10/world/asia/10china.html.

5. Calum MacLeod, "China's Economic Stimulus Plan Targets Its Infrastructure,"
   USA Today, November 11, 2008. www.usatoday.com/money/world/2008-11
   -11-China_N.htm.

6. "Who We Are," AECOM web site. www.aecom.com/About/36/89/index.html.

7. "AECOM Reports 29% Growth in Revenue, Backlog of $9.2 Billion for
   Second Quarter of Fiscal Year 2009," AECOM Technology Corporation press
   release, May 7, 2009. http://finance.yahoo.com/news/AECOM-Reports-29
   -Growth-in-bw-15162825.html?.v=4.

8. "AECOM Reports 31% Growth in Diluted Earnings per Share, Backlog
   of $9.0 Billion for First Quarter of Fiscal Year 2009," AECOM Technology
   Corporation press release, February 10, 2009. http://investors.aecom.com/
   phoenix.zhtml?c=131318&p=irol-newsArticle&ID=1254851&highlight=.

9. Company profile, Fluor web site. www.fluor.com/about_fluor/corporate_
   information/Pages/profile.aspx.

10. Projects page, Fluor web site. www.fluor.com/projects/Pages/default.aspx.

11. Granite Construction web site. www.graniteconstruction.com.

12. State Street Global Advisors web site. www.spdrs.com.

13. Barclays Global Investors web site. www.ishares.com.

14. Invesco PowerShares Capital Management LLC web site. www.powershares.com.

15. Ibid.

Chapter 6: The Green Movement: Alternative Energy

1. "Fact Sheet on the Three Mile Island Accident," United States Nuclear Regulatory
   Commission, March 2009. www.nrc.gov/reading-rm/doc-collections/fact-sheets/
   3mile-isle.html.

2. Time for Change web site. http://timeforchange.org/pros-and-cons-of
   -nuclear-power-and-sustainability.

3. Elisabeth Rosenthal, "Italy Embraces Nuclear Power," *New York Times*, May 23,
   2008. www.nytimes.com/2008/05/23/world/europe/23nuke.html?ref=europe.

4. "Sweden Reverses Its Nuclear Phaseout," World Nuclear News, February 5, 2009. www.world-nuclear-news.org/newsarticle.aspx?id=24606.

5. "Nuclear Power in France," World Nuclear Association web site, June 2009. www.world-nuclear.org/info/inf40.html.

6. "Nuclear Power in China," World Nuclear Association web site, June 16, 2009. www.world-nuclear.org/info/inf63.html.

7. "Nuclear Power in India," World Nuclear Association web site, May 2009. www.world-nuclear.org/info/inf53.html.

8. "World Nuclear Power Reactors 2008–09 and Uranium Requirements," World Nuclear Association web site, June 1, 2009. www.world-nuclear.org/info/reactors.html.

9. AREVA company web site. www.areva.com/servlet/group-en.html.

10. AREVA company description, Hoovers web site. www.hoovers.com/areva/--ID__104852--/free-co-profile.xhtml.

11. "Africa's Largest Uranium Mine Gets the Go-Ahead," World Nuclear News, January 6, 2009. www.world-nuclear-news.org/newsarticle.aspx?id=24247.

12. Steven Mufson, "Expansive Energy Bill Advances in Congress," *Washington Post*, June 18, 2009. www.washingtonpost.com/wp-dyn/content/article/2009/06/17/AR2009061701699.html?hpid=moreheadlines.

13. Exelon company web site. www.exeloncorp.com/aboutus/.

14. Exelon company web site. www.exeloncorp.com/ourcompanies/powergen/nuclear/.

15. Ibid.

16. Van Eck Securities Corporation web site. www.vaneck.com/index.cfm?cat = 3192&cGroup=ETF&tkr=KWT&LN=3_02.

17. "Solar Energy ETF (KWT)," Van Eck Securities Corporation web site, 2009. www.vaneck.com/sld/vaneck//offerings/factsheets/KWT_FactSheet.pdf.

18. "Fast Solar Energy Facts," Solarbuzz web site, March 2009. www.solarbuzz.com/FastFactsIndustry.htm.

19. Ibid.

20. Company overview, First Solar company web site. www.firstsolar.com/company_overview.php.

21. "First Solar Strikes Middle East Supply Deal," Associated Press, January 15, 2009. www.cnbc.com/id/28679715.

22. Q-Cells company web site. www.q-cells.com/en/home/index.html.

23. MEMC Electronic Materials, Inc. company profile, Hoovers web site. www.hoovers.com/memc-electronic-materials/--ID__44021--/free-co-profile.xhtml.

24. Eric Savitz, "Solar: What Happens When Polysilicon Prices Collapse?," *Barron's*, February 12, 2009. http://blogs.barrons.com/techtraderdaily/2009/02/12/solar-what-happens-when-polysilicon-prices-collapse/?mod=yahoobarrons.

25. "20% Wind Energy by 2030 Increasing Wind Energy's Contribution to U.S. Electricity Supply," U.S. Department of Energy report, July 2008. www.20percentwind.org/20p.aspx?page=Overview.

26. Pickens Plan company web site. www.pickensplan.com/oilimports/.

27. "Wind Energy Fast Facts," American Wind Energy Association web site, 2009. www.awea.org/newsroom/pdf/Fast_Facts.pdf.

28. "U.S. and China in Race to the Top of Global Wind Industry," American Wind Energy Association press release, February 2, 2009. www.awea.org/newsroom/releases/us_and_china_race_to_top_of_wind_energy_02Fed09.html.

29. DMI Industries web site. www.dmiindustries.com/company.asp.

30. "Annual Report 2008: No. 1 in Modern Energy with Wind Power at the Top of the Energy Agenda," Vestas Wind Systems A/S company press release, February 11, 2009. www.vestas.com/files//Filer/EN/Investor/Company_announcements/2009/090211-CA_UK-04.pdf.

31. "First Trust ISE Global Wind Energy Index Fund (FAN)," list of holdings as of June 24, 2009. www.ftportfolios.com/Retail/etf/ETFholdings.aspx?Ticker=FAN.

Chapter 7: The Long-Term Bull Market for Commodities

1. Kitco company web site. www.kitco.com.

2. "NYSE Arca Gold Miners Index (GDM)," Van Eck company web site fund overview. www.vaneck.com/index.cfm?cat=3193&cGroup=INDEX&tkr=GDX&LN=3-03.

3. Royal Gold company reports. www.royalgold.com.

4. Freeport-McMoRan Copper and Gold, Inc. 2008 Annual Report. www.fcx.com/ir/AR/2008/FCX_AR_2008.pdf.

5. Alcoa company reports. www.alcoa.com/global/en/home.asp.

6. Simon Romero, "In Bolivia, Untapped Bounty Meets Nationalism," *New York Times*, February 2, 2009. www.nytimes.com/2009/02/03/world/americas/03lithium.html?_r=2&hp=&pagewanted=all.

7. FMC Corp. (FMC) company profile. http://finance.yahoo.com/q/co?s=FMC.

8. FMC Corporation reports. www.fmclithium.com.

9. "SQM Reports Earnings for the First Quarter 2009," SQM Company earnings report, April 28, 2009. www.sqm.com/aspx/en/Default.aspx.

10. BHP Billiton company profile. www.bhpbilliton.com/.

11. "NYSE Arca Steel Index (STEEL)," Van Eck company web site fund overview. www.vaneck.com/index.cfm?cat=3193&cGroup=INDEX&tkr=SLX&LN =3-03.

12. Syngenta company reports. www.syngenta.com/en/media/index.html.

13. "Agribusiness ETF (MOO)," Van Eck company web site fund overview. www .vaneck.com/index.cfm?cat=3192&cGroup=ETF&tkr=MOO&LN=3-02.

Chapter 8: Health Care and the Emergence of the Baby Boomers

1. National HealthCare Corporation company reports. www.nhccare.com/ press.cfm.

2. "Amedisys Reports Record Fourth Quarter Revenue and Net Income," Amedisys, Inc. press release, February 17, 2009. www.amedisys.com/pdf/ 021709_AMED_Q4_Earnings.pdf.

3. "Investor Fact Sheet," September 22, 2008. http://media.corporate-ir.net/ media_files/irol/17/176872/FactSheetSept2008.pdf.

4. NuVasive company reports. www.nuvasive.com/.

5. iShares company reports. www.ishares.com.

6. Gilead company reports. www.gilead.com.

7. "SPDR S&P Biotech ETF (XBI)," State Street Global Advisors web site. https://www.spdrs.com/product/fund.seam?ticker=XBI.

8. "Quick Facts: Highlights of the ASAPS 2008 Statistics on Cosmetic Surgery," American Society for Aesthetic Plastic Surgery 2008 reports. www.surgery .org/download/2008QFacts.pdf.

9. "Allergan Reports Fourth Quarter 2008 Operating Results and Announces Restructuring," Allergan, Inc. web site. http://agn.client.shareholder.com/ earningsreleasedetail.cfm?ReleaseID=363526.

10. "Myriad Genetics, Inc. Reports Results for Second Quarter of Fiscal 2009," Myriad Genetics press release, February 3, 2009. http://finance.yahoo.com/ news/Myriad-Genetics-Inc-Reports-iw-14232429.html.

11. Affiliated Managers Group company reports. www.amg.com/about/ structure_diagram.aspx.

12. "Affiliated posts 4Q loss; lower cash net income," Associated Press, January 28, 2009. www.fool.com/news/associated-press/2009/01/28/affiliated-posts -4q-loss-lower-cash-net-income.aspx.

Chapter 10: Finding the Next Brazil: Investing in Frontier Markets

1. "Kazakhstan Seen Preparing to Devalue Currency," January 28, 2009. Radio Free Europe/Radio Liberty. www.rferl.org/content/Kazakhstan_Seen_ Preparing_To_Devalue_Currency/1375909.html.

2. International Monetary Fund publication. www.imf.org/external/pubs/ ft/weo/2008/02/pdf/c2.pdf.

3. "Nigeria Forecast, Outlook for 2009–10," *Economist*, May 27, 2009. www .economist.com/Countries/Nigeria/profile.cfm?folder=Profile-Forecast.

4. David Nellor, "Nigeria Needs Sustained Reforms to Build on Success," International Monetary Fund, February 15, 2008. www.imf.org/external/ pubs/ft/survey/so/2008/CAR021508A.htm.

5. International Monetary Fund publication. Op. cit.

6. "Vietnam Forecast, Outlook for 2009–10," *Economist*, May 26, 2009. www .economist.com/Countries/Vietnam/profile.cfm?folder=Profile-Forecast.

7. "Kazakhstan Forecast, Outlook for 2009–10," *Economist*, June 9, 2009. www .economist.com/Countries/Kazakhstan/profile.cfm?folder=Profile-Forecast.

8. International Monetary Fund publication. Op. cit.

9. MSCI Barra Frontier Markets and Indices report, June 2009. www.mscibarra .com/products/indices/fm/MSCI_Frontier_Markets_FactSheet.pdf.

10. "Kuwait Forecast, Outlook for 2009–10," *Economist*, May 15, 2009. www .economist.com/Countries/Kuwait/profile.cfm?folder=Profile-Forecast.

11. Kuwait Stock Exchange web site. www.kuwaitse.com/PORTAL/History/ MarketIndex.aspx.

12. International Monetary Fund publication. Op. cit.

13. "United Arab Emirates Forecast, Outlook for 2009–10," *Economist*, May 26, 2009. www.economist.com/countries/UnitedArabEmirates/profile.cfm?folder =Profile-Forecast.

14. Invesco PowerShares Capital Management company reports. www.invesco powershares.com/products/overview.aspx?ticker=PMNA.

15. Claymore Securities, Inc. company reports. www.claymore.com/etf/fund/ frn/holdings.

16. "Dow Jones Africa Titans 50 Index (DJAFK)," Van Eck company web site fund overview. www.vaneck.com/index.cfm?cat=3193&cGroup=INDEX&tkr =AFK&LN=3-03.

17. "SPDR S&P Emerging Europe ETF (GUR) Fund Overview," State Street Global Advisors web site. www.spdrs.com/product/fund.seam?ticker=gur.

Chapter 11: Peak Oil: Making Money with Oil at $100

1. Suncor Energy company reports. www.suncor.com/default.aspx?cid=70& lang=1.

2. Suncor Energy Inc. company description, Hoovers web site. www.hoovers .com/suncor/--ID__53524--/free-co-profile.xhtml.

3. "Petro-Canada at a Glance," Petro Canada press release, March 2009. www .suncor.com/doc.aspx?id=451.

4. Imperial Oil company profile. www.imperialoil.com/Canada-English/ThisIs/Profile/TI_P_CorporateProfile.asp.

5. Imperial Oil Limited company description, Hoovers web site. www.hoovers.com/imperial-oil/--ID__42419--/free-co-profile.xhtml.

6. "Coast to Coast Operations: Oil Sands," Imperial Oil company web site. www.imperialoil.com/Canada-English/ThisIs/Operations/TI_O_OilSands.asp.

7. "Canadian Natural Resources Limited Announces First Shipment of Synthetic Crude Oil from Horizon," Imperial Oil company press release, March 20, 2009. http://finance.yahoo.com/news/Canadian-Natural-Resources-iw-1469/912.html.

8. "Canadian Natural's Earnings More Than Double," TheStreet.com, March 6, 2009. www.thestreet.com/_yahoo/story/10468658/1/canadian-naturals-earnings-more-than-double.html?cm_ven=YAHOO&cm_cat=FREE&cm_ite=NA.

9. ExxonMobil company reports. www.exxonmobil.com/Corporate/about_what.aspx.

10. "Oil Winners and Losers: ExxonMobil," TheStreet.com, April 6, 2009. www.thestreet.com/_yahoo/story/10482706/1/oil-winners-and-losers-exxon-mobil.html?cm_ven=YAHOO&cm_cat=FREE&cm_ite=NA.

11. Petrobras company reports. www2.petrobras.com.br/ingles/ads/ads_Petrobras.html.

12. "Petrobras' Important Gas Discovery in Sao Paulo," Seeking Alpha, January 28, 2009. http://seekingalpha.com/article/116909-petrobras-important-gas-discovery-in-sao-paulo.

13. Jason Simpkins, "Will Brazil Be the New Saudi Arabia?" Seeking Alpha, March 18, 2009. http://seekingalpha.com/article/126579-will-brazil-be-the-new-saudi-arabia.

14. Pethokoukis, James, "Range Resources Shares Poised to Take Off—Barron's," Reuters, June 14, 2009. www.reuters.com/article/marketsNews/idAFN1413212620090614?rpc=44.

15. Invesco PowerShares company reports. www.invescopowershares.com/products/overview.aspx?ticker=DBE.

Chapter 12: The ETF Explosion

1. Ron Rowland, "How Many ETFs Are There Anyway?" Invest with an Edge, January 22, 2009. http://investwithanedge.com/how-many-etfs-are-there-anyway.

2. "Dodge & Cox International Stock (DODFX)," company profile at Yahoo! Finance web site. http://finance.yahoo.com/q/hp?s=DODFX.

3. The Growth Fund of America (growth fund) detailed fund information, American Funds web site. https://www.americanfunds.com/funds/details.htm?fundGroupNumber=5&fundClassNumber=0-returns-expenses.

4. Fund details, iShares web site, March 31, 2009. http://us.ishares.com/content/stream.jsp?url=/content/repository/material/fact_sheet/jke.pdf&mimeType=application/pdf.

5. Invesco PowerShares company reports. www.invescopowershares.com/products/overview.aspx?ticker=DBC.

6. Invesco PowerShares company reports. www.invescopowershares.com/products/overview.aspx?ticker=DBP.

7. Invesco PowerShares company reports. www.invescopowershares.com/products/overview.aspx?ticker=PCY.

Index